Literature for Teaching
A Guide for Choosing Solo Vocal Repertoire
from a Developmental Perspective

Christopher Arneson, DMA
With Lauren Athey-Janka

Inside View Press

Literature for Teaching
A Guide for Choosing Solo Vocal Repertoire from a Developmental Perspective

Copyright © (2014) by Christopher Arneson and Inside View Press
All rights reserved

No part of this book may be reproduced, stored in a retrieval system, or transmitted by any means, electronic, mechanical, photocopying, recording, or otherwise, without written permission from the author and publisher.

ISBN: 978-0-9905073-0-7

Inside View Press
Delaware, OH

www.InsideViewPress.com

Printed in the United States of America

Acknowledgments

Thanks to my colleagues Scott McCoy, Lindsey Christiansen, Margaret Cusack, Thomas Faracco, Sharon Sweet, Marvin Keenze, Laura Brooks Rice, Elem Eley and Nova Thomas.

Thanks to the graduate students in my Literature for Teaching courses at Westminster Choir College of Rider University.

Thanks to Jennifer Newmann for compiling and formatting the original index and for helping me flesh out the early drafts of this book. There have been significant changes since we started this project, but your work was indispensable.

Thanks to Lauren Athey-Janka for organizing, writing, editing, hand holding, and creating hundreds of rubrics with me during the wee hours at Panera restaurants across South Jersey.

Thanks to Paul E. Wright, my most important mentor and music teacher.

Thanks to my dad.

For Bugga

Literature for Teaching
A Guide for Choosing Solo Vocal Repertoire from a Developmental Perspective

Table of Contents

Forward	ix
Introduction	1
Student Profiling	1
Sample Evaluation Forms	4
Repertoire Ideas	5
Evaluating Repertoire	6
Categorizing Repertoire	8
Developing a Difficulty Rating System with Rubrics	11
Using the Rubrics	
Deh, rendetemi (Francesco Provenzale)	16
Come Away Death (Roger Quilter)	22
I am in Need of Music (Ben Moore)	28
Kommen und Scheiden (Fanny Mendelssohn Hensel)	34
Ein goldenes Kettlein (Joseph Marx)	40
Organizing Repertoire	46
Developing a Teaching Plan Using Repertoire	46
Special Considerations	47
Very Young Students	47
Preteen/Precollege	48
University/Developing Professionals	48
Mature Adult Singers	49
Transitioning Voices	49
The Young Bass	50
Special Needs Singers	50
Other Repertoire Considerations	50
Operatic Arias	50
Musical Theater	51
20th & 21st Century Music	52
The How-to Chapter	53
Songs for Improving Registration	54
Songs for Improving Breathing and Breath Support	60
Songs for Improving Phonation and Resonance	62
Songs for Improving Articulation	66
Songs for Encouraging Expression	68
Songs that are Melodically/Harmonically Accessible	69
The 'Hook' Song	72
Examples for practicing repertoire evaluation	73
Encouraging Success through Sequencing of Songs	85

Suggested Repertoire for Technical Issues — 86

- Articulation — 86
- Breathing — 96
- Registration — 106
- Resonance — 116
- Support — 126
- Transition from alto to soprano — 136
- Transition from baritone to tenor — 146

Suggested Repertoire by Genre — 156

- Baroque Arias — 156
- Beginning Bass — 166
- Easier Songs by Important Composers — 176

Song and Aria Index for a Variety of Technical Goals and Genres — 186

- Agility — 186
- Articulation — 187
- Breathing — 188
- Legato — 190
- Registration — 192
- Resonance — 193
- Support — 194
- Transition from alto to soprano — 195
- Transition from baritone to tenor — 197
- Baroque arias — 197
- Beginning Bass — 198
- Characterization — 199
- Easier operatic arias for baritone — 200
- Easier operatic arias for bass — 200
- Easier operatic arias for mezzo — 200
- Easier operatic arias for soprano — 201
- Easier operatic arias for tenor — 201
- Easier songs by important composers — 202
- Harmonically interesting songs — 203
- Humorous songs — 203
- Rhythmic interest — 204

Bibliography of Reference Sources — 205

Song & Aria Title index — 211

Composer index — 227

About the Author — 237

Forward

When I graduated with my bachelor's degree, my teacher, Roberta Schlosser gave me a copy of Sergius Kagen's *Music for the Voice,* as a gift. Kagen was a student of Marcella Sembrich, who introduced him to much of the solo vocal repertoire that appears in his seminal text. Roberta Schlosser was a student of the Metropolitan Opera soprano Josephine Antoine, who also studied with Sembrich. Later, when I went to Rutgers, I was introduced to Valorie Goodall, who had studied with Berton Coffin, who authored *Singers Repertoire*, another important reference book. When Valorie retired, she gave me most of her vocal music collection, some of which originally belonged to Mr. Coffin.

At Rutgers, I also met Judith Nicosia, who is a walking encyclopedia of solo vocal repertoire and who possesses what I estimate to be one of the most significant libraries in the western hemisphere. Repertoire has always been on my mind. Judith and I were invited to teach *Repertoire from a Developmental Perspective* for the New York Singing Teachers Association's Professional Development Program. Later, I developed my own course, *Literature for Teaching*, in which dozens of graduate students have studied the repertoire I learned from Schlosser and Kagen and Sembrich and Coffin and Nicosia. This book is a natural outgrowth of this lineage of which I am exceedingly proud.

Christopher Arneson, June 2014

Introduction

One of the biggest challenges for voice teachers is choosing repertoire that meets a pedagogical end without exceeding the student's ability. Very often, colleges train their undergraduate students to become teachers of singing without teaching them how to evaluate and select repertoire. As a result, these new teachers turn to repertoire they sang during their own training—repertoire that may not be suitable for the unique technical issues of their current students. The most extensive problem is the assignment of repertoire that is too difficult (not musically, but technically), and that is not aligned with the teacher's pedagogical goals.

The intent of this book is to give you tools for selecting age and skill appropriate repertoire for your students that will help you achieve your pedagogical goals for them. We will explore some key topics:

- How to evaluate your student's current skill level
- How to evaluate repertoire and determine difficulty level
- How to use repertoire as a tool to improve technical skills
- How to create a long term repertoire plan for your students that will foster growth of their singing and lead to the assignment of more difficult repertoire, such as operatic arias
- How to broaden your own repertoire knowledge

We have included an index, which provides examples of songs intended for specific technical challenges.

Student Profiles

Before you can select repertoire, you need to get to know the student, the voice, previous musical experiences and pre-established skill sets, so that you can determine short and long term goals and decide upon repertoire that will help to achieve those goals. Aural evaluation of singers is a challenging skill that takes time and practice to develop. Pedagogy students in graduate programs are encouraged to begin developing these skills early on through the creation of student evaluation profiles and the use of audio and video recordings. They are asked to assess singers in these recordings to hone their listening and evaluating skills when developing repertoire assignments and then to apply those skills to their own students. It is important to remember that there is no right or wrong answer. The intent is not to diagnose issues at this point, it is to learn, listen to the sound, watch the actions and then evaluate what is seen and heard.

What can you quantify?

The first step to creating a profile of the students is to evaluate what you see when they are singing:

- How is the student's natural posture when talking?
- When he starts to sing, are his feet a shoulder's width apart?
- Are the knees bent slightly?
- Is the sternum held high with the shoulders relaxed?
- Is the face looking straight ahead or angled up or down?

- How free is the student's body when singing?

The majority of young singers have at least one area of tension when they are singing:
- Where does your student "hold" tension?
- Start your observation at the toes and work your way up. Are the knees locked?
- Is the posterior jutted out?
- Is the back arched?
- Do the arms pull away from the body?
- Are fingers tense or rigid?
- Are the elbows locked?
- Are shoulders locked in a shrug?
- Does the jaw rotate to one side?
- Are veins protruding from the neck?
- Is the chin protruding?
- Are the eyebrows lifted, wrinkling the forehead?

All of these are symptoms of tension in various areas of the body that will need to be addressed as lessons progress.

Once you've evaluated a singer's body while singing and where tension lies, pay close attention to how she is breathing:
- Are the shoulders moving up and down, or are they in a relaxed position?
- Is the student pushing the abdomen out when inhaling, or is it expanding naturally?
- Is the chest expanded freely or is there tension creeping up the chest into the neck?
- Is she able to sing a two-measure phrase in common time on a single breath?
- How about a four-measure phrase?
- Is the inhalation silent or noisy?
- Can he exhale without making a sound?
- How about when the student is engaged in conversation?
- Is breathing the same for talking and singing?
- Is the speaking breath more efficient than the singing breath?

Next, evaluate the sound the student makes when singing simple vocalises. Instead of starting with things that are wrong, identify factual information:
- What is the singer's total range?
- What part of his vocal range is strongest?
- Which notes are weaker than the others?
- Are the registers "mixed," or is there a significant register shift?
- If there is a significant register shift, on which pitch does that shift occur?
- Where is the voice the purest?
- Where does it sound forced?
- Does the voice move freely or is there weightiness to it?

After you have evaluated the quantifiable parts of the singing voice, move to the subjective. Remember that there is no right or wrong answer to these questions; these are your

personal impressions of the voice in front of you, using the collective input of all the singers you've heard and worked with in the past. Start by asking yourself how you would describe the color of the voice:
- Is it warm?
- Dark?
- Round?
- Bright?

Comparing the sound of a voice to other, non-musical images creates connections to emotions that can lead you to repertoire choices later.

What about the size of the voice?
- Is the sound big?
- Is there a natural resonance that will cut through an orchestra?
- Are there cues that a larger voice may be uncovered after a solid technique is acquired and when they are older?
- Is the voice vibrant?
    - Is the speed of the vibrato fast or slow?
    - Is the vibrato consistent in speed across the range?

Now that you have some general impressions about the student's posture, alignment, respiration, breath management, phonation and resonance, it's time to see what the student knows about music:
- Is the student able to match random pitches played on the piano?
- How difficult a pattern can she repeat?
- Does she have any musicianship skills?
- Can she read music?
- Can she sight read a basic melody?
- When asked to sing a simple song, is the student intuitively musical, or does she just sing the notes on the page with no sense of line or emphasis on important words or climactic sections?

Of all the evaluation tools discussed, perhaps the most important information comes from asking questions of the student:
- Why does the student want to study voice?
- What are the goals for the lessons?
- Is there an affinity for certain kinds of music?
- Is there a desire to sing classical music, show-tunes, jazz, pop, country or other genres?
- Was there prior musical education either in school or through private study?
- Does he play an instrument?
- What is her performing experience?
- Are there any fears of speaking or singing in public?
- How does the student present himself during conversation?

- Are there signs of poor self-confidence, such as staring at the floor or over your head when speaking?

It is critical to determine students' goals for being in your studio. Not every voice student has aspirations to star at the Metropolitan Opera. It is important to know why your students want to learn to sing better, and what it is they want to sing, so that you make repertoire choices that are appropriate for their interests, as well as their skills.

Here is a student evaluation and observation form, which can help you organize this information.

Student Profile and Evaluation Form

Student Name _____

Years of Singing _____

Musical Interests (Genres) _____

Instruments Played (How long?) _____

Extracurricular Activities _____

Why take singing lessons? (If applicable) _____

Assumed Voice Type _____

Observation and Evaluation Form

Posture/Body Alignment _____

Breathing _____

Phonation/Tone Quality _____

Registration _____

Resonance _____

Articulation _____

Diction _____

Pitch Memory/Intonation _____

Sight-Singing Skills _____

Expressivity/Musical Intuition _____

Repertoire Ideas

Genres _____

Difficulty _____

Languages _____

Other Comments _____

_____

_____

_____

_____

_____

_____

Evaluating Repertoire

Now that you have gathered information about your student's voice, you can start to think about repertoire. Not all songs are created equally. Choosing the right repertoire for each student requires some detailed analysis. The analysis protocol takes into consideration a number of things. What do you see the first time you look at a piece of music? How do we make sense of the music without playing through it? There are many elements to consider when choosing repertoire. It is much easier to evaluate whether or not a piece will be potentially helpful for your student when you know what to look for.

The Basics

The first thing to notice when you look at a piece will be the basic information, starting with the name of the composer and, possibly, the birth and death dates (depending on the publication). General periods of composition, composer output, and historical context are also helpful. Other things to consider might be the language of the text or the length of the piece.

Basic Musical elements

Clues about a song are found in its basic framework. If you have very little time, these elements will be the key to helping you decide whether or not to look further into a piece of music.

The first musical element to look at is the key or mode of the piece. Each key possesses different properties, different energy and mood, and different aural requirements for the musician. In terms of vocal development, certain keys may be easier for one Fach versus another to sing, or even one student over another of similar voice timbre.

Perhaps the most important element when considering a piece for a young singer is the range of the vocal line. For a beginning singer, it is ideal for a song to have a range of an octave or less. Consider the tessitura of the piece. For beginning singers, look for pieces that stay around a comfortable middle range, with lines that extend outward.

On a non-tonal level, one can get a good sense of a piece simply by looking at the meter, rhythms and tempi. Is the piece written in simple or complex meter? Are there meter changes in the piece? The same questions should be considered when looking at rhythms. How many notes are there per bar, on average? Are there rhythmic patterns that repeat? Are the rhythms easy to read? This is important to consider, because many pieces can look either easier or more complicated than they actually are. For a beginning student, looking at a piece with challenging rhythms or a non-traditional time signature may cause some unnecessary anxiety, so appearance should be considered. The solution may be as easy as finding a different arrangement or publisher.

Next, consider how fast or slow the composer expects the singer to execute those rhythm and meter changes. Is the tempo unrelentingly fast with many notes per bar, as in much of Handel and Scarlatti's florid writing? Is the tempo slow and drawn out? Different meters have an effect on the tone, timbre, and breadth of singers' voices. For instance, triple meter in a moderate tempo can be extremely effective for encouraging lightness in the voice and good breath flow.

You also can learn a lot about a piece simply by looking at its form. Different forms have been favored in different eras of music. How long is the song? Does it have any repeating sections? Does the piece require ornamentation? Is the ornamentation already written in? Is the poem strophic? In most cases, a song with repeating patterns, either melodic or rhythmic, will be easier to teach and learn than one that is through-composed and evolving constantly throughout the piece.

Melodic elements

It is important to take a detailed look at the vocal line. What is the intervallic structure? What are the properties of the phrases? Is the piece primarily driven by melody or text?

When thinking of beginning singers, look at phrase length. Is it possible to break up phrases and insert breaths? Do the phrases build upon each other? Is there a pattern in the way the phrases are organized? Are there sequences? Consider which direction the phrases go; are they mostly ascending or descending? Look for melodic or intervallic patterns, as these will make your work easier when breaking the piece into manageable sections.

A small range is best when choosing repertoire for a beginning singer. By the same token, pieces with primarily small intervallic leaps or common interval patterns will lead to greater success for beginning singers. Melodic lines that move mostly stepwise should also be considered. Conversely, a line that has many large leaps may be more difficult to learn. Look for the intervals that are most common in the piece and whether there are any tricky leaps. Vocal fold coordination is more difficult in non-diatonic intervals. A piece with difficult patterns or large leaps could be used as an opportunity to teach musicianship to your students, but proceed with caution and ensure that they are not left feeling frustrated if they cannot accomplish difficult passages quickly. Musicianship training is important for your students and should be incorporated into their warm-ups and repertoire; there will be more discussion on that subject in a later chapter.

Once you have taken the vocal line apart, consider the melodic writing as a whole. Does the melodic line reflect the intent and mood of the poetry? Could it express the story without words, or is it primarily supportive of the text? Is the writing syllabic or melismatic? Is the melody memorable?

Harmonic elements

Harmony can make a seemingly simple piece sound extremely complicated. It can also be the support a singer needs to get through a passage that is difficult in other ways. On a visual level, it is easy to scan a page for accidentals and marked key changes. These will be your first indications of how complex the harmony is. There are other things to consider. Are there many accidentals? How are key changes dealt with? How fast are the harmonic changes? Are harmonic changes in the vocal line supported by the accompaniment? In that vein, for a young singer, it will be important that the accompaniment be as supportive as possible. In the most supportive instances, the vocal line will be doubled in the piano. If that is not the case, is the harmony supportive of the melodic line? Remember, the more supportive the harmony, the more easily the student will be able to sing the music expressively.

Expressive Considerations

Vocal music is a marriage of music and text. Once you have evaluated the piece from a musical standpoint, it is important to consider aspects such as language, meaning, and expression.

Language considerations might include questions such as: Does the piece have a lot of text? How does the composer treat the text? Is the writing primarily syllabic or lyric? Every language has its difficulties when it comes to singing. What challenges could this pose for your singer? For instance, are the vowel sounds familiar or mostly foreign (i.e. not familiar to produce, such as the German *ichlaut* or *achlaut*). Does the language lend itself to legato singing (e.g. Italian or French), or is it consonant-driven (e.g. German and English)?

Much of the traditional canon is not appropriate for a young singer. Take this into consideration when choosing repertoire for your beginning singers. If the text is difficult for the singer to connect to, it will be difficult to encourage the singer to be expressive. You should look at the poetry in depth, if possible, before assigning a piece of music:

- Who is speaking in the poem?
    - A narrator?
    - A character?
- Is that character male or female?
- To whom is the character speaking?
- What is the subject of the poem?
- Are the poetry and language easy to understand or are they dated, obscure, or flowery?

You should also consider what type of text it is. Does it encourage outward expression, or is it more contemplative? All of these considerations will determine how well your student will connect with a piece of music (this will be different for each student) when it comes time to join expression and musicality.

When considering the text of a song, it is important to keep the specific student in mind. Selecting a song that is outside of the realm of experience for the student can result in difficulty connecting to the lyrics. Without that connection, the student will attempt to manufacture a sound instead of expressing the lyrical line organically. For that reason, it is best that a teacher get to know the student so that repertoire selections align not only with the technical ability of the student, but also with his emotional maturity.

Other considerations

Once you have determined that you like a piece and will find it useful for your student, there are some other practical things to consider. For instance, is the piece available in other keys if the tessitura is too high or too low? Is the piece available in an easier or more authentic arrangement from a different publisher? Where can you find the piece (which volumes or where online)?

Categorizing Repertoire

While some teachers are blessed with opportunities to work with professional singers who come to the studio just to polish repertoire or prepare for a new role at a large opera house, the majority of us work with children, young adults in the academic setting and amateur singers, all of whom have gaps in technique. The use of repertoire to meet a pedagogical end is critical in creating and meeting goals set by you and your student. Where evaluating repertoire requires an in-depth look into the musical aspects of a song, categorizing repertoire requires the application of pedagogical knowledge of vocal skills that can be addressed by the elements found in a piece.

Technical goals

Breathing

Respiration and breath management are the foundations of good singing. Insufficient inhalation and inefficient exhalation lead to many other technical issues. Repertoire selection must include songs that will help you correct these issues. As you review a piece, notice the phrase length:

- Is the singer given time to breathe?
- Do the rests indicate the need for a catch breath?
- Are the phrases uneven or regularly patterned?
- Can you establish a breathing pattern within the song?
- Can you break longer phrases apart to add breaths at first and then remove them as the student learns to better manage breath?
- Does the tempo of the song help the student learn to use breath efficiently, or is it so slow that the student is merely trying to survive to the end of the phrase instead of singing in a lyrical, legato manner?

Phonation

Phonation is the manner of closure of the vocal folds and the duration of the closure in each vibratory cycle, which determines the quality of the sound produced. The onset of phonation is often a source of great struggle for singers, as they must find a balance between two extremes of onset: pressed (formerly called a glottal attack) or breathy. When evaluating repertoire to address phonation issues, it is important to evaluate the text of the piece. Do phrases begin with consonants that will aid students in vocal onset, or with vowels that will expose technical issues?

What about phrase endings? Do the last words of phrases end with vowels that might encourage abrupt glottal closure or consonants that close with the teeth or tongue? The amount of time available to breathe between phrases also is critical, as a student with onset issues needs to have enough time to breathe with the same position as the opening word requires. Look for songs that contain sustained notes to encourage vowel purity and vowel sequencing to influence resonance.

Registration

Registers often are an acoustical phenomenon, but can have a physiologic component as well. Smooth transitions between registers establish a balanced tone across the range. This results in the ability to create a variety of dynamics and colors, which leads to effective communication of thought or emotion. Before selecting music, it is important to consider which voice type you are dealing with. Where does the voice "break" naturally? Does the singer mix the registers seamlessly, or does she sing all in chest (or head) voice? Vowels are the most important tool for working on registration. Be mindful of which vowels are most common in the piece and where they fall in the singer's range. Look at the vowel sequences in songs – if you are working with a chest-voice-dominant singer who needs to add more head voice, songs containing vowels such as [u] will help with that transition. If your singer is head-voice-dominant and needs to mix more chest voice into the sound, songs that contain words with the [a] vowel will help engage a stronger mix in that direction. Other questions to ask: What is the tessitura of the piece? Do ascending or descending phrases approach the passaggio? How are high and low notes approached? Is there sufficient time to breathe when changing registers?

Songs selected to improve registration should have limited range in the melodic line. For females, the melody should contain pitches between the passaggi; for males, pitches below the passaggio are more helpful. Look for songs where the melody skips over the passaggio and songs where the singer has the opportunity to reset the breath regularly. Melodic lines that descend stepwise will encourage bringing head resonance down into the lower range, and are less fatiguing than ones with ascending motion. Dotted rhythms and staccati encourage lightening of the voice, while a song or aria that is more speech-like in the lower range can encourage the chest voice to assist with the middle range.

Articulation

Articulation is defined as the act or process of speaking or expressing in words. As singers, articulation is the means by which we communicate the lyrics of a song to our audience. It is that goal of communication, of making the story understood, that often leads to great tension in singing. However, just as articulation can lead to tension, it can also be used as a tool to eliminate tension in the vocal tract. Neutralizing articulation can also be a means of negating regional accent in performance. Questions to consider when looking for songs with articulation in mind include:
- Is the song lyric or syllabic?
- How "wordy" are the lyrics?
- What is the language of the piece?
- Which vowels are most common in the text?
- What is the pitch range of the song?
- Are there diphthongs?
- Are there many consonants?
- Pure vowels or mixed vowels?
- What is the tempo and mood of the piece?

Articulation can be a gateway to correcting other issues as well; for example, [k] raises the soft palate while [g] lowers the larynx.

Expression

Communication with an audience should be the primary goal of any singer. It is important to select music that does not exceed a student's ability to communicate the message. While some students have natural acting ability that allows them to express emotions they have not yet fully experienced themselves, it is far more likely that your younger students will not be able to connect with many themes found in vocal music. This is not to say that songs like *Nun hast du mir den ersten Schmerz getan* from Schumann's *Frauenliebe und Leben* cannot be used to meet other pedagogical ends, but it is unlikely that an 18-year old can identify with the pain and despair associated with the death of a spouse.

So what should you look for when considering a piece to work on expressivity? First, review the text/poetry of the song:
- How difficult are the words to enunciate?
- Is the poetry direct or symbolic?
- Will the singer be able to understand the lyrical meaning?

- Is the singer a specific character in the story or does he/she play the role of narrator?
- What is the subject matter of the poetry?

Next, look at the style or era of the song and poetry:
- Is the material relevant to the singer?
- Can the story be made more modern to reach a younger student?

Some singers have difficulty connecting to the emotional essence of a song such as Nymphs and Shepherds (Purcell).

Application

While it is important to spend time evaluating all the musical, technical and expressive elements of a piece, there are key elements that can help you determine the difficulty of a song and which technical skills it will develop. Concentrating on these key elements through the use of a rubric and organizing completed rubrics into a notebook will give you quick and easy access to a variety of songs to address a variety of skills.

Developing a Difficulty Rating System with Rubrics

The Rubric

A rubric is a simple tool that provides basic information for a piece and ranks the difficulty of certain fundamental skills found in the piece. At the top of your rubric, you should include the song title, composer, and publisher so that you can easily find the song in your collection. Including the voice part(s) that can sing the piece, the language of the text and the range/tessitura of the song (in all keys the song is available) will allow you to scan the rubric and make a quick decision regarding whether (or not) the piece is appropriate for your student, regardless of the technical difficulty.

The second section of the rubric is where you make decisions about the difficulty of the work, based on your review of the entire piece, while answering the questions we discussed earlier in this chapter. There is no right or wrong musical element to include in a rubric; the skills you list should be those that you believe are most important.

The four sample rubrics were created by graduate students in my Literature for Teaching course, but were inspired by an article that appeared in the NATS *Journal of Singing* in January/February 2002 by John Nix.[1] The students used a numeric ranking for each skill set deemed important for consideration when evaluating music, but the specific areas they chose to evaluate varied based on their experience in the studio. In all four examples, the rank of the lowest number is applied to beginning skills, and the highest number to advanced skills. The *other notes* section might include additional information on the challenges identified in the numeric rank section.[2]

---

[1] Nix, John. "Criteria for Selecting Repertoire." *Journal of Singing*, Volume 58, issue 3, January/February 2002.
[2] Nota Bene: You will find that after you train your eye and your mind to evaluate repertoire, using rubrics, you will be able to do without them. I now use a simple system of rating using a scale of 1-4. However, I would not be able to do this if I had not first used rubrics to evaluate hundreds of songs and arias. If you think you can evaluate repertoire by simply scanning for the above-

Rubric 1

Title Composer
Composition Date Genre
Language Tempo Key(s)

	Beginning 1	Moderate 2	Advanced 3	Exceptionally Difficult 4	Score
Fundamental Objective/ Criteria	For beginning level instruction to aid in developing good basic vocal production.	For further development of vocal technique.	High level of technical ability needed to adequately perform.	Superb technical ability required to sufficiently study and perform.	
Tessitura					
Melodic Line/Interval Leaps					
Breathing					
Rhythm					
Piano Accompaniment					
Poetic Text/Thematic Material					
Overall Difficulty Level					

mentioned criteria, test yourself. Use a rubric for a song that you like to assign. Is it really as easy as you thought? "Silent Noon," by Ralph Vaughn Williams, and Barber's "Sure on this Shining Night" are two examples of songs that often are assigned to younger singers and which, when evaluated in detail, are found to be difficult from a technical perspective.

Rubric 2

Title _____

   *from*_____

Composer_____

Score, Anthology, or Book_____

Editor_____ Year_____

Key_____

Language_____

Range _____ to _____

Tessitura _____ to _____

Voice Type_____

Tempo_____

Lyrical or Conversational_____

Student Level   Beginner   Intermediate   Advanced

	Simple		Moderate		Difficult
Rhythms	1	2	3	4	5
Intervallic Leaps	1	2	3	4	5
Phrase Length	1	2	3	4	5
Vowel Sequence	1	2	3	4	5
Character	1	2	3	4	5
Text/Poetry	1	2	3	4	5
Diction	1	2	3	4	5
Accompaniment Support/Double	1	2	3	4	5
Accompaniment Playable/Fakeable	1	2	3	4	5
Language	1	2	3	4	5
Other:	1	2	3	4	5
	1	2	3	4	5
	1	2	3	4	5

Rubric 3

Song Title _____

Composer _____

Publisher _____

Voice Part _____

Language _____

Range _____ Tessitura _____

	Beginner		Intermediate		Advanced
Registration	1	2	3	4	5
Accompaniment Support	1	2	3	4	5
Articulation	1	2	3	4	5
Text Interpretation	1	2	3	4	5
Phrase Length	1	2	3	4	5
Range	1	2	3	4	5
Tempo	1	2	3	4	5
Rhythm	1	2	3	4	5
Diction / Language	1	2	3	4	5
Lyrical Flow	1	2	3	4	5
Melismas	1	2	3	4	5
Other notes					
					Final Rating

Rubric 4
Rubric for Grading Repertoire

Scale of 1-5
Total score: 12-28 points easy, 28-44 points moderate, 44-60 points difficult

Technical Issue Addressed	Problem Solving Questions	Scale 1-5
Accompaniment	Is the accompaniment utilitarian, supportive, independent, etc.? Is the accompaniment part of the story line? Is the accompaniment descriptive (e.g. water figures, spinning wheel)?	
Characterization/acting	Is the character appropriate to the student's dramatic capacity or life experiences? Will the student benefit from portraying this type of character?	
Diction/articulation	Consideration of challenging consonant clusters. Closed position or difficult consonants on challenging pitches? Student's knowledge of French, Italian, Russian, German, etc. language or diction?	
Dynamics	Is the singer expected to sing a pianissimo high note? Are the markings pedagogically helpful (e.g. crescendo on held notes to assist in breath energy and/or vibrancy)?	
Melismatic phrases	Beginning or advanced melismas/melismatic phrases present? Appoggiatura? Dotted rhythms?	
Musical considerations	Through composed? Strophic? Accessible harmonic language? Tonal? An enjoyable melody?	
Range/tessitura	How are high notes approached (e.g. dramatically)? Is the range too vast? Is the tessitura too low or high? Can a young singer sit in that particular part of the voice for that long without fatiguing?	
Registration	Does the piece assist in working through passaggio issues? Will the student carry weight up? Helpful vowels in an underdeveloped part of the student's voice? Etc.	
Respiration	Are phrase lengths accessible? Will the breaths allow for renewal of positioning?	
Text setting	Syllabic, Patter Song, Lyric? Does the text setting assist in memorization?	
Vowels & vowel sequences	Observation of vowels in passaggio. Will vowel patterns assist in correcting vocal faults? Front to back, tongue position, etc.?	
Words: Poetry/lyrics/libretto	Is this accessible poetry? Is the story age appropriate? Will the text make the memorization process difficult?	
Total score:		

Using the Rubrics

Example 1: *Aria di Armidoro: Deh, rendetemi*
from *La Stellidaura vendicata* by Francesco Provenzale

This is an accessible and beautiful aria for an advanced beginner or intermediate student. It's appropriate for a medium or low voice in the key analyzed. The singer must be secure enough to sing without the vocal line constantly being doubled in the accompaniment. In the medium-low key, this piece may be given to a mezzo or a young countertenor. This aria is dated 1640-1700.

- **Registration:** The range of this piece stays within an octave, and the tessitura is mostly middle voice in the medium-low key for medium or lower voices.
- **Vowels &Vowel Sequences:** Many Italian vowels are presented to work through in the middle voice. Diphthongs and a triphthongs are found.
- **Text Setting:** The text setting is often syllabic. A triphthong is found on an eighth note, which may be tricky for a beginning student. The text has a delicate feeling, requiring seamless articulation.
- **Respiration:** The tempo is sustained and may be sung slowly, but phrase lengths are accessible and not particularly long. Occasional catch breaths are needed. The rhythmically driven accompaniment may assist with breath energy.
- **Diction/Articulation:** The text is somewhat quick. The teacher can work through articulation, paying special attention to Italian dental consonants [l], [r], [d], [t] and [n]. Some consonant clusters can be tricky (e.g. [nd]). Double consonants must also be addressed.
- **Musical Considerations:** The melody is straightforward and accessible, although its form is AB. The subdued text requires a singer with controlled and quiet singing. Appoggiatura and dotted rhythms prevent the singer from oversinging.
- **Accompaniment:** The voice is quite independent. The rhythmically driven accompaniment is excellent for respiration, but the singer must sing a legato melody over quick and arpeggiated chords.
- **Melismatic phrases:** Dotted rhythms and a triplet are found, but this is very simple and helpful for a younger singer.
- **Poetry/Lyrics/Libretto:** The mature and melancholy text may be better suited for a more mature singer.
- **Dynamics:** Controlled and quiet singing is required.
- **Range/Tessitura:** The range is within an octave and the tessitura sits mostly in the middle voice.
- **Characterization/Acting:** A deep sense of melancholy is required.

Example 1: *Deh, rendetemi*

Rubric 1

Title: ***Aria di Armidoro: Deh, rendetemi***
    from *La Stellidaura vendicata*
Composer: Francesco Provenzale   Composition Date: 1640-1700
Genre: operatic arias suitable for young singers   Language: Italian
Tempo: *Andante un poco mosso*   Key: E minor

	Beginning 1	Moderate 2	Advanced 3	Exceptionally Difficult 4	Score
Fundamental Objective/ Criteria	For beginning level instruction to aid in developing good basic vocal production.	For further development of vocal technique.	High level of technical ability needed to adequately perform.	Superb technical ability required to sufficiently study and perform.	
Tessitura		X			2
Melodic Line/Interval Leaps		X			2
Breathing			X		3
Rhythm		X			2
Piano accompaniment			X		3
Poetic Text/Thematic Material			X		3
Overall Difficulty Level					**15**

Rubric 2

Piece: ***Aria di Armidoro: Deh, rendetemi***
  From: *Stellidaura vendicata*

Composer: Francesco Provenzale   Year: 1640-1700

Score, Anthology, or Book: Classic Italian Songs for School and Studio in Three Volumes, Volume II, Medium Low

Publisher: Oliver Ditson Company

Key: E minor   Language: Italian

Range: D-sharp to D   Tessitura: E to C

Voice Type: Mezzo Soprano or Contralto   Tempo: *Andante un poco mosso*

Lyric or Conversational: Lyric   Student Level: Intermediate

	Simple	Moderate	Difficult
Rhythms	2		
Intervallic Leaps	2		
Phrase Length		3	
Vowel Sequence		3	
Character	2		
Text/Poetry		3	
Diction	2		
Accompaniment -Support/Double		3	
Accompaniment -Playable/Fakeable			4
Language		3	
Total			27

Rubric 3

Song Title: ***Aria di Armidoro: Deh, rendetemi***
    from: *Stellidaura vendicata*
Composer: Francesco Provenzale
Publisher: Oliver Ditson Company
Voice Part: Mezzo Soprano or Countertenor
Language: Italian
Range: D-sharp to D
Tessitura: E to C

	Beginner		Intermediate		Advanced
Registration		2			
Accompaniment Support			3		
Articulation			3		
Text Interpretation			3		
Phrase Length			3		
Range		2			
Tempo		2			
Rhythm		2			
Diction/ Language			3		
Lyrical Flow		2			
Melismas	1				

Other notes: Advanced Beginning or Intermediate piece

Final Rating: 26

Rubric 4

Aria di Armidoro: Deh, rendetemi
from *Stellidaura vendicata*
by Francesco Provenzale

Scale of 1-5
Total score: 12-28 points easy, 28-44 points moderate, 44-60 points difficult

Technical Issue Addressed	Problem Solving Questions	Scale 1-5
Accompaniment	Is the accompaniment utilitarian, supportive, independent, etc.? Is the accompaniment part of the story line? Is the accompaniment descriptive (e.g. water figures, spinning wheel)?	3
Characterization/acting	Is the character appropriate to the student's dramatic capacity or life experiences? Will the student benefit from portraying this type of character?	2
Diction/articulation	Consideration of challenging consonant clusters. Closed position or difficult consonants on challenging pitches? Student's knowledge of French, Italian, Russian, German, etc. language or diction?	3
Dynamics	Is the singer expected to sing a pianissimo high note? Are the markings pedagogically helpful (e.g. crescendo on held notes to assist in breath energy and/or vibrancy)?	2
Melismatic phrases	Beginning or advanced melismas/melismatic phrases present? Appoggiatura? Dotted rhythms?	1
Musical considerations	Through composed? Strophic? Accessible harmonic language? Tonal? An enjoyable melody?	3
Range/tessitura	How are high notes approached (e.g. dramatically)? Is the range too vast? Is the tessitura too low or high? Can a young singer sit in that particular part of the voice for that long without fatiguing?	2
Registration	Does the piece assist in working through passaggio issues? Will the student carry weight up? Helpful vowels in an underdeveloped part of the student's voice? Etc.	2
Respiration	Are phrase lengths accessible? Will the breaths allow for renewal of positioning?	3
Text setting	Syllabic, Patter Song, Lyric? Does the text setting assist in memorization?	2
Vowels & vowel sequences	Observation of vowels in passaggio. Will vowel patterns assist in correcting vocal faults? Forward to back, tongue position, etc.?	2
Words: Poetry/lyrics/libretto	Is this accessible poetry? Is the story age appropriate? Will the text make the memorization process difficult?	3
Total score:		28

Using the Rubrics

Example 2: **Come Away Death** by Rodger Quilter

Many of Rodger Quilter's songs are excellent for younger students. The melody of this song is beautiful, and the accompaniment is varied and never intrusive. His prosody is excellent; he uses great texts and sets them well, but it should be noted that the poems are often truncated. He utilizes a diatonic melodic language.

- **Registration:** The dotted rhythms can assist in releasing tension and bulk. The [o] vowels are excellent for registration. The skips and leaps can be tricky.
- **Vowels &Vowel Sequences:** There are tricky vowels for certain parts of the voice, including the words "slain" and "weep" on higher pitches. This song presents an excellent opportunity to work on English diphthongs.
- **Text Setting:** The text setting is mostly syllabic and accessible.
- **Respiration:** There are phrases with no rests or pauses to breathe. Occasional catch breaths are needed. There is a long phrase at the end of the song.
- **Diction/Articulation:** This repertoire is sung with British-inflected dialect. The text is set syllabically. Consonant clusters must be addressed: [sl] and [fl].
- **Musical Considerations:** Control is needed, as dynamic markings of *p*, *f*, and crescendos are indicated. Good musicianship is needed, as the voice is independent.
- **Accompaniment:** The piano adds other interest, such as echoes, countermelodies and arpeggios. The piano does not double the melody.
- **Melismatic phrases:** Only simple triplets are found.
- **Poetry/Lyrics/Libretto:** Shakespeare can be difficult for a young singer to interpret, but this text is accessible and straightforward.
- **Dynamics:** A lyrical and sustained quality is present throughout the piece. *p* and *f* and crescendos are marked.
- **Range/Tessitura:** If using the higher key, the tessitura can be high at times. The leaps and range are difficult.
- **Characterization/Acting:** Research is needed for texts of Shakespeare.

Example 2: Come Away Death

Rubric 1

Title: **Come Away Death**
   from *Three Shakespeare Songs*, Op. 6 (First set)
Composer: Rodger Quilter   Composition Date: published in 1955
Genre: British Song   Language: English, British-received
Tempo: Poco andante   Key: C minor

	Beginning 1	Moderate 2	Advanced 3	Exceptionally Difficult 4	Score
Fundamental Objective/ Criteria	For beginning level instruction to aid in developing good basic vocal production.	For further development of vocal technique.	High level of technical ability needed to adequately perform.	Superb technical ability required to sufficiently study and perform.	
Tessitura			X		3
Melodic Line/Interval Leaps			X		3
Breathing		X			2
Rhythm		X			2
Piano Accompaniment		X			2
Poetic Text/Thematic Material		X			2
Overall Difficulty Level					**14**

Rubric 2

Piece: **Come Away Death**
From: *Three Shakespeare Songs*, Op. 6 (First set)

Composer: Rodger Quilter   Year: published in 1955

Score, Anthology, or Book: Roger Quilter, 55 Songs

Publisher: Hal Leonard

Key: C minor   Language: English, British-inflected

Range: C to E-flat   Tessitura: E-flat to C

Voice Type: medium or medium high voice   Tempo: Poco andante

Lyric or Conversational: Lyric   Student Level: Intermediate

	Simple	Moderate	Difficult
Rhythms	2		
Intervallic Leaps		4	
Phrase Length	2		
Vowel Sequence		3	
Character	2		
Text/Poetry	2		
Diction	2		
Accompaniment -Support/Double		3	
Accompaniment -Playable/Fakeable		3	
Language		3	
Total			26

Rubric 3

Song Title: **Come Away Death**
    from *Three Shakespeare Songs*, Op. 6 (First set)
Composer: Rodger Quilter
Publisher: Hal Leonard
Voice Part: Medium or Medium High Voice
Language: English, British- received
Range: C to E-flat
Tessitura: E-flat to C

	Beginner		Intermediate		Advanced
Registration			3		
Accompaniment Support			3		
Articulation			3		
Text Interpretation		2			
Phrase Length		2			
Range			3		
Tempo		2			
Rhythm		2			
Diction/ Language			3		
Lyrical Flow			3		
Melismas	1				

Other notes: Intermediate to advanced intermediate piece

Final Rating: 27

Rubric 4

Come Away Death
   from *Three Shakespeare Songs*, Op. 6 (First set)
by Rodger Quilter

Scale of 1-5
Total score: 12-28 points easy, 28-44 points moderate, 44-60 points difficult

Technical Issue Addressed	Problem Solving Questions	Scale 1-5
Accompaniment	Is the accompaniment utilitarian, supportive, independent, etc.? Is the accompaniment part of the story line? Is the accompaniment descriptive (e.g. water figures, spinning wheel)?	2
Characterization/acting	Is the character appropriate to the student's dramatic capacity or life experiences? Will the student benefit from portraying this type of character?	1
Diction/articulation	Consideration of challenging consonant clusters. Closed position or difficult consonants on challenging pitches? Student's knowledge of French, Italian, Russian, German, etc. language or diction?	2
Dynamics	Is the singer expected to sing a pianissimo high note? Are the markings pedagogically helpful (e.g. crescendo on held notes to assist in breath energy and/or vibrancy)?	3
Melismatic phrases	Beginning or advanced melismas/melismatic phrases present? Appoggiatura? Dotted rhythms?	1
Musical considerations	Through composed? Strophic? Accessible harmonic language? Tonal? An enjoyable melody?	3
Range/tessitura	How are high notes approached (e.g. dramatically)? Is the range too vast? Is the tessitura too low or high? Can a young singer sit in that particular part of the voice for that long without fatiguing?	3
Registration	Does the piece assist in working through passaggio issues? Will the student carry weight up? Helpful vowels in an underdeveloped part of the student's voice? Etc.	3
Respiration	Are phrase lengths accessible? Will the breaths allow for renewal of positioning?	4
Text setting	Syllabic, Patter Song, Lyric? Does the text setting assist in memorization?	2
Vowels & vowel sequences	Observation of vowels in passaggio. Will vowel patterns assist in correcting vocal faults? Forward to back, tongue position, etc.?	3
Words: Poetry/lyrics/libretto	Is this accessible poetry? Is the story age appropriate? Will the text make the memorization process difficult?	2
Total score:		**29**

Using the Rubrics

Example 3: I am in Need of Music by Ben Moore

This piece will promote good habits in classical singing, while exploring and performing a heartfelt text. American English is difficult, because the singer may bring a regional dialect to the pronunciation. Because of the nature of American English, a consonant driven language, articulation must be carefully observed. Approach the diction as you would a foreign language, especially if the student is struggling with diphthongs, spread or overly closed vowels, or strange pronunciation of words and consonants. Articulation habits from the study of this song will benefit the student. The work required on intervals in this song may be useful for coordination of registration. This piece is not for the beginner, as seen in the rubrics below. It was written for Deborah Voigt, after all.

- **Registration:** Difficult skips and leaps must be studied. The approach to high notes requires a skilled singer. High notes are approached either from an ascending interval or starting right on the note.
- **Vowels &Vowel Sequences:** English diphthongs may require attention. Certain vowels on higher notes may prove to be difficult, for example [u] on a high G.
- **Text Setting:** The text setting is not always syllabic; it can be tricky to maintain a seamless legato.
- **Respiration:** Long lines exist throughout the song, and catch breaths are needed at times.
- **Diction/Articulation:** American [r] and [l] may compromise vowel space for singers.
- **Musical Considerations:** Various dynamics are indicated, including *p*, *f* and crescendo; excellent control and technique is needed. The voice is independent, and there are accidentals throughout. Musicianship skills are non-negotiable with this repertoire.
- **Accompaniment:** The piano adds other interest and does not double the melody.
- **Melismatic phrases:** Triplets and complicated rhythms are found.
- **Poetry/Lyrics/Libretto:** The accessible poetry is beautiful.
- **Dynamics:** A lyrical, sustained and expansive quality is needed. The dynamic range is wide.
- **Range/Tessitura:** The leaps and intervals are very tricky, and the range is wide.
- **Characterization/Acting:** This Elizabeth Bishop poem is inspiring.

Example 3: I am in Need of Music

Rubric 1

Title: **I am in Need of Music**
Composer: Ben Moore
Genre: Contemporary American Song
Tempo: Adagietto, with quiet intensity

Composition Date: published in 2004
Language: American English
Key: C minor

	Beginning 1	Moderate 2	Advanced 3	Exceptionally Difficult 4	Score
Fundamental Objective/ Criteria	For beginning level instruction to aid in developing good basic vocal production.	For further development of vocal technique.	High level of technical ability needed to adequately perform.	Superb technical ability required to sufficiently study and perform.	
Tessitura			X		3
Melodic Line/Interval Leaps				X	4
Breathing				X	4
Rhythm			X		3
Piano Accompaniment			X		3
Poetic Text/Thematic Material		X			2
Overall Difficulty Level					19

Rubric 2

Piece: **I am in Need of Music**
Composer: Ben Moore   Year: published in 2004

Score, Anthology, or Book: BEN MOORE 14 Songs Medium High Voice and Piano

Publisher: G. Schirmer, Inc. Distributed by Hal Leonard

Key: C minor   Language: American English

Range: B-flat to G, expansive octave   Tessitura: E-flat to E-flat,

Voice Type: medium high voice   Tempo: Adagietto, with quiet intensity

Lyric or Conversational: Lyric   Student Level: Advanced

	Simple	Moderate	Difficult
Rhythms		4	
Intervallic Leaps		4	
Phrase Length			5
Vowel Sequence		3	
Character	2		
Text/Poetry	2		
Diction		3	
Accompaniment -Support/Double		4	
Accompaniment -Playable/Fakeable			5
Language		3	
Total			**35**

Rubric 3

Song Title:	**I am in Need of Music**	
Composer:	Ben Moore	
Publisher:	G. Schirmer, Inc. Distributed by Hal Leonard	
Voice Part:	Medium or Medium High Voice	
Language:	American English	
Range:	B-flat to G, expansive	
Tessitura:	E-flat to E-flat, octave	

	Beginner		Intermediate		Advanced
Registration				4	
Accompaniment Support				4	
Articulation			3		
Text Interpretation		2			
Phrase Length		2			
Range					5
Tempo				4	
Rhythm				4	
Diction/ Language			3		
Lyrical Flow				4	
Melismas			3		

Other notes: Intermediate to advanced-intermediate piece

Final Rating: 38

Rubric 4

I am in Need of Music
by Ben Moore

Scale of 1-5
Total score: 12-28 points easy, 28-44 points moderate, 44-60 points difficult

Technical Issue Addressed	Problem Solving Questions	Scale 1-5
Accompaniment	Is the accompaniment utilitarian, supportive, independent, etc.? Is the accompaniment part of the story line? Is the accompaniment descriptive (e.g. water figures, spinning wheel)?	4
Characterization/acting	Is the character appropriate to the student's dramatic capacity or life experiences? Will the student benefit from portraying this type of character?	2
Diction/articulation	Consideration of challenging consonant clusters. Closed position or difficult consonants on challenging pitches? Student's knowledge of French, Italian, Russian, German, etc. language or diction?	3
Dynamics	Is the singer expected to sing a pianissimo high note? Are the markings pedagogically helpful (e.g. crescendo on held notes to assist in breath energy and/or vibrancy)?	4
Melismatic phrases	Beginning or advanced melismas/melismatic phrases present? Appoggiatura? Dotted rhythms?	3
Musical considerations	Through composed? Strophic? Accessible harmonic language? Tonal? An enjoyable melody?	4
Range/tessitura	How are high notes approached (e.g. dramatically)? Is the range too vast? Is the tessitura too low or high? Can a young singer sit in that particular part of the voice for that long without fatiguing?	4
Registration	Does the piece assist in working through passaggio issues? Will the student carry weight up? Helpful vowels in an underdeveloped part of the student's voice? Etc.	4
Respiration	Are phrase lengths accessible? Will the breaths allow for renewal of positioning?	5
Text setting	Syllabic, Patter Song, Lyric? Does the text setting assist in memorization?	2
Vowels & vowel sequences	Observation of vowels in passaggio. Will vowel patterns assist in correcting vocal faults? Forward to back, tongue position, etc.?	3
Words: Poetry/lyrics/libretto	Is this accessible poetry? Is the story age appropriate? Will the text make the memorization process difficult?	2
Total score:		40

Using the Rubrics

Example 4: *Kommen und Scheiden* by Fanny Mendelssohn Hensel

The rhythmic accompaniment drives this song, helping the singer to find breath energy through vowels and consonants. Starting a high f-sharp on [z] will provoke a closed position; this must be addressed. The larger intervals in this piece require space that must not be compromised by the German consonants. Leaps must be made on the breath (supported), and the use of the wrong articulation muscles could interfere with this technique. A relaxed jaw and articulation with the lips, teeth and tongue are required. Long vocal lines with little time to breathe make breath management a priority, so care must be taken not to waste air on consonants. Pronunciation of German consonants at ends of long phrases is difficult.

- **Registration:** Leaps and arpeggios are found throughout song. [ɛ] and [e] vowels are present in passaggio.
- **Vowels &Vowel Sequences:** Vowels on higher pitches may be difficult: [i], [ɛ] and [e]. Vowel to vowel connection must be observed. Vowels may look difficult on the page for a younger student: ü, eu, ö,
- **Text Setting:** Difficult and advanced articulation throughout the song demands attention, including leaps and eighth notes.
- **Respiration:** Technically advanced leaps and long lines are found throughout.
- **Diction/Articulation:** The text setting is mostly syllabic throughout; pay careful attention to pronunciation on leaps and eighth note syllabic settings.
- **Musical Considerations:** The singer does not enter on a downbeat. Triplets and piano doubling are present throughout entire song.
- **Accompaniment:** The vocal line is doubled in the utilitarian accompaniment.
- **Melismatic phrases:** Triplets and piano doubling are present throughout the entire song.
- **Poetry/Lyrics/Libretto:** The accessible and charming poetry has a melancholy ending.
- **Dynamics:** *p* and *f* singing, diminuendos on high notes and crescendos require a student with significant skills.
- **Range/Tessitura:** Large leaps and skips are common. The piece sits high and in the passaggio.
- **Characterization/Acting:** The music guides the character through the emotions.

Example 4: *Kommen und Scheiden*

Rubric 1

Title: *Kommen und Scheiden*

Composer: Fanny Mendelssohn Hensel   Composition Date: 1896

Genre: Lieder   Language: German

Tempo: Allegretto   Key: A Major

	Beginning 1	Moderate 2	Advanced 3	Exceptionally Difficult 4	Score
Fundamental Objective/ Criteria	For beginning level instruction to aid in developing good basic vocal production.	For further development of vocal technique.	High level of technical ability needed to adequately perform.	Superb technical ability required to sufficiently study and perform.	
Tessitura			X		3
Melodic Line/Interval Leaps			X		3
Breathing			X		3
Rhythm		X			2
Piano Accompaniment		X			2
Poetic Text/Thematic Material	X				1
Overall Difficulty Level					**14**

Rubric 2

Piece: ***Kommen und Scheiden***
Composer: Fanny Mendelssohn Hensel   Year: 1896

Score, Anthology, or Book: 16 Songs, Fanny Mendelssohn Hensel, High

Publisher: Alfred Publishing Co., Inc.

Key: A Major   Language: German

Range: E to F-sharp   Tessitura: E to E

Voice Type: medium high or high voice   Tempo: Allegretto

Lyric or Conversational: Lyric   Student Level: Intermediate

	Simple	Moderate	Difficult
Rhythms	2		
Intervallic Leaps		3	
Phrase Length		3	
Vowel Sequence			5
Character	1		
Text/Poetry	1		
Diction		3	
Accompaniment -Support/Double	2		
Accompaniment -Playable/Fakeable	2		
Language		3	
Total			**25**

Rubric 3

Song Title: ***Kommen und Scheiden***
Composer: Fanny Mendelssohn Hensel
Publisher: Alfred Publishing Co., Inc.
Voice Part: Medium High or High Voice
Language: German
Range: E to F-sharp
Tessitura: E to E

	Beginner		Intermediate		Advanced
Registration				4	
Accompaniment Support	1				
Articulation			3		
Text Interpretation	1				
Phrase Length			3		
Range			3		
Tempo		2			
Rhythm		2			
Diction/Language			3		
Lyrical Flow				4	
Melismas		2			

Other notes: Intermediate to advanced-intermediate piece
Final Rating: 28

Rubric 4

Kommen und Scheiden
by Fanny Mendelssohn Hensel

Scale of 1-5
Total score: 12-28 points easy, 28-44 points moderate, 44-60 points difficult

Technical Issue Addressed	Problem Solving Questions	Scale 1-5
Accompaniment	Is the accompaniment utilitarian, supportive, independent, etc.? Is the accompaniment part of the story line? Is the accompaniment descriptive (e.g. water figures, spinning wheel)?	1
Characterization/acting	Is the character appropriate to the student's dramatic capacity or life experiences? Will the student benefit from portraying this type of character?	1
Diction/articulation	Consideration of challenging consonant clusters. Closed position or difficult consonants on challenging pitches? Student's knowledge of French, Italian, Russian, German, etc. language or diction?	4
Dynamics	Is the singer expected to sing a pianissimo high note? Are the markings pedagogically helpful (e.g. crescendo on held notes to assist in breath energy and/or vibrancy)?	3
Melismatic phrases	Beginning or advanced melismas/melismatic phrases present? Appoggiatura? Dotted rhythms?	1
Musical considerations	Through composed? Strophic? Accessible harmonic language? Tonal? An enjoyable melody?	3
Range/tessitura	How are high notes approached (e.g. dramatically)? Is the range too vast? Is the tessitura too low or high? Can a young singer sit in that particular part of the voice for that long without fatiguing?	4
Registration	Does the piece assist in working through passaggio issues? Will the student carry weight up? Helpful vowels in an underdeveloped part of the student's voice? Etc.	4
Respiration	Are phrase lengths accessible? Will the breaths allow for renewal of positioning?	4
Text setting	Syllabic, Patter Song, Lyric? Does the text setting assist in memorization?	3
Vowels & vowel sequences	Observation of vowels in passaggio. Will vowel patterns assist in correcting vocal faults? Forward to back, tongue position, etc.?	5
Words: Poetry/lyrics/libretto	Is this accessible poetry? Is the story age appropriate? Will the text make the memorization process difficult?	1
Total score:		**34**

Using the Rubrics

Example 5: *Ein goldenes Kettlein* by Joseph Marx

Ein goldenes Kettlein is a beautiful song with legato sections that allow for relaxed articulation. The faster and syllabic text setting requires attention. The melodic leaps are especially difficult because space must be prepared, and singers cannot allow German consonants to compromise the space required by vowels. Leaps must be made on the breath, and the use of the wrong articulation muscles could interfere with this technique. Higher pitches in this piece often begin with tricky consonants. Singers must be taught to pronounce German with as little effort as possible. Due to the range and varied dynamics, this song is recommended for an advanced-intermediate or advanced student.

- **Registration:** A solid technique is essential for the large range and leaps, especially up to high pitches.
- **Vowels &Vowel Sequences:** A few difficult vowels in the passaggio and above are found, especially ü on a high G-sharp.
- **Text Setting:** This is not a melodic setting of text; syllabic settings of the text on eighth and sixteenth notes can take away from the legato line.
- **Respiration:** Longer lines and catch breaths make this an advanced piece.
- **Diction/Articulation:** This piece is mostly syllabic in consonant-heavy German. Attention to articulation is crucial on tricky leaps and difficult consonants on high pitches, [k], [tr], [s], [n], [g].
- **Musical Considerations:** This through-composed piece includes a great number of accidentals. The melody is not simple, albeit beautiful. *p* and *f* singing, as well as crescendos and diminuendos are vital for the story.
- **Accompaniment:** The accompaniment often doubles the voice, but is busy and full of accidentals.
- **Melismatic phrases:** Not applicable.
- **Poetry/Lyrics/Libretto:** This is accessible but mature poetry.
- **Dynamics:** The melody and story demand *p* and *f* singing with diminuendos and crescendos.
- **Range/Tessitura:** The large leaps and expansive range require a technically advanced singer.
- **Characterization/Acting:** This text is mature but accessible.

Example 5: *Ein goldnes Kettlein*

Rubric 1

Title: *Ein goldenes Kettlein*
Composer: Joseph Marx   Composition Date: 1958

Genre: Lieder   Language: German

Tempo: Fließend   Key: A Major

	Beginning 1	Moderate 2	Advanced 3	Exceptionally Difficult 4	Score
Fundamental Objective/ Criteria	For beginning level instruction to aid in developing good basic vocal production.	For further development of vocal technique.	High level of technical ability needed to adequately perform.	Superb technical ability required to sufficiently study and perform.	
Tessitura				X	4
Melodic Line/Interval Leaps				X	4
Breathing			X		3
Rhythm			X		3
Piano Accompaniment			X		3
Poetic Text/Thematic Material			X		3
Overall Difficulty Level					**20**

Rubric 2

Piece: *Ein goldenes Kettlein*

Composer: Joseph Marx   Year: 1958

Score, Anthology, or Book: Songs of Joseph Marx, High Voice

Publisher: Hal Leonard

Key: A Major   Language: German

Range: D-sharp to G-sharp, expansive   Tessitura: F-sharp to F-sharp

Voice Type: high voice   Tempo: Fließend

Lyric or Conversational: Lyric   Student Level: Advanced Intermediate to Advanced

	Simple	Moderate	Difficult
Rhythms		3	
Intervallic Leaps			5
Phrase Length		3	
Vowel Sequence		4	
Character		3	
Text/Poetry		3	
Diction		4	
Accompaniment -Support/Double		4	
Accompaniment -Playable/Fakeable			5
Language		3	
Total			**37**

Rubric 3

Song Title: *Ein goldenes Kettlein*
Composer: Joseph Marx
Publisher: Hal Leonard
Voice Part: High Voice
Language: German
Range: D-sharp to G-sharp, expansive
Tessitura: F-sharp to F-sharp

	Beginner		Intermediate		Advanced
Registration					5
Accompaniment Support			3		
Articulation				4	
Text Interpretation			3		
Phrase Length			3		
Range					5
Tempo			3		
Rhythm			3		
Diction/ Language				4	
Lyrical Flow					5
Melismas	1				

Other notes: Intermediate to advanced-intermediate piece

Final Rating: 39

Rubric 4

Ein goldenes Kettlein
by Joseph Marx

Scale of 1-5
Total score: 12-28 points easy, 28-44 points moderate, 44-60 points difficult

Technical Issue Addressed	Problem Solving Questions	Scale 1-5
Accompaniment	Is the accompaniment utilitarian, supportive, independent, etc.? Is the accompaniment part of the story line? Is the accompaniment descriptive (e.g. water figures, spinning wheel)?	3
Characterization/acting	Is the character appropriate to the student's dramatic capacity or life experiences? Will the student benefit from portraying this type of character?	3
Diction/articulation	Consideration of challenging consonant clusters. Closed position or difficult consonants on challenging pitches? Student's knowledge of French, Italian, Russian, German, etc. language or diction?	4
Dynamics	Is the singer expected to sing a pianissimo high note? Are the markings pedagogically helpful (e.g. crescendo on held notes to assist in breath energy and/or vibrancy)?	3
Melismatic phrases	Beginning or advanced melismas/melismatic phrases present? Appoggiatura? Dotted rhythms?	1
Musical considerations	Through composed? Strophic? Accessible harmonic language? Tonal? An enjoyable melody?	4
Range/tessitura	How are high notes approached (e.g. dramatically)? Is the range too vast? Is the tessitura too low or high? Can a young singer sit in that particular part of the voice for that long without fatiguing?	5
Registration	Does the piece assist in working through passaggio issues? Will the student carry weight up? Helpful vowels in an underdeveloped part of the student's voice? Etc.	5
Respiration	Are phrase lengths accessible? Will the breaths allow for renewal of positioning?	3
Text setting	Syllabic, Patter Song, Lyric? Does the text setting assist in memorization?	4
Vowels & vowel sequences	Observation of vowels in passaggio. Will vowel patterns assist in correcting vocal faults? Forward to back, tongue position, etc.?	3
Words: Poetry/lyrics/libretto	Is this accessible poetry? Is the story age appropriate? Will the text make the memorization process difficult?	3
Total score:		41

Organizing repertoire

Once you have evaluated a number of pieces, you will need to find a way to catalog repertoire in your personal library for easy access. There are as many options for cataloging repertoire as there are songs to include, so personal preference plays a big part in your choices. Here are a few suggestions:

By Fach

If you have a large collection of repertoire, the quickest way to organize your collection is by Fach. You might prefer to have a bookshelf for each major Fach (Soprano, Mezzo, Tenor, Baritone, Bass). Your rubrics can be printed out and placed in a three-ring binder with dividers for each Fach, or you could save them on the computer in subfolders by Fach.

By Style/Era

Some examples include: Musical Theater, Pop, Rock, Baroque, Classical, or other genres. You also might use these as a sub-category.

By Level of Difficulty

Songs for beginners, intermediate and advanced singers can be separated. It may take a while, but if you give each piece a level as you assign it, you gradually can compile your repertoire in this way.

Developing a Teaching Plan Using Repertoire

Typically, a student will present with a number of technical deficiencies, which can be tackled through repertoire. Issues of breath, resonance, articulation and support can be addressed systematically and require prioritizing. In my own teaching, I have utilized a flow chart for the various components of vocal technique. These components are ordered according to the function and interrelation of the systems of voice production. Consider the following list, which is prioritized:

1. Relaxation, Posture, Alignment
2. Respiration
3. Phonation
4. Support
5. Registration
6. Resonance
7. Articulation

This list can be used to assist you in deciding which of the areas of study you wish to address first, through repertoire choices. While it is not necessary to follow this order, it is necessary to consider how the various functions or systems of the voice interact. Articulation problems, for instance, can be a result of poor breath management. It is possible to assign repertoire to deal with a breathing issue, and/or it is possible to assign repertoire to deal with an articulation issue, or both. It is imperative that teachers identify technical challenges and create a plan *before* assigning repertoire. Choosing pieces that help solve these challenges takes time, but ultimately makes acquisition of technique much more efficient. Begin with easier pieces and move to more difficult songs.

Creating Vocalises

It is important to present the repertoire in an interesting way that makes it appealing for the student. Next, it is effective to create vocalises based on the more challenging sections of each song assigned. Creating vocalises, which are assigned in advance of the repertoire, can foster self-assurance in the student. Vocalises that include the vowel sequences of the text, the dynamic markings of the phrases, the general melodic contour, and possibly the underlying harmony, can help pave the way to technical success.

Context

A brief discussion of the composer, the socio-political environment surrounding the song, and anecdotes can help a student take interest in the music being assigned. Give listening assignments at this point, and ask the student to create a "song profile."

Practice Plan

Presenting a practice plan for the new repertoire that encourages students to focus on one area or component at a time can also facilitate effective learning. Separating rhythm and melody and text at first, for instance, can make complicated vocal coordination more efficient. Text should be read without consideration of rhythm and melody, as a monologue or poem. Singing the melody on solfege is very beneficial. How many times a day should your student practice? How should the practice time be broken up?

Special Considerations

It has been said before but bears repeating: No two students are alike, and teachers need to teach to the specific skills and abilities of the individual student. However, most students can be grouped into one of the following categories:

Very young students

While most children start their private music education with Suzuki violin instruction or piano lessons, increasing numbers of parents are enrolling their young children in singing lessons as part of their after-school activities.

So how do you choose repertoire for younger children? Obviously they are too immature to start learning opera arias. Perhaps the best part of teaching very young children is their uncanny ability to memorize anything and everything quickly. Use this to your benefit in furthering their overall musical ability. The elementary school years are the ideal time to work on musicianship skills: basic ear training, pitch matching, rhythm repetition and note reading, for example. Older elementary students can be taught sight singing and basic harmony identification as well. If you teach very young students, reach out to their school music teachers to see what skills have been taught and expand from there.

Repertoire for very young children should be simple in structure with supportive accompaniment. Folk songs, Disney tunes, familiar tunes and various musical theater collections for children, which are widely available in various anthologies, are all good resources. For older elementary students, explore musical theater shows available in "Junior" versions, where the keys have been altered to fit the range and tessitura of children.

Preteen/Precollege

The preteen and teenage years are difficult for both young men and women, as the body is continually changing and growing. It is important to use repertoire that addresses vocal issues and does not harm the student's perception of self. Encouragement and support are important during these sensitive years.

Most preteen boys are considered soprano, alto, cambiata or baritone. Teenage boys will eventually settle into a general Fach in their mid to late teenage years. There will be significant breaks in the voice, but young men can successfully and happily sing through these changes as long as the teacher is flexible and understanding of their limited ranges. Choosing repertoire with a small range and comfortable tessitura is best for the student. Be flexible with the key of the piece chosen. One week the key of C Major might be best for a particular piece of music; the next week, D Major could be the only key that works. Allow for the students to sing an octave, fifth or third above or below the written melody; the vocal line may be altered as needed. At this time, the music must cater to the needs of the student. Assigning repertoire can be a challenge. Fortunately, there are vocal books available for the changing voice, musical theater books for teenage boys, and folk songs with limited ranges in various voice types (low, medium-low, medium, medium-high, high). For their later teenage years, accessible classical repertoire is available in various beginning anthologies for all voice types.

Although changes in young women's voices are less dramatic than that of young men, the challenges are still difficult. Preteen girls will experience register breaks, fatigue, and breathiness from both hormonal stages and underdevelopment of the phonation muscles. For most preteen girls, the head voice is weak, especially in a culture where popular music is chest-voice-dominant. It is wise to choose repertoire that facilitates vocal, musical and emotional development and allows her to feel confident despite the vocal changes she is facing. Folk songs with limited or appropriate ranges, musical theater pieces for teenage girls and simple classical songs in various languages with supported accompaniment are accommodating for this age group.

University singers & developing professionals

While university singers and developing professionals might not seem like a special consideration, they do present unique needs that should be discussed. These students experience significant stress in their daily lives as musicians. Juries, ensemble requirements, opera and musical theater audition pressures, peer analysis – all these situations compounded with school work and being away from family (some for the first time) can result in stress that influences their advancement in the studio. It is important as teachers of singing to guide our students with professional aspirations in all areas of career development. This includes developing confidence in their repertoire.

Mature adult singers

Teaching older students can be a rewarding opportunity for a voice instructor. Understanding the instrument will allow men and women to continue singing as long as they possibly can. Many of these students have been singing their entire lives and may continue to perform in their later years in church or community choirs, opera, or musical theater companies.

In many ways, your older students will follow a similar lesson plan to your very youngest students. Private music lessons give these students an opportunity to learn, or re-learn, basic skills that will help to improve their vocal and musical abilities. Work to instill confidence in students by teaching them how to read music, hear intervals, identify key changes, and even sight-sing.

Discuss repertoire choices to see what type of music they would enjoy singing. Look for collections of Big Band Favorites and to musical theater songs from the 1940s, 50s, and 60s. For students who are involved in a church choir, teach hymns so that technique is carried into their into their Sunday repertoire. Classical repertoire should be chosen with accessible melodies and supportive accompaniment.

Singers who are transitioning from one voice type to another
Perhaps the most difficult situation is a change of Fach. Many singers identify themselves by their Fach: changing from alto to soprano or baritone to tenor is more than changing repertoire; it's a change of identity. This is why it's so important for teachers to avoid rushing to label a student before it is truly necessary. It is perfectly acceptable for a young woman with a good ear for harmony to sing alto in choir while working on soprano art songs in lessons. Until students are ready to prepare arias for recitals or auditions for opera companies, there really is no need to label them with specific voice types.

Alto (or Mezzo) to Soprano
When you are working with a young woman transitioning from alto to soprano, the first steps will include re-balancing the middle range (passaggio) by bringing the head voice down and encouraging a lighter tone. You will likely need to dispel a fear of high notes, so avoiding songs with sustained high notes is a wise move. Songs with melismas and rhythmic passages can help lighten tone quality, and those that just touch rather than sustain upper pitches can help to build a singer's confidence. Suggestions are made for repertoire choices for these singers, as well as others, in the song index.

Baritone to Tenor
Similar to an alto transitioning to soprano, a young man transitioning from baritone to tenor will need to re-balance the middle range/passaggio and lighten his tone, as well as gain confidence that he can sing higher notes. The student also will need to transition to a brighter color across the range. Songs requiring flexible articulation are helpful in avoiding a laryngeal position that is not too low.

The Young Bass
A true bass is very rare. Basses have a different vocal color than baritones and bass-baritones, and there is a tendency for bass voices to be less flexible than higher voices because of the thickness of the vocal folds. As a result, young basses want to make their sound darker than necessary. This can lead to register violations and trouble balancing the middle and upper ranges.

Finding repertoire for a baby bass can be difficult and often requires transposition. Things to look for in repertoire include dotted rhythms, vowels [o], [u], [i] (or mixed vowels) around the passaggio to allow the voice to turn over, and masculine text (yet appropriate for the age range). A good range for pieces for a young bass would be A2 to A3.

Special Needs Singers
In both the academic setting and the private studio, a voice teacher may be presented

with the opportunity to teach special needs students or students with various disorders and disabilities. Many singers who face special challenges have an innate love of music and are especially receptive to what voice lessons have to offer. All people deserve an outlet for their creative side, and participation in music activities provides an outstanding opportunity for special learners to be a part of the action. It is important to remain flexible, as every student, even students with the same diagnosed disability, will have varying levels of needs.

Students with learning challenges should be taught individualized practice strategies to effectively learn repertoire. Some students may struggle to master technique and repertoire in traditional ways, so they need to be accommodated in whatever way possible. For example, some students may need to be taught repertoire aurally, rather than learning notes and lyrics from written music. It is important to learn about the singer's reading ability. Assigning a reading level that enables the learner to decode words and draw inference for understanding and sequencing is not always possible. You will need to engage your singers in conversation about the text if their ability to read for understanding and comprehension is compromised. Folk song texts are easy to understand and usually follow a predictable pattern. Look for these qualities in musical theater and classical repertoire for beginning students.

The lines and spaces of the musical staff present focus and visual distractions for many special learners and often hamper progress. Singing and speaking by rote or imitation phrase-by-phrase or responding to a recording of the teacher's voice is very beneficial for students with dyslexia. Separating text from musical rhythms and pitch is helpful. Students can learn to read rhythms with words, but it's important to explain how one word can stretch over several notes and that words have syllables, which may or may not have different rhythmic and melodic features. Getting the student "off the page" as soon as possible is imperative. Present the student with a roadmap to learn the texts. Sequencing may be applied to teaching and learning repertoire:

1. Have students repeat after you measure by measure.
2. Repeat the text with students until it is almost memorized.
3. Speak the text using the rhythm of the melody.
4. Speak the text in rhythm, using ascending or descending pitches that follow the melody.
5. Apply the text to the melody.
6. Combine measure by measure, phrase by phrase.

Other Repertoire Considerations

Operatic Arias

Before one can establish whether a student's voice is light or lyric or dramatic, there is a stage when it is very difficult to assign operatic arias. Arias should be graduated and diversified according to the technical and expressive difficulties they pose. The indexes provided in this book suggest easier arias suitable for collegiate singers, which are good replacements for those from the standard repertoire that so widely are assigned in colleges, universities and private studios. If we analyze these arias, such as *Deh vieni, non tardar*, *Porgi amor*, *Voi che sapete*, or *Se vuol ballare*, we find that they actually exceed the technical abilities of many young singers.

Musical Theater

The call of Broadway to young singers across the United States has never been stronger. All across America, high schools are mounting musical theater productions and creating local stars with dreams of "making it" in New York. Interest in musical theater has resulted in TV shows, including *Pushing Daisies*, *Glee*, and *Smash*, and movie productions of Broadway hits such as *Les Miserables* and *The Sound of Music*. Many private studios are full of students who want to learn to sing like a Broadway star.

Musical theater repertoire has significant benefits. The speech-derived production assists with resonance, tone and overall production. For many students, there is an instant engagement to the music and its more modern sound. The repertoire covers a wide variety of subject areas and can help develop characterization skills.

When assigning repertoire, be reminded of our first commitment—to do no harm. Avoid teaching belting techniques until you have received adequate training from an experienced teacher of belting. Musical theater repertoire written before 1970 focuses more on legit singing. Contemporary musical theater repertoire often requires belting or chest-voice-dominant singing. Musical Theater is not a single vocal style, but encompasses the entire gamut from classical to rock-and-roll.

For the beginning classical student who may have experience singing other genres of music, it is advantageous to assign a classical piece and a musical theater piece that will achieve the same goal. Goals of technique and expression can be carried into both pieces. This is especially beneficial for the crossover student (see example 6a-b).

Sebben, crudele and *Many a New Day* are two examples that inform each other in vocal studies. Both songs are marked *grazioso* and have various ascending leaps and chromaticism.

Example 6a: *Sebben crudele*

Example 6b: Many a New Day

The wider leaps in Many a New Day can be sung more effectively when prepared by the stepwise ascending and descending lines in *Sebben, crudele*.

20th & 21st Century

Not all modern repertoire is inaccessible, and much of it is unexplored. Composers to consider when looking for current works include:
- Ricky Ian Gordon – pop/musical theater influenced
- William Finn – pop/musical theater crossover
- Maury Yeston – musical theater crossover
- Jake Heggie – jazz influenced
- Richard Hundley – a number of beautiful, accessible songs
- Lori Laitman – generally for more advanced students
- Libby Larsen – a wide variety of difficulty levels

The How-To Chapter

Choosing the right repertoire for each student requires some detailed analysis. The analysis protocol takes into consideration seven musical values:
- melodic contour
- phrasing
- language
- rhythm
- accompaniment
- harmonic language
- dynamics

Each of these values could be utilized in a difficulty rating system.

Melodic Contour

The melodic contour may be the most significant indicator of a song's difficulty. Narrow ranges make fewer vocal demands than wider ranges. High tessitura challenges the student's ability to sing a unified scale. Disjunct motion further stretches basic vocal skills.

Phrasing

Phrasing places demands on another basic vocal skill: breath management. Most young singers have no difficulty singing four- to six-second phrases. They experience moderate difficulty in singing phrases of six to ten seconds in length; only more advanced singers can manage the breath demands of phrases lasting ten seconds or longer. Some fast songs leave little time to breathe, thereby adding value to this element.

Rhythm

Melodies of moderate speed, with minimal demands placed upon articulation, present fewer difficulties to a young singer, while melodies requiring either fast or sustained articulation present more challenges. Changing meters, cross rhythms, hemeolas, and other rhythmic devices add to the overall rhythmic complexity of a song.

Text

Issues of articulation, including jaw, tongue and lip tension, can be corrected with carefully chosen texts. Voiced and unvoiced consonants, pure vowels, diphthongs, syllabic and vocalic text settings, elisions, and onsets and offsets are just a few things to be considered in this area. Assignment of foreign language texts requires additional consideration. The various subsystems of voice (respiratory, phonatory, articulatory, etc.) are greatly affected by a singer's knowledge of the meaning of the text. Specific mastery of translation is essential for efficient vocal function. In other words, rhythm, respiration and diction are adversely affected if the singer does not have a clear mental picture of each word he is singing.

Accompaniment

Accompaniment patterns generally fall into three categories: imitative, supportive, and independent. Accompaniments that mirror the melody, exactly or approximately, simplify the task of singing the melody. Patterns that support the melodic line without imitating the melody require young singers to be more musically autonomous. Independent, even antagonistic, accompaniments require the singer's musical self-reliance.

Harmonic language

The harmonic language of a song—diatonic chromatic, or atonal—plays an important role in the ability of a young singer to successfully perform it. The more complex the harmonic language, the more developed must be the young singer's musicianship. Singers' comprehension of the harmonic language can help them achieve a wider variety of vocal colors and understand the overall structure of the piece.

Dynamics

If singers are to perform as the composer intended, dynamics must play a part in the equation. It is important to consider how dynamics can affect vocal functions. For example, the teacher who is striving to balance registration in a young voice will do well to consider the dynamics required by the composer in a given song or aria.

Songs for Improving Registration

This analysis protocol also takes into consideration six technical values: Breath, Support, Phonation, Registration, Resonance, and Articulation. Additionally, emotional expression and several other areas are evaluated.

Things to look for:

A limited range is helpful when working through registration issues. Look for melodies that work between the passaggi for females, and below the passaggio for males, as well as melodies that skip over the passaggi. Accommodating repertoire will allow the singer to reset the breath regularly. Descending stepwise lines are less fatiguing and encourage bringing head resonance down into the lower pitches. When selecting repertoire, be mindful of which vowels are most common and where they fall in the singer's range. For example, [u] is primarily a head-dominant vowel, whereas [a] is primarily a chest-dominant vowel. A piece that requires a more speech-like approach in the lower range could be helpful for accessing chest voice to strengthen the middle range. Dotted rhythms and staccati encourage lightening of the voice.

Caro mio ben by Giuseppe Giordani

Scale of 1-5
Total score: 12-28 points easy, 28-44 points moderate, 44-60 points difficult

Technical Issue Addressed	Problem Solving Questions	Scale 1-5
Accompaniment	Is the accompaniment utilitarian, supportive, independent, etc.? Is the accompaniment part of the story line? Is the accompaniment descriptive (e.g. water figures, spinning wheel)?	2
Characterization/acting	Is the character appropriate to the student's dramatic capacity or life experiences? Will the student benefit from portraying this type of character?	2
Diction/articulation	Consideration of challenging consonant clusters. Closed position or difficult consonants on challenging pitches? Student's knowledge of French, Italian, Russian, German, etc. language or diction?	3
Dynamics	Is the singer expected to sing a pianissimo high note? Are the markings pedagogically helpful (e.g. crescendo on held notes to assist in breath energy and/or vibrancy)?	3
Melismatic phrases	Beginning or advanced melismas/melismatic phrases present? Appoggiatura? Dotted rhythms?	1
Musical considerations	Through composed? Strophic? Accessible harmonic language? Tonal? An enjoyable melody?	2
Range/tessitura	How are high notes approached (e.g. dramatically)? Is the range too vast? Is the tessitura too low or high? Can a young singer sit in that particular part of the voice for that long without fatiguing?	2
Registration	Is the accompaniment utilitarian, supportive, independent, etc.? Is the accompaniment part of the story line? Is the accompaniment descriptive (e.g. water figures, spinning wheel)?	3
Respiration	Are phrase lengths accessible? Will the breaths allow for renewal of positioning?	2
Text setting	Syllabic, Patter Song, Lyric? Does the text setting assist in memorization?	2
Vowels & vowel sequences	Observation of vowels in passaggio. Will vowel patterns assist in correcting vocal faults? Forward to back, tongue position, etc.?	3
Words: Poetry/lyrics/libretto	Is this accessible poetry? Is the story age appropriate? Will the text make the memorization process difficult?	2
Total score:		27

The downward motion of the vocal line helps develop the middle register and blend it with the upper. The rising melodic sequence of the B section gives time for singers to reset the breath before ascending. The vowel sequencing naturally helps registration. TIP: To build confidence in your students, take patterns out of the songs you assign and use them as vocalises.

Example 7: *Caro mio ben*

Lydia by Gabriel Fauré

Scale of 1-5
Total score: 12-28 points easy, 28-44 points moderate, 44-60 points difficult

Technical Issue Addressed	Problem Solving Questions	Scale 1-5
Accompaniment	Is the accompaniment utilitarian, supportive, independent, etc.? Is the accompaniment part of the story line? Is the accompaniment descriptive (e.g. water figures, spinning wheel)?	2
Characterization/acting	Is the character appropriate to the student's dramatic capacity or life experiences? Will the student benefit from portraying this type of character?	2
Diction/articulation	Consideration of challenging consonant clusters. Closed position or difficult consonants on challenging pitches? Student's knowledge of French, Italian, Russian, German, etc. language or diction?	3
Dynamics	Is the singer expected to sing a pianissimo high note? Are the markings pedagogically helpful (e.g. crescendo on held notes to assist in breath energy and/or vibrancy)?	3
Melismatic phrases	Beginning or advanced melismas/melismatic phrases present? Appoggiatura? Dotted rhythms?	2
Musical considerations	Through composed? Strophic? Accessible harmonic language? Tonal? An enjoyable melody?	3
Range/tessitura	How are high notes approached (e.g. dramatically)? Is the range too vast? Is the tessitura too low or high? Can a young singer sit in that particular part of the voice for that long without fatiguing?	2
Registration	Does the piece assist in working through passaggio issues? Will the student carry weight up? Helpful vowels in an underdeveloped part of the student's voice? Etc.	2
Respiration	Are phrase lengths accessible? Will the breaths allow for renewal of positioning?	4
Text setting	Syllabic, Patter Song, Lyric? Does the text setting assist in memorization?	3
Vowels & vowel sequences	Observation of vowels in passaggio. Will vowel patterns assist in correcting vocal faults? Forward to back, tongue position, etc.?	2
Words: Poetry/lyrics/libretto	Is this accessible poetry? Is the story age appropriate? Will the text make the memorization process difficult?	2
Total score:		**30**

This is an excellent piece for working through the passaggio in male voices. The vowel sequences are especially helpful when balancing registration. Also, frequent closed vowels in the higher range are ideal (as shown in Example 8). The range is one octave. The tessitura is medium high, and there are steps and small skips throughout. The dynamics vary from *p* to *mf*. The French is not extremely difficult, but is syllabic and fairly wordy and requires some prior knowledge of the language for ease of articulation. The vocal line is doubled in the piano, building confidence in an insecure musician.

Example 8: *Lydia*

Mädchen mit dem Rothen Mündchen by Robert Franz

Scale of 1-5
Total score: 12-28 points easy, 28-44 points moderate, 44-60 points difficult

Technical Issue Addressed	Problem Solving Questions	Scale 1-5
Accompaniment	Is the accompaniment utilitarian, supportive, independent, etc.? Is the accompaniment part of the story line? Is the accompaniment descriptive (e.g. water figures, spinning wheel)?	3
Characterization/acting	Is the character appropriate to the student's dramatic capacity or life experiences? Will the student benefit from portraying this type of character?	2
Diction/articulation	Consideration of challenging consonant clusters. Closed position or difficult consonants on challenging pitches? Student's knowledge of French, Italian, Russian, German, etc. language or diction?	3
Dynamics	Is the singer expected to sing a pianissimo high note? Are the markings pedagogically helpful (e.g. crescendo on held notes to assist in breath energy and/or vibrancy)?	3
Melismatic phrases	Beginning or advanced melismas/melismatic phrases present? Appoggiatura? Dotted rhythms?	1
Musical considerations	Through composed? Strophic? Accessible harmonic language? Tonal? An enjoyable melody?	2
Range/tessitura	How are high notes approached (e.g. dramatically)? Is the range too vast? Is the tessitura too low or high? Can a young singer sit in that particular part of the voice for that long without fatiguing?	3
Registration	Does the piece assist in working through passaggio issues? Will the student carry weight up? Helpful vowels in an underdeveloped part of the student's voice? Etc.	2
Respiration	Are phrase lengths accessible? Will the breaths allow for renewal of positioning?	2
Text setting	Syllabic, Patter Song, Lyric? Does the text setting assist in memorization?	2
Vowels & vowel sequences	Observation of vowels in passaggio. Will vowel patterns assist in correcting vocal faults? Forward to back, tongue position, etc.?	3
Words: Poetry/lyrics/libretto	Is this accessible poetry? Is the story age appropriate? Will the text make the memorization process difficult?	2
Total score:		**28**

Mädchen mit dem Rothen Mündchen is an intermediate lied, available in many keys. When in G minor, the octave range makes it an ideal song for dealing with registration. The descending melodic line assists in bringing the head voice down into the middle voice. The phrases are short. The dynamic indications, especially where the composer asks for a crescendo as the line descends, are beneficial in balancing registration. The piece also aids in legato and resonance.

Example 9: *Mädchen mit dem Rothen Mündchen*

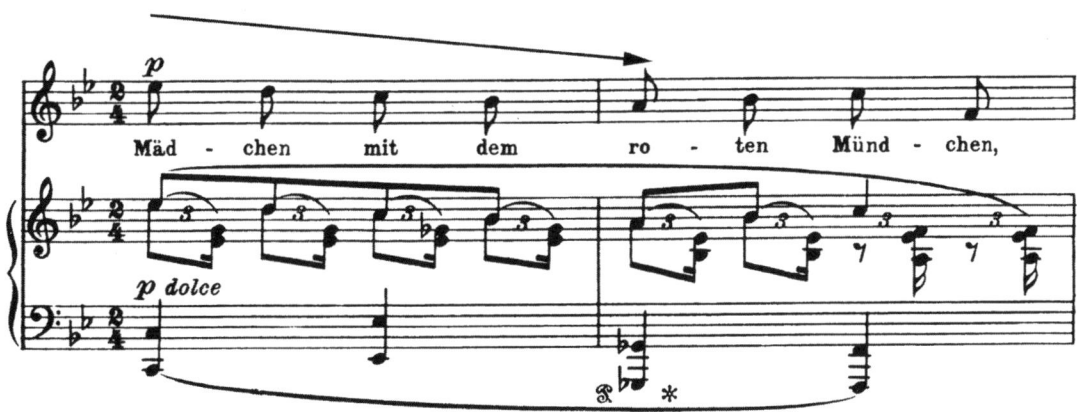

Ch'io mai vi possa by G.F. Handel

Scale of 1-5
Total score: 12-28 points easy, 28-44 points moderate, 44-60 points difficult

Technical Issue Addressed	Problem Solving Questions	Scale 1-5
Accompaniment	Is the accompaniment utilitarian, supportive, independent, etc.? Is the accompaniment part of the story line? Is the accompaniment descriptive (e.g. water figures, spinning wheel)?	3
Characterization/acting	Is the character appropriate to the student's dramatic capacity or life experiences? Will the student benefit from portraying this type of character?	2
Diction/articulation	Consideration of challenging consonant clusters. Closed position or difficult consonants on challenging pitches? Student's knowledge of French, Italian, Russian, German, etc. language or diction?	3
Dynamics	Is the singer expected to sing a pianissimo high note? Are the markings pedagogically helpful (e.g. crescendo on held notes to assist in breath energy and/or vibrancy)?	2
Melismatic phrases	Beginning or advanced melismas/melismatic phrases present? Appoggiatura? Dotted rhythms?	4
Musical considerations	Through composed? Strophic? Accessible harmonic language? Tonal? An enjoyable melody?	3
Range/tessitura	How are high notes approached (e.g. dramatically)? Is the range too vast? Is the tessitura too low or high? Can a young singer sit in that particular part of the voice for that long without fatiguing?	4
Registration	Is the accompaniment utilitarian, supportive, independent, etc.? Is the accompaniment part of the story line? Is the accompaniment descriptive (e.g. water figures, spinning wheel)?	3
Respiration	Are phrase lengths accessible? Will the breaths allow for renewal of positioning?	3
Text setting	Syllabic, Patter Song, Lyric? Does the text setting assist in memorization?	2
Vowels & vowel sequences	Observation of vowels in passaggio. Will vowel patterns assist in correcting vocal faults? Forward to back, tongue position, etc.?	3
Words: Poetry/lyrics/libretto	Is this accessible poetry? Is the story age appropriate? Will the text make the memorization process difficult?	2
Total score:		34

Ch'io mai vi possa from *Siroe* is an early Italian Aria for an intermediate soprano. The range G4 to E-flat5 serves the pedagogical purpose of registration, with descending scales and the alternating ascending and descending melodic idea (Example 10a). Most of the vowels in the upper passaggio are helpful. Breath, flexibility and ornamentation are also explored. Be sure to assign this aria to a mature musician, as tuning may be difficult with the changing tonality in the middle sections. Large leaps and melismatic writing require a secure technique (Example 10).

Example 10a: *Ch'io mai vi possa*

Example 10b: *Ch'io mai vi possa*

Songs for Improving Breathing and Support

Things to look for:

Choose repertoire with phrases where it is easy to add breaths and then take them out gradually, as the singer is ready. The singer needs enough time to reset the breath between phrases. Notice the structure where the phrase lengths build, such as two, two-bar phrases followed by a four-bar phrase. Triplet rhythms are helpful, as the breath energizes and moves. Mixed meters make it difficult for young singers to predict breath timing.

Caro mio ben by Giuseppe Giordani

Scale of 1-5
Total score: 12-28 points easy, 28-44 points moderate, 44-60 points difficult

Technical Issue Addressed	Problem Solving Questions	Scale 1-5
Accompaniment	Is the accompaniment utilitarian, supportive, independent, etc.? Is the accompaniment part of the story line? Is the accompaniment descriptive (e.g. water figures, spinning wheel)?	2
Characterization/acting	Is the character appropriate to the student's dramatic capacity or life experiences? Will the student benefit from portraying this type of character?	2
Diction/articulation	Consideration of challenging consonant clusters. Closed position or difficult consonants on challenging pitches? Student's knowledge of French, Italian, Russian, German, etc. language or diction?	3
Dynamics	Is the singer expected to sing a pianissimo high note? Are the markings pedagogically helpful (e.g. crescendo on held notes to assist in breath energy and/or vibrancy)?	3
Melismatic phrases	Beginning or advanced melismas/melismatic phrases present? Appoggiatura? Dotted rhythms?	1
Musical considerations	Through composed? Strophic? Accessible harmonic language? Tonal? An enjoyable melody?	2
Range/tessitura	How are high notes approached (e.g. dramatically)? Is the range too vast? Is the tessitura too low or high? Can a young singer sit in that particular part of the voice for that long without fatiguing?	2
Registration	Does the piece assist in working through passaggio issues? Will the student carry weight up? Helpful vowels in an underdeveloped part of the student's voice? Etc.	3
Respiration	Are phrase lengths accessible? Will the breaths allow for renewal of positioning?	2
Text setting	Syllabic, Patter Song, Lyric? Does the text setting assist in memorization?	2
Vowels & vowel sequences	Observation of vowels in passaggio. Will vowel patterns assist in correcting vocal faults? Forward to back, tongue position, etc.?	3
Words: Poetry/lyrics/libretto	Is this accessible poetry? Is the story age appropriate? Will the text make the memorization process difficult?	2
Total score:		27

The rising melodic sequence of the B section gives time for singers to reset their breath before ascending. Add breaths, and then take them out as ability improves. As shown in Example 11, initially breathing can be managed as: *Il tuo fedel*, (breath) *sospira ognor*, (breath) *Cessa crudel* (breath) *tanto rigor!* As skill is developed, that strategy can change to: *Il tuo fedel sospira ognor,* (breath) *Cessa crudel, tanto rigor!*

Example 11: *Caro mio ben*

Songs for Improving Phonation and Resonance

Things to look for:

Sustained notes and good vowel sequencing give the singer time to adjust and enhance resonance. For the voice that is lacking in focus, you can use songs with specific combinations of vowels and consonants to remedy this issue. Search for songs that encourage balanced onsets. A singer who displays an aspirated onset would be greatly assisted by the [m], [n] and [v] preceding consonants in the opening phrases, as well as the gentle melodic ascent. Consider using language as a tool to encourage the resonance you are trying to cultivate. Each language is unique, in terms of where it resonates. Speaking Italian feels very different from speaking German. Onsets are of extreme importance, as are offsets.

Lydia by Gabriel Fauré

Scale of 1-5
Total score: 12-28 points easy, 28-44 points moderate, 44-60 points difficult

Technical Issue Addressed	Problem Solving Questions	Scale 1-5
Accompaniment	Is the accompaniment utilitarian, supportive, independent, etc.? Is the accompaniment part of the story line? Is the accompaniment descriptive (e.g. water figures, spinning wheel)?	2
Characterization/acting	Is the character appropriate to the student's dramatic capacity or life experiences? Will the student benefit from portraying this type of character?	2
Diction/articulation	Consideration of challenging consonant clusters. Closed position or difficult consonants on challenging pitches? Student's knowledge of French, Italian, Russian, German, etc. language or diction?	3
Dynamics	Is the singer expected to sing a pianissimo high note? Are the markings pedagogically helpful (e.g. crescendo on held notes to assist in breath energy and/or vibrancy)?	3
Melismatic phrases	Beginning or advanced melismas/melismatic phrases present? Appoggiatura? Dotted rhythms?	2
Musical considerations	Through composed? Strophic? Accessible harmonic language? Tonal? An enjoyable melody?	3
Range/tessitura	How are high notes approached (e.g. dramatically)? Is the range too vast? Is the tessitura too low or high? Can a young singer sit in that particular part of the voice for that long without fatiguing?	2
Registration	Does the piece assist in working through passaggio issues? Will the student carry weight up? Helpful vowels in an underdeveloped part of the student's voice? Etc.	2
Respiration	Are phrase lengths accessible? Will the breaths allow for renewal of positioning?	4
Text setting	Syllabic, Patter Song, Lyric? Does the text setting assist in memorization?	3
Vowels & vowel sequences	Observation of vowels in passaggio. Will vowel patterns assist in correcting vocal faults? Forward to back, tongue position, etc.?	2
Words: Poetry/lyrics/libretto	Is this accessible poetry? Is the story age appropriate? Will the text make the memorization process difficult?	2
Total score:		30

Long, sustained notes help teach vowel purity. The vowel sequence within the text influences resonance; here, it would bring focus to the sound. Nasal vowels can assist in teaching focus: *Lydia* (a is held) sur tes rose joues (u is held). *Lydia* also assists in teaching articulation. Again, the French is not extremely difficult, but is syllabic and fairly wordy and requires some prior knowledge of the language for ease of articulation. Observe the number of syllables in Example 12, and the legato that is required.

Example 12: *Lydia*

Non vogl'io se non vederti by Giuseppe Giordani

Scale of 1-5
Total score: 12-28 points easy, 28-44 points moderate, 44-60 points difficult

Technical Issue Addressed	Problem Solving Questions	Scale 1-5
Accompaniment	Is the accompaniment utilitarian, supportive, independent, etc.? Is the accompaniment part of the story line? Is the accompaniment descriptive (e.g. water figures, spinning wheel)?	2
Characterization/acting	Is the character appropriate to the student's dramatic capacity or life experiences? Will the student benefit from portraying this type of character?	2
Diction/articulation	Consideration of challenging consonant clusters. Closed position or difficult consonants on challenging pitches? Student's knowledge of French, Italian, Russian, German, etc. language or diction?	3
Dynamics	Is the singer expected to sing a pianissimo high note? Are the markings pedagogically helpful (e.g. crescendo on held notes to assist in breath energy and/or vibrancy)?	2
Melismatic phrases	Beginning or advanced melismas/melismatic phrases present? Appoggiatura? Dotted rhythms?	2
Musical considerations	Through composed? Strophic? Accessible harmonic language? Tonal? An enjoyable melody?	2
Range/tessitura	How are high notes approached (e.g. dramatically)? Is the range too vast? Is the tessitura too low or high? Can a young singer sit in that particular part of the voice for that long without fatiguing?	2
Registration	Does the piece assist in working through passaggio issues? Will the student carry weight up? Helpful vowels in an underdeveloped part of the student's voice? Etc.	2
Respiration	Are phrase lengths accessible? Will the breaths allow for renewal of positioning?	3
Text setting	Syllabic, Patter Song, Lyric? Does the text setting assist in memorization?	3
Vowels & vowel sequences	Observation of vowels in passaggio. Will vowel patterns assist in correcting vocal faults? Forward to back, tongue position, etc.?	3
Words: Poetry/lyrics/libretto	Is this accessible poetry? Is the story age appropriate? Will the text make the memorization process difficult?	2
Total score:		**28**

The text, with its various consonants and vowel combinations, is ideal to help develop a resonant core. The variety of voiced consonants is perfect for teaching balanced onset.

Example 13: *Non vogl'io se non vederti*

Si, tra i ceppi by G. F. Handel

Scale of 1-5
Total score: 12-28 points easy, 28-44 points moderate, 44-60 points difficult

Technical Issue Addressed	Problem Solving Questions	Scale 1-5
Accompaniment	Is the accompaniment utilitarian, supportive, independent, etc.? Is the accompaniment part of the story line? Is the accompaniment descriptive (e.g. water figures, spinning wheel)?	3
Characterization/acting	Is the character appropriate to the student's dramatic capacity or life experiences? Will the student benefit from portraying this type of character?	3
Diction/articulation	Consideration of challenging consonant clusters. Closed position or difficult consonants on challenging pitches? Student's knowledge of French, Italian, Russian, German, etc. language or diction?	3
Dynamics	Is the singer expected to sing a pianissimo high note? Are the markings pedagogically helpful (e.g. crescendo on held notes to assist in breath energy and/or vibrancy)?	2
Melismatic phrases	Beginning or advanced melismas/melismatic phrases present? Appoggiatura? Dotted rhythms?	4
Musical considerations	Through composed? Strophic? Accessible harmonic language? Tonal? An enjoyable melody?	3
Range/tessitura	How are high notes approached (e.g. dramatically)? Is the range too vast? Is the tessitura too low or high? Can a young singer sit in that particular part of the voice for that long without fatiguing?	4
Registration	Does the piece assist in working through passaggio issues? Will the student carry weight up? Helpful vowels in an underdeveloped part of the student's voice? Etc.	4
Respiration	Are phrase lengths accessible? Will the breaths allow for renewal of positioning?	4
Text setting	Syllabic, Patter Song, Lyric? Does the text setting assist in memorization?	3
Vowels & vowel sequences	Observation of vowels in passaggio. Will vowel patterns assist in correcting vocal faults? Forward to back, tongue position, etc.?	4
Words: Poetry/lyrics/libretto	Is this accessible poetry? Is the story age appropriate? Will the text make the memorization process difficult?	3
Total Score:		40

Si, tra i ceppi is an early Italian Aria in C Major, suitable for a baritone or bass. The reiterated [a], as shown in Example 14, requires consistent balance in resonance on a variety of pitches. Descending phrases assist the middle voice. The tessitura lies between B2 and D4. The large intervallic leaps are more suitable for an intermediate to advanced student. Style is taught, as well as agility and ornamentation.

Example 14: *Si, tra i ceppi*

Songs for Improving Articulation

Things to look for:

If students are ready, challenge them with lots of text. Or, select a piece that allows them to enjoy and explore the way the language works. Consider how certain consonants help the voice. For example, [k] raises the soft palate and [g] lowers the larynx. The jaw and the tongue should operate independently. Aim to unite articulation with vowel production.

Bei der Wiege by Felix Mendelssohn

Example 15: *Bei der Wiege*

Scale of 1-5
Total score: 12-28 points easy, 28-44 points moderate, 44-60 points difficult

Technical Issue Addressed	Problem Solving Questions	Scale 1-5
Accompaniment	Is the accompaniment utilitarian, supportive, independent, etc.? Is the accompaniment part of the story line? Is the accompaniment descriptive (e.g. water figures, spinning wheel)?	2
Characterization/acting	Is the character appropriate to the student's dramatic capacity or life experiences? Will the student benefit from portraying this type of character?	1
Diction/articulation	Consideration of challenging consonant clusters. Closed position or difficult consonants on challenging pitches? Student's knowledge of French, Italian, Russian, German, etc. language or diction?	4
Dynamics	Is the singer expected to sing a pianissimo high note? Are the markings pedagogically helpful (e.g. crescendo on held notes to assist in breath energy and/or vibrancy)?	2
Melismatic phrases	Beginning or advanced melismas/melismatic phrases present? Appoggiatura? Dotted rhythms?	1
Musical considerations	Through composed? Strophic? Accessible harmonic language? Tonal? An enjoyable melody?	2
Range/tessitura	How are high notes approached (e.g. dramatically)? Is the range too vast? Is the tessitura too low or high? Can a young singer sit in that particular part of the voice for that long without fatiguing?	2
Registration	Does the piece assist in working through passaggio issues? Will the student carry weight up? Helpful vowels in an underdeveloped part of the student's voice? Etc.	2
Respiration	Are phrase lengths accessible? Will the breaths allow for renewal of positioning?	3
Text setting	Syllabic, Patter Song, Lyric? Does the text setting assist in memorization?	4
Vowels & vowel sequences	Observation of vowels in passaggio. Will vowel patterns assist in correcting vocal faults? Forward to back, tongue position, etc.?	3
Words: Poetry/lyrics/libretto	Is this accessible poetry? Is the story age appropriate? Will the text make the memorization process difficult?	1
Total score:		27

This syllabic piece requires the singer to pronounce quickly on 8th and 16th notes, as shown in Example 15. German consonants can bring about issues in breath management if articulated incorrectly. Vowel to vowel connection can be difficult with syllabic settings and consonant clusters. Make sure the tongue is free, the lips are rounded, the space is adequate, and the laryngeal position is free and somewhat stabilized. Take care that the student's jaw is free during articulation. Coordinating this type of articulation (which must also be worked through in English) requires specific and detailed instruction. Practice [n] to [k] (*von kommen*) by instructing student to pronounce [n] with tongue then [k] by the molars with only the tongue. Another issue with this piece is articulation of consonants at *p* dynamic levels and controlled singing. A young student may still be in the process of learning to sing quietly with appropriate breath energy.

Songs for Encouraging Expression

Things to look for:
Songs that are narrative, or texts that have clear narrators, are helpful to beginning storytellers. Songs that are funny or outwardly emotional in some way, or that have a personal connection to the student, also are useful. Songs that appear more difficult than they actually are can be attractive to students.

I Wish it so by Marc Blitzstein from the musical *Juno*

Scale of 1-5
Total score: 12-28 points easy, 28-44 points moderate, 44-60 points difficult

Technical Issue Addressed	Problem Solving Questions	Scale 1-5
Accompaniment	Is the accompaniment utilitarian, supportive, independent, etc.? Is the accompaniment part of the story line? Is the accompaniment descriptive (e.g. water figures, spinning wheel)?	2
Characterization/acting	Is the character appropriate to the student's dramatic capacity or life experiences? Will the student benefit from portraying this type of character?	1
Diction/articulation	Consideration of challenging consonant clusters. Closed position or difficult consonants on challenging pitches? Student's knowledge of French, Italian, Russian, German, etc. language or diction?	2
Dynamics	Is the singer expected to sing a pianissimo high note? Are the markings pedagogically helpful (e.g. crescendo on held notes to assist in breath energy and/or vibrancy)?	2
Melismatic phrases	Beginning or advanced melismas/melismatic phrases present? Appoggiatura? Dotted rhythms?	1
Musical considerations	Through composed? Strophic? Accessible harmonic language? Tonal? An enjoyable melody?	2
Range/tessitura	How are high notes approached (e.g. dramatically)? Is the range too vast? Is the tessitura too low or high? Can a young singer sit in that particular part of the voice for that long without fatiguing?	3
Registration	Does the piece assist in working through passaggio issues? Will the student carry weight up? Helpful vowels in an underdeveloped part of the student's voice? Etc.	3
Respiration	Are phrase lengths accessible? Will the breaths allow for renewal of positioning?	2
Text setting	Syllabic, Patter Song, Lyric? Does the text setting assist in memorization?	1
Vowels & vowel sequences	Observation of vowels in passaggio. Will vowel patterns assist in correcting vocal faults? Forward to back, tongue position, etc.?	2
Words: Poetry/lyrics/libretto	Is this accessible poetry? Is the story age appropriate? Will the text make the memorization process difficult?	1
Total score:		22

There are varied dynamic levels, meter changes, ritards, diminuendos, and crescendos, which help to develop expression and emotional connection, as can be seen from the excerpt in Example 16. These markings written in for the singer will guide the student. The accompaniment is straightforward and helpful for the singer. This song has accessible lyrics and an engaging storyline.

Example 16: I Wish it So

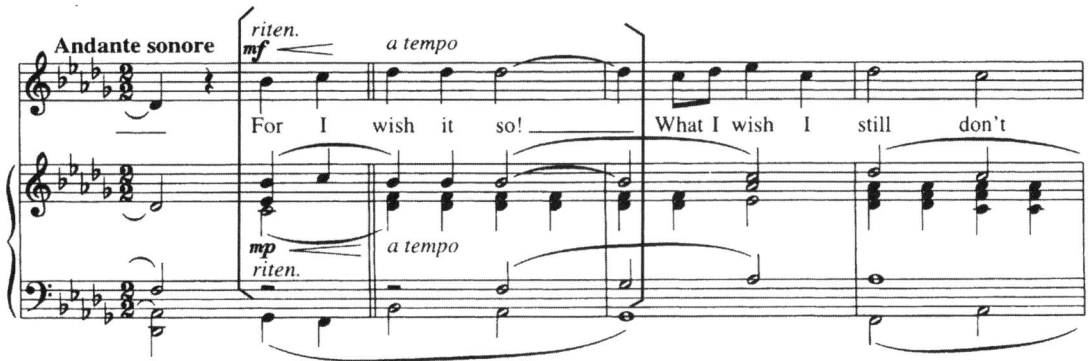

Songs that are Melodically/Harmonically Accessible

Things to look for:
 Well-known and lyrical melodies with simple and supportive accompaniments are best for building a musical ear and confidence. Intervallic leaps of a major third or less are the least difficult. Remember: Simple melodies allow you and your student to focus on technical aspects. If the singer knows where the harmony is going, he will find breath management more accessible.

Greensleeves arranged by Philip Kern

Example 17: Greensleeves

Scale of 1-5
Total score: 12-28 points easy, 28-44 points moderate, 44-60 points difficult

Technical Issue Addressed	Problem Solving Questions	Scale 1-5
Accompaniment	Is the accompaniment utilitarian, supportive, independent, etc.? Is the accompaniment part of the story line? Is the accompaniment descriptive (e.g. water figures, spinning wheel)?	1
Characterization/acting	Is the character appropriate to the student's dramatic capacity or life experiences? Will the student benefit from portraying this type of character?	2
Diction/articulation	Consideration of challenging consonant clusters. Closed position or difficult consonants on challenging pitches? Student's knowledge of French, Italian, Russian, German, etc. language or diction?	2
Dynamics	Is the singer expected to sing a pianissimo high note? Are the markings pedagogically helpful (e.g. crescendo on held notes to assist in breath energy and/or vibrancy)?	2
Melismatic phrases	Beginning or advanced melismas/melismatic phrases present? Appoggiatura? Dotted rhythms?	1
Musical considerations	Through composed? Strophic? Accessible harmonic language? Tonal? An enjoyable melody?	1
Range/tessitura	How are high notes approached (e.g. dramatically)? Is the range too vast? Is the tessitura too low or high? Can a young singer sit in that particular part of the voice for that long without fatiguing?	3
Registration	Does the piece assist in working through passaggio issues? Will the student carry weight up? Helpful vowels in an underdeveloped part of the student's voice? Etc.	3
Respiration	Are phrase lengths accessible? Will the breaths allow for renewal of positioning?	3
Text setting	Syllabic, Patter Song, Lyric? Does the text setting assist in memorization?	3
Vowels & vowel sequences	Observation of vowels in passaggio. Will vowel patterns assist in correcting vocal faults? Forward to back, tongue position, etc.?	3
Words: Poetry/lyrics/libretto	Is this accessible poetry? Is the story age appropriate? Will the text make the memorization process difficult?	2
Total score:		26

Observe the simplicity of the melody. It is a widely known tune and allows the teacher to address registration and/or phonation through dotted rhythms and a natural 6/8 lilt. In addition, the melody does not include any large intervallic leaps.

The Metropolitan Tower by Lori Laitman

Scale of 1-5
Total score: 12-28 points easy, 28-44 points moderate, 44-60 points difficult

Technical Issue Addressed	Problem Solving Questions	Scale 1-5
Accompaniment	Is the accompaniment utilitarian, supportive, independent, etc.? Is the accompaniment part of the story line? Is the accompaniment descriptive (e.g. water figures, spinning wheel)?	1
Characterization/acting	Is the character appropriate to the student's dramatic capacity or life experiences? Will the student benefit from portraying this type of character?	1
Diction/articulation	Consideration of challenging consonant clusters. Closed position or difficult consonants on challenging pitches? Student's knowledge of French, Italian, Russian, German, etc. language or diction?	2
Dynamics	Is the singer expected to sing a pianissimo high note? Are the markings pedagogically helpful (e.g. crescendo on held notes to assist in breath energy and/or vibrancy)?	3
Melismatic phrases	Beginning or advanced melismas/melismatic phrases present? Appoggiatura? Dotted rhythms?	1
Musical considerations	Through composed? Strophic? Accessible harmonic language? Tonal? An enjoyable melody?	3
Range/tessitura	How are high notes approached (e.g. dramatically)? Is the range too vast? Is the tessitura too low or high? Can a young singer sit in that particular part of the voice for that long without fatiguing?	2
Registration	Does the piece assist in working through passaggio issues? Will the student carry weight up? Helpful vowels in an underdeveloped part of the student's voice? Etc.	2
Respiration	Are phrase lengths accessible? Will the breaths allow for renewal of positioning?	4
Text setting	Syllabic, Patter Song, Lyric? Does the text setting assist in memorization?	1
Vowels & vowel sequences	Observation of vowels in passaggio. Will vowel patterns assist in correcting vocal faults? Forward to back, tongue position, etc.?	2
Words: Poetry/lyrics/libretto	Is this accessible poetry? Is the story age appropriate? Will the text make the memorization process difficult?	2
Total score:		24

    This beautiful melody sits in the middle voice for a soprano, who sings about her first love. The piano often doubles the voice, as shown in Example 18. Decrescendos and crescendos are marked and tempo indications are exacting, assisting the singer in creating vivid characterization.

Examle 18: Metropolitan Tower

The 'Hook' Song

It is important that students get to sing music that they like. This does not have to be true for all of the material you assign students, but it helps. A 'hook' song is any song that will get students interested in what you are trying to teach them. This could also be a song that sounds harder than it actually is, allowing students to feel that they are working on challenging repertoire. There are many elements that could 'hook' a student: an interesting or funny text, a familiar or enticing melody or a modern-sounding aesthetic. How many classical art songs have a pop flair to them?

Examples:

    Song: *El tra la la y el punteado* (Granados)
    Hook: Flirty text, Spanish flair

    Song: In My Life (Lennon & Mcartney)
    Hook: Beatles song.

    Song: Parting (Thomas Pasatieri)
    Hook: Modern and sounds profound

    Song: Let's Call the Whole Thing Off (Gershwin)
    Hook: Witty text, part of a movie with Ginger Rogers and Fred Astaire

    Song: Happy Working Song from the film *Enchanted*
    Hook: From a popular, modern movie.

Let's See What You've Learned

Why might this song be pedagogically helpful for a young singer? Grade the song in the rubric shown to determine your answer.

Widmung by Robert Franz

Scale of 1-5
Total score: 12-28 points easy, 28-44 points moderate, 44-60 points difficult

Technical Issue Addressed	Problem Solving Questions	Scale 1-5
Accompaniment	Is the accompaniment utilitarian, supportive, independent, etc.? Is the accompaniment part of the story line? Is the accompaniment descriptive (e.g. water figures, spinning wheel)?	
Characterization/acting	Is the character appropriate to the student's dramatic capacity or life experiences? Will the student benefit from portraying this type of character?	
Diction/articulation	Consideration of challenging consonant clusters. Closed position or difficult consonants on challenging pitches? Student's knowledge of French, Italian, Russian, German, etc. language or diction?	
Dynamics	Is the singer expected to sing a pianissimo high note? Are the markings pedagogically helpful (e.g. crescendo on held notes to assist in breath energy and/or vibrancy)?	
Melismatic phrases	Beginning or advanced melismas/melismatic phrases present? Appoggiatura? Dotted rhythms?	
Musical considerations	Through composed? Strophic? Accessible harmonic language? Tonal? An enjoyable melody?	
Range/tessitura	How are high notes approached (e.g. dramatically)? Is the range too vast? Is the tessitura too low or high? Can a young singer sit in that particular part of the voice for that long without fatiguing?	
Registration	Does the piece assist in working through passaggio issues? Will the student carry weight up? Helpful vowels in an underdeveloped part of the student's voice? Etc.	
Respiration	Are phrase lengths accessible? Will the breaths allow for renewal of positioning?	
Text setting	Syllabic, Patter Song, Lyric? Does the text setting assist in memorization?	
Vowels & vowel sequences	Observation of vowels in passaggio. Will vowel patterns assist in correcting vocal faults? Forward to back, tongue position, etc.?	
Words: Poetry/lyrics/libretto	Is this accessible poetry? Is the story age appropriate? Will the text make the memorization process difficult?	
Total score:		

Widmung's descending melodies help facilitate the mixing of head voice and chest voice (measures 1-2). The dotted rhythms remedy hyper-phonation (measures 5, 7, 9). The melody is doubled in the accompaniment (throughout). Pitches that approach the lower passaggio are sung on closed vowels (measure 9), which would be helpful for male registration. The range of this piece does not extend past one octave.

Example 19: *Widmung*

Some More Practice

How might this piece have a negative pedagogical impact? Grade the song in the rubric shown, to determine your answer.

Quella fiamma che m'accende by Benedetto Marcello

Scale of 1-5
Total score: 12-28 points easy, 28-44 points moderate, 44-60 points difficult

Technical Issue Addressed	Problem Solving Questions	Scale 1-5
Accompaniment	Is the accompaniment utilitarian, supportive, independent, etc.? Is the accompaniment part of the story line? Is the accompaniment descriptive (e.g. water figures, spinning wheel)?	
Characterization/acting	Is the character appropriate to the student's dramatic capacity or life experiences? Will the student benefit from portraying this type of character?	
Diction/articulation	Consideration of challenging consonant clusters. Closed position or difficult consonants on challenging pitches? Student's knowledge of French, Italian, Russian, German, etc. language or diction?	
Dynamics	Is the singer expected to sing a pianissimo high note? Are the markings pedagogically helpful (e.g. crescendo on held notes to assist in breath energy and/or vibrancy)?	
Melismatic phrases	Beginning or advanced melismas/melismatic phrases present? Appoggiatura? Dotted rhythms?	
Musical considerations	Through composed? Strophic? Accessible harmonic language? Tonal? An enjoyable melody?	
Range/tessitura	How are high notes approached (e.g. dramatically)? Is the range too vast? Is the tessitura too low or high? Can a young singer sit in that particular part of the voice for that long without fatiguing?	
Registration	Does the piece assist in working through passaggio issues? Will the student carry weight up? Helpful vowels in an underdeveloped part of the student's voice? Etc.	
Respiration	Are phrase lengths accessible? Will the breaths allow for renewal of positioning?	
Text setting	Syllabic, Patter Song, Lyric? Does the text setting assist in memorization?	
Vowels & vowel sequences	Observation of vowels in passaggio. Will vowel patterns assist in correcting vocal faults? Forward to back, tongue position, etc.?	
Words: Poetry/lyrics/libretto	Is this accessible poetry? Is the story age appropriate? Will the text make the memorization process difficult?	
Total score:		

The music includes intervallic leaps of more than a major third (measures 14 & 16). The accompaniment does not double the melody and is sparse (measure 16) at times. Climactic phrases within the song approach or lie within the passaggio (measure 18).

Example 20: *Quella fiamma*

Some More Practice

What is unhelpful about this piece? Grade the song in the rubric shown to determine your answer.

Après un Rêve by Gabriel Fauré

Scale of 1-5
Total score: 12-28 points easy, 28-44 points moderate, 44-60 points difficult

Technical Issue Addressed	Problem Solving Questions	Scale 1-5
Accompaniment	Is the accompaniment utilitarian, supportive, independent, etc.? Is the accompaniment part of the story line? Is the accompaniment descriptive (e.g. water figures, spinning wheel)?	
Characterization/acting	Is the character appropriate to the student's dramatic capacity or life experiences? Will the student benefit from portraying this type of character?	
Diction/articulation	Consideration of challenging consonant clusters. Closed position or difficult consonants on challenging pitches? Student's knowledge of French, Italian, Russian, German, etc. language or diction?	
Dynamics	Is the singer expected to sing a pianissimo high note? Are the markings pedagogically helpful (e.g. crescendo on held notes to assist in breath energy and/or vibrancy)?	
Melismatic phrases	Beginning or advanced melismas/melismatic phrases present? Appoggiatura? Dotted rhythms?	
Musical considerations	Through composed? Strophic? Accessible harmonic language? Tonal? An enjoyable melody?	
Range/tessitura	How are high notes approached (e.g. dramatically)? Is the range too vast? Is the tessitura too low or high? Can a young singer sit in that particular part of the voice for that long without fatiguing?	
Registration	Does the piece assist in working through passaggio issues? Will the student carry weight up? Helpful vowels in an underdeveloped part of the student's voice? Etc.	
Respiration	Are phrase lengths accessible? Will the breaths allow for renewal of positioning?	
Text setting	Syllabic, Patter Song, Lyric? Does the text setting assist in memorization?	
Vowels & vowel sequences	Observation of vowels in passaggio. Will vowel patterns assist in correcting vocal faults? Forward to back, tongue position, etc.?	
Words: Poetry/lyrics/libretto	Is this accessible poetry? Is the story age appropriate? Will the text make the memorization process difficult?	
Total score:		

Observe phrase structure as well as the accompaniment, which does not double the voice and could be difficult for the young singer to follow musically. The melody ascends and the dynamics increase into the passaggio (measures 17-18). The song could be rhythmically difficult for the young singer. The melody contains chromatic passages (measures 6-7). There are intervallic leaps of greater than a perfect fifth (measure 20).

Example 21: *Après un Rêve*

Some More Practice

How might this song help you to teach a female singer? Are there any other positive or negative aspects of this song? Grade the song in the rubric shown to determine your answer.

In My Own Little Corner by Richard Rodgers

Scale of 1-5
Total score: 12-28 points easy, 28-44 points moderate, 44-60 points difficult

Technical Issue Addressed	Problem Solving Questions	Scale 1-5
Accompaniment	Is the accompaniment utilitarian, supportive, independent, etc.? Is the accompaniment part of the story line? Is the accompaniment descriptive (e.g. water figures, spinning wheel)?	
Characterization/acting	Is the character appropriate to the student's dramatic capacity or life experiences? Will the student benefit from portraying this type of character?	
Diction/articulation	Consideration of challenging consonant clusters. Closed position or difficult consonants on challenging pitches? Student's knowledge of French, Italian, Russian, German, etc. language or diction?	
Dynamics	Is the singer expected to sing a pianissimo high note? Are the markings pedagogically helpful (e.g. crescendo on held notes to assist in breath energy and/or vibrancy)?	
Melismatic phrases	Beginning or advanced melismas/melismatic phrases present? Appoggiatura? Dotted rhythms?	
Musical considerations	Through composed? Strophic? Accessible harmonic language? Tonal? An enjoyable melody?	
Range/tessitura	How are high notes approached (e.g. dramatically)? Is the range too vast? Is the tessitura too low or high? Can a young singer sit in that particular part of the voice for that long without fatiguing?	
Registration	Does the piece assist in working through passaggio issues? Will the student carry weight up? Helpful vowels in an underdeveloped part of the student's voice? Etc.	
Respiration	Are phrase lengths accessible? Will the breaths allow for renewal of positioning?	
Text setting	Syllabic, Patter Song, Lyric? Does the text setting assist in memorization?	
Vowels & vowel sequences	Observation of vowels in passaggio. Will vowel patterns assist in correcting vocal faults? Forward to back, tongue position, etc.?	
Words: Poetry/lyrics/libretto	Is this accessible poetry? Is the story age appropriate? Will the text make the memorization process difficult?	
Total score:		

The range of this song is within an octave. The tessitura lies between E4 and A4, which is particularly helpful for mixing chest and head voice and is not too high. There is an intervallic leap of a perfect fourth (A4 to D5, in measure 10 of the excerpt), which may require special instruction. Tip: Musical Theater songs use a more speech-driven quality that can help the young singer learn to mix more chest voice into her middle range.

Example 22: In My Own Little Corner

Final Test

How might this song be helpful for male registration? Are there any other positive or negative aspects of this song? Grade the song in the rubric shown to determine your answer.

Edelweiss by Rodgers and Hammerstein

Scale of 1-5
Total score: 12-28 points easy, 28-44 points moderate, 44-60 points difficult

Technical Issue Addressed	Problem Solving Questions	Scale 1-5
Accompaniment	Is the accompaniment utilitarian, supportive, independent, etc.? Is the accompaniment part of the story line? Is the accompaniment descriptive (e.g. water figures, spinning wheel)?	
Characterization/acting	Is the character appropriate to the student's dramatic capacity or life experiences? Will the student benefit from portraying this type of character?	
Diction/articulation	Consideration of challenging consonant clusters. Closed position or difficult consonants on challenging pitches? Student's knowledge of French, Italian, Russian, German, etc. language or diction?	
Dynamics	Is the singer expected to sing a pianissimo high note? Are the markings pedagogically helpful (e.g. crescendo on held notes to assist in breath energy and/or vibrancy)?	
Melismatic phrases	Beginning or advanced melismas/melismatic phrases present? Appoggiatura? Dotted rhythms?	
Musical considerations	Through composed? Strophic? Accessible harmonic language? Tonal? An enjoyable melody?	
Range/tessitura	How are high notes approached (e.g. dramatically)? Is the range too vast? Is the tessitura too low or high? Can a young singer sit in that particular part of the voice for that long without fatiguing?	
Registration	Does the piece assist in working through passaggio issues? Will the student carry weight up? Helpful vowels in an underdeveloped part of the student's voice? Etc.	
Respiration	Are phrase lengths accessible? Will the breaths allow for renewal of positioning?	
Text setting	Syllabic, Patter Song, Lyric? Does the text setting assist in memorization?	
Vowels & vowel sequences	Observation of vowels in passaggio. Will vowel patterns assist in correcting vocal faults? Forward to back, tongue position, etc.?	
Words: Poetry/lyrics/libretto	Is this accessible poetry? Is the story age appropriate? Will the text make the memorization process difficult?	
Total score:		

Helpful Elements

This song is easily transposed and could be used to teach mixed voice to the young male. The range of this song is less than an octave. The tessitura lies between F3 and C4, which would be helpful for the changing voice or the lower-voice male. The song teaches legato. The melody is mostly scalar and contains intervallic leaps of less than a perfect fourth. There is an intervallic leap of a perfect fifth (F3 to C4), which may require special instruction.

Unhelpful Elements

The melody ascends to middle-C (C_4), where most of the vowels are open. Tuning the arpeggiated figures in the melodic line might present difficulties. This may create challenges for balancing registration.

Example 23: Edelweiss

Are Musical Theater Songs Sometimes Preferable to Traditional Repertoire?

Observe the similarities/dissimilarities between this song and the previous one. Grade the song in the rubric shown to determine your answer.

Vittoria, vittoria! by Giacomo Carissimi

Scale of 1-5
Total score: 12-28 points easy, 28-44 points moderate, 44-60 points difficult

Technical Issue Addressed	Problem Solving Questions	Scale 1-5
Accompaniment	Is the accompaniment utilitarian, supportive, independent, etc.? Is the accompaniment part of the story line? Is the accompaniment descriptive (e.g. water figures, spinning wheel)?	
Characterization/acting	Is the character appropriate to the student's dramatic capacity or life experiences? Will the student benefit from portraying this type of character?	
Diction/articulation	Consideration of challenging consonant clusters. Closed position or difficult consonants on challenging pitches? Student's knowledge of French, Italian, Russian, German, etc. language or diction?	
Dynamics	Is the singer expected to sing a pianissimo high note? Are the markings pedagogically helpful (e.g. crescendo on held notes to assist in breath energy and/or vibrancy)?	
Melismatic phrases	Beginning or advanced melismas/melismatic phrases present? Appoggiatura? Dotted rhythms?	
Musical considerations	Through composed? Strophic? Accessible harmonic language? Tonal? An enjoyable melody?	
Range/tessitura	How are high notes approached (e.g. dramatically)? Is the range too vast? Is the tessitura too low or high? Can a young singer sit in that particular part of the voice for that long without fatiguing?	
Registration	Does the piece assist in working through passaggio issues? Will the student carry weight up? Helpful vowels in an underdeveloped part of the student's voice? Etc.	
Respiration	Are phrase lengths accessible? Will the breaths allow for renewal of positioning?	
Text setting	Syllabic, Patter Song, Lyric? Does the text setting assist in memorization?	
Vowels &vowel sequences	Observation of vowels in passaggio. Will vowel patterns assist in correcting vocal faults? Forward to back, tongue position, etc.?	
Words: Poetry/lyrics/libretto	Is this accessible poetry? Is the story age appropriate? Will the text make the memorization process difficult?	
Total score:		

Helpful Elements

The song demonstrates a limited range. The singer is afforded many opportunities to breathe. Brief passages of coloratura could help the singer develop agility and/or a lighter mechanism. The accompaniment often doubles the melody.

Unhelpful Elements

The tessitura may be difficult to sustain. There are multiple instances where the singer is requested to sing a louder dynamic level while entering the passaggio. The melody ascends more often than it descends, which might not be helpful.

Example 24: *Vittoria, mio core*

Encouraging Success through Sequencing of Songs

Consider choosing two or three songs at once that build toward your goal. Assign the first piece, and only assign the next piece when the student has mastered the first one. This will allow the student to build skill sets as he studies singing and will foster confidence (which is integral to learning). The songs could be related by key, subject matter and poetry, and common melodic, rhythmic, or metrical patterns. Songs with similar technical challenges, once mastered, could be followed by an easier aria (see index), and then perhaps some phrases from a more difficult aria. Once the phrases are mastered, they can be reinserted onto the body of the aria, which can then be studied in its entirety.

Below is a sample of a song sequence that will lead to an aria:
1. Have you see but a white lily grow (Anonymous, attributed to Ben Johnson)
2. Fairest Isle, All Isles Excelling (Henry Purcell)
3. Caro Laccio, Dolce Nodo (Francesco Gasparini)
4. Selve, voi che le speranze (Salvator Rosa)
5. Lascia ch'io pianga (G.F Handel)

Selected Analyzed Songs from the Index

We have analyzed 200 songs from various categories of the index with a rating scale of 11-55 points. Technical issues included in the analyses are: Articulation, Breathing, Registration, Resonance, Support, Alto to Soprano, and Baritone to Tenor. Genres included in the analyses are: Baroque, Beginning Bass, and Easier Songs by Important Composers.[3]

---

[3] Nota Bene: In the rubrics that follow, Diction refers to the idiomatic pronunciation of the language. Articulation refers to the coordination of the musles of the tongue and jaw. The category Lyrical Flow refers to how difficult it may be to sustain legato as written.

Suggested Repertoire for Technical Issues

Articulation

Song Title:	**Anthem**
Composer:	Anderson & Ulvaeus, Tim Rice
Key:	D Major
Tessitura:	F-sharp3 to D4
Publisher/Edition:	Selections from *Chess*, Hal Leonard
Typically Sung By:	Baritone
Challenges:	Registration is very difficult
Other info:	Belter's song

Total: 39

	Beginning		Intermediate		Advanced
	1	2	3	4	5
Registration					X
Accompaniment support				X	
Articulation				X	
Text interpretation			X		
Phrase Length			X		
Range					X
Tempo		X			
Rhythm			X		
Diction/Language				X	
Lyrical Flow				X	
Melismas		X			

Articulation

Song Title:	***Arie aus dem Spiegel von Arcadien***
Composer:	Arnold Schoenberg
Key:	A Major
Tessitura:	F-sharp4 to F-sharp5
Publisher/Edition:	Brettl-Lieder, Belmont
Typically Sung By:	Mezzo, Tenor, Baritone
Challenges:	Interludes of vocalisms on "bum," difficult piece
Other info:	Humorous, strophic nature

Total: 43

	Beginning		Intermediate		Advanced
	1	2	3	4	5
Registration					X
Accompaniment support				X	
Articulation					X
Text interpretation				X	
Phrase Length				X	
Range					X
Tempo			X		
Rhythm			X		
Diction/Language				X	
Lyrical Flow					X
Melismas	X				

Articulation

Song Title:	**Bread and Cherries**				
Composer:	Ivor Gurney				
Key:	G Major				
Tessitura:	G4 to E5			Total: 37	
Publisher/Edition:	Bury St. Edmonds				
Typically Sung By:	Soprano				
Challenges:	Rhythmic lilting syncopation, consonant clusters				
Other info:	More difficult than it appears				

	Beginning		Intermediate		Advanced
	1	2	3	4	5
Registration				X	
Accompaniment support			X		
Articulation				X	
Text interpretation		X			
Phrase Length			X		
Range				X	
Tempo		X			
Rhythm			X		
Diction/Language				X	
Lyrical Flow				X	
Melismas				X	

Articulation

Song Title:	*Cantique*				
Composer:	Natalie Boulanger				
Key:	F Major				
Tessitura:	F4 to F5			Total: 25	
Publisher/Edition:	available on IMSLP.org				
Typically Sung By:	Soprano, Tenor				
Challenges:	Sustained pianissimo ascending				
Other info:	Female composer, sounds more difficult than it is				

	Beginning		Intermediate		Advanced
	1	2	3	4	5
Registration			X		
Accompaniment support			X		
Articulation		X			
Text interpretation			X		
Phrase Length			X		
Range		X			
Tempo		X			
Rhythm		X			
Diction/Language		X			
Lyrical Flow		X			
Melismas	X				

Articulation

Song Title:	**Early in the Morning**
Composer:	Ned Rorem
Key:	B-flat Major
Tessitura:	F4 to D-flat5
Publisher/Edition:	Ned Rorem 50 Collected Songs, High Voice, Boosey & Hawkes, Hal Lenoard
Typically Sung By:	Various
Challenges:	Syllabic text, exposed vocal line, breath work
Other info:	Good intro to French language sounds

Total: 33

	Beginning		Intermediate		Advanced
	1	2	3	4	5
Registration			X		
Accompaniment support			X		
Articulation				X	
Text interpretation				X	
Phrase Length			X		
Range			X		
Tempo		X			
Rhythm			X		
Diction/Language				X	
Lyrical Flow			X		
Melismas	X				

Articulation

Song Title:	**El Caballito**
Composer:	Silvestra Revueltas
Key:	A Major
Tessitura:	F-sharp4 to E5
Publisher/Edition:	The Art Song in Latin America: Selected Works by 20th Century Composers, Pendragon Press
Typically Sung By:	Various
Challenges:	Complex rhythms
Other info:	Spanish language

Total: 28

	Beginning		Intermediate		Advanced
	1	2	3	4	5
Registration			X		
Accompaniment support			X		
Articulation			X		
Text interpretation			X		
Phrase Length		X			
Range			X		
Tempo		X			
Rhythm			X		
Diction/Language			X		
Lyrical Flow		X			
Melismas	X				

Articulation

Song Title: ***El tra la la y el punteado***
Composer: Enrique Granados
Key: A Major
Tessitura: E3 to E4
Publisher/Edition: Anthology of Spanish Song, High Voice, Hal Leonard
Typically Sung By: Soprano
Challenges: Rapid articulation
Other info: Character piece

Total: 33

	Beginning		Intermediate		Advanced
	1	2	3	4	5
Registration			X		
Accompaniment support				X	
Articulation				X	
Text interpretation		X			
Phrase Length			X		
Range			X		
Tempo			X		
Rhythm			X		
Diction/Language				X	
Lyrical Flow			X		
Melismas	X				

Articulation

Song Title: **Green Finch and Linnet Bird**
Composer: Stephen Sondheim
Key: F Major
Tessitura: G4 to D5
Publisher/Edition: Musical Theatre for Classical Singers, Soprano, Hal Leonard
Typically Sung By: Soprano
Challenges: Chromatic, Larger intervals
Other info: Challenging tessitura, more difficult than it looks

Total: 39

	Beginning		Intermediate		Advanced
	1	2	3	4	5
Registration				X	
Accompaniment support				X	
Articulation				X	
Text interpretation			X		
Phrase Length			X		
Range				X	
Tempo			X		
Rhythm			X		
Diction/Language				X	
Lyrical Flow			X		
Melismas				X	

Articulation

Song Title:	**I Bought me a Cat**				
Composer:	Aaron Copland				
Key:	F Major				
Tessitura:	F4 to C5				Total: 28
Publisher/Edition:	Old American Songs, Book 1, Boosey and Hawkes				
Typically Sung By:	Various				
Challenges:	Tricky rhythms, syncopation, sparse accompaniment				
Other info:	Animal noises				

	Beginning		Intermediate		Advanced
	1	2	3	4	5
Registration		X			
Accompaniment support			X		
Articulation				X	
Text interpretation			X		
Phrase Length		X			
Range		X			
Tempo		X			
Rhythm			X		
Diction/Language			X		
Lyrical Flow			X		
Melismas	X				

Articulation

Song Title:	**I Feel Pretty**				
Composer:	Leonard Bernstein and Stephen Sondheim				
Key:	F Major/ G Major				Total: 36
Tessitura:	C4 to A5				
Publisher/Edition:	Musical Theatre for Classical Singers, Soprano, Hal Leonard				
Typically Sung By:	Soprano				
Challenges:	Fast paced, lots of text				
Other info:	Good crossover piece				

	Beginning		Intermediate		Advanced
	1	2	3	4	5
Registration				X	
Accompaniment support			X		
Articulation				X	
Text interpretation		X			
Phrase Length			X		
Range				X	
Tempo			X		
Rhythm			X		
Diction/Language				X	
Lyrical Flow			X		
Melismas			X		

Articulation

Song Title:	**I Whistle a Happy Tune**
Composer:	Richard Rodgers
Key:	B-flat Major
Tessitura:	F4 to B-flat5
Publisher/Edition:	The Singer's Musical Theatre Anthology, Soprano, Vol. 2, Hal Leonard
Typically Sung By:	Soprano, Mezzo Soprano
Challenges:	Must be able to whistle, British dialect
Other info:	Scalar motion, supported vocal line, develops middle voice

Total: 24

	Beginning		Intermediate		Advanced
	1	2	3	4	5
Registration		X			
Accompaniment support		X			
Articulation			X		
Text interpretation		X			
Phrase Length		X			
Range		X			
Tempo		X			
Rhythm		X			
Diction/Language			X		
Lyrical Flow			X		
Melismas	x				

Articulation

Song Title:	**Lion Tamer**
Composer:	Stephen Schwartz
Key:	D-flat Major
Tessitura:	D4 to B-flat4
Publisher/Edition:	Stephen Schwartz Songbook, W. Brothers
Typically Sung By:	Medium Voice
Challenges:	Unusual time signature, disjunct intervals
Other info:	Shows vulnerability

Total: 35

	Beginning		Intermediate		Advanced
	1	2	3	4	5
Registration				X	
Accompaniment support			X		
Articulation				X	
Text interpretation			X		
Phrase Length			X		
Range				X	
Tempo			X		
Rhythm			X		
Diction/Language			X		
Lyrical Flow				X	
Melismas	X				

Articulation

Song Title:	**Mr. Snow**	
Composer:	Rodgers & Hammerstein	Total: 27
Key:	G Major	
Tessitura:	D4 to D4	
Publisher/Edition:	The Singer's Musical Theatre Anthology, Soprano, Vol. 2, Hal Leonard	
Typically Sung By:	Soprano, Mezzo Soprano	
Challenges:	Lengthy, speech-like recitative quality, dialect	
Other info:	Blending registration in lower passaggio	

	Beginning		Intermediate		Advanced
	1	2	3	4	5
Registration			X		
Accompaniment support		X			
Articulation			X		
Text interpretation		X			
Phrase Length			X		
Range			X		
Tempo		X			
Rhythm		X			
Diction/Language			X		
Lyrical Flow			X		
Melismas	X				

Articulation

Song Title:	**Nine of the Clock**	
Composer:	Ivor Gurney	
Key:	G Major	
Tessitura:	G4 to D5	Total: 37
Publisher/Edition:	Oxford University Press	
Typically Sung By:	Soprano, Mezzo Soprano	
Challenges:	Sophisticated language, catch breaths throughout	
Other info:	Expressive communication needed musically and dramatically	

	Beginning		Intermediate		Advanced
	1	2	3	4	5
Registration				X	
Accompaniment support				X	
Articulation			X		
Text interpretation			X		
Phrase Length				X	
Range				X	
Tempo			X		
Rhythm				X	
Diction/Language				X	
Lyrical Flow			X		
Melismas	X				

Articulation

Song Title: ***Nun lass uns Frieden Schliessen***
Composer: Hugo Wolf
Key: E-flat Major
Tessitura: B-flat4 to E-flat5
Publisher/Edition: Hugo Wolf, 60 Songs for Voice and Piano, International Music Co.
Typically Sung By: Mezzo Soprano, Soprano
Challenges: Difficult entrances, syncopation, difficult leaps
Other info: Helpful for expression and breath management

Total: 41

	Beginning		Intermediate		Advanced
	1	2	3	4	5
Registration				X	
Accompaniment support				X	
Articulation				X	
Text interpretation				X	
Phrase Length				X	
Range				X	
Tempo				X	
Rhythm				X	
Diction/Language				X	
Lyrical Flow				X	
Melismas	X				

Articulation

Song Title: ***Per pieta, bell'idol mio***
Composer: Vincenzo Bellini
Key: E-flat Major
Tessitura: A4 to A-flat5
Publisher/Edition: 15 Composizioni Da Camara for High Voice and Piano, Ricordi, Hal Leonard
Typically Sung By: Soprano, Tenor
Challenges: Large intervallic leaps
Other info: Dotted rhythms, helpful for legato and breath

Total: 40

	Beginning		Intermediate		Advanced
	1	2	3	4	5
Registration				X	
Accompaniment support			X		
Articulation				X	
Text interpretation		X			
Phrase Length			X		
Range					X
Tempo				X	
Rhythm				X	
Diction/Language				X	
Lyrical Flow				X	
Melismas			X		

Articulation

Song Title: ***Petit oiseau***
Composer: Hector Berlioz
Key: F minor
Tessitura: F3 to E-flat4
Publisher/Edition: Berlioz, 15 Songs with Piano, Barenreiter
Typically Sung By: Tenor, Baritone
Challenges: Fast modulation
Other info: Sustained

Total: 39

	Beginning		Intermediate		Advanced
	1	2	3	4	5
Registration				X	
Accompaniment support			X		
Articulation				X	
Text interpretation			X		
Phrase Length				X	
Range				X	
Tempo		X			
Rhythm				X	
Diction/Language				X	
Lyrical Flow				X	
Melismas			X		

Articulation

Song Title: **Spick and Span**
Composer: Theodore Chanler
Key: F Major
Tessitura: F4 to C5
Publisher/Edition: G. Schirmer, Inc.
Typically Sung By: Soprano, Mezzo Soprano, Baritone
Challenges: Crisp articulation
Other info: Humorous

Total: 28

	Beginning		Intermediate		Advanced
	1	2	3	4	5
Registration			X		
Accompaniment support				X	
Articulation			X		
Text interpretation		X			
Phrase Length		X			
Range			X		
Tempo		X			
Rhythm			X		
Diction/Language			X		
Lyrical Flow		X			
Melismas	X				

Articulation

Song Title:	***Toglietemi la vita ancor***	
Composer:	Alessandro Scarlatti	
Key:	F Minor	**Total: 33**
Tessitura:	F3 to C4	
Publisher/Edition:	Italian Songs of the 17th and 18th Centuries for Voice and Piano (Luigi Dallapiccola), Vol. II, Low, International Music Company	
Typically Sung By:	Various	
Challenges:	Articulatory Demands	
Other info:	Very dramatic	

	Beginning		Intermediate		Advanced
	1	2	3	4	5
Registration			X		
Accompaniment support		X			
Articulation				X	
Text interpretation		X			
Phrase Length			X		
Range			X		
Tempo		X			
Rhythm			X		
Diction/Language				X	
Lyrical Flow				X	
Melismas			X		

Articulation

Song Title:	***Zéphyr***	
Composer:	Claude Debussy	
Key:	B minor	**Total: 41**
Tessitura:	G-sharp4 to E5	
Publisher/Edition:	Songs of Claude Debussy, Vol. I: High Voice, Hal Leonard	
Typically Sung By:	Higher voice	
Challenges:	Vocal line independent	
Other info:	Sustained	

	Beginning		Intermediate		Advanced
	1	2	3	4	5
Registration					X
Accompaniment support				X	
Articulation					X
Text interpretation				X	
Phrase Length			X		
Range					X
Tempo			X		
Rhythm			X		
Diction/Language				X	
Lyrical Flow				X	
Melismas	X				

Breathing

Song Title: ***Adieu!***
Composer: Gabriel Fauré
Key: E Major
Tessitura: F-sharp4 to E5
Publisher/Edition: 30 Fauré Songs, Medium Voice, Kagen
Typically Sung By: Mezzo Soprano or Soprano (medium voice)
Challenges: Long phrases, ascending lines
Other info: Ascending melody ending in passaggio

Total: 35

	Beginning		Intermediate		Advanced
	1	2	3	4	5
Registration				X	
Accompaniment support				X	
Articulation				X	
Text interpretation			X		
Phrase Length			X		
Range				X	
Tempo		X			
Rhythm			X		
Diction/Language				X	
Lyrical Flow			X		
Melismas	X				

Breathing

Song Title: ***Ballade des gros dindons***
Composer: Emmanuel Chabrier
Key: F Major
Tessitura: B3 to F5
Publisher/Edition: Chabrier, Recueil de melodies, Kalmus Classic
Typically Sung By: Baritone, Mezzo Soprano
Challenges: Long French Phrases, large range
Other info: Humorous

Total: 36

	Beginning		Intermediate		Advanced
	1	2	3	4	5
Registration				X	
Accompaniment support				X	
Articulation				X	
Text interpretation			X		
Phrase Length			X		
Range				X	
Tempo		X			
Rhythm			X		
Diction/Language				X	
Lyrical Flow			X		
Melismas		X			

Breathing

Song Title:	**Blind**
Composer:	John Ireland
Key:	D dorian
Tessitura:	D3 to A3
Publisher/Edition:	Stainer & Bell
Typically Sung By:	Baritone
Challenges:	Dark subject matter
Other info:	Interesting harmonies

Total: 24

	Beginning		Intermediate		Advanced
	1	2	3	4	5
Registration		X			
Accompaniment support		X			
Articulation		X			
Text interpretation		X			
Phrase Length		X			
Range		X			
Tempo		X			
Rhythm			X		
Diction/Language		X			
Lyrical Flow			X		
Melismas		X			

Breathing

Song Title:	**Come Again, Sweet Love**
Composer:	John Dowland
Key:	F Major
Tessitura:	F4 to C5
Publisher/Edition:	McGraw-Hill
Typically Sung By:	Various
Challenges:	Syncopated rhythm respresents panting and sighing emotional figure
Other info:	Dotted figures, ornament on final cadence

Total: 30

	Beginning		Intermediate		Advanced
	1	2	3	4	5
Registration			X		
Accompaniment support			X		
Articulation			X		
Text interpretation			X		
Phrase Length		X			
Range		X			
Tempo		X			
Rhythm			X		
Diction/Language			X		
Lyrical Flow			X		
Melismas			X		

Breathing

Song Title: ***Date abbiento al mio dolore***
Composer: Stefano Donaudy
Key: G Major
Tessitura: G4 to E5
Publisher/Edition: Ricordi
Typically Sung By: Soprano, Tenor
Challenges: Difficult ending passage, difficult registration
Other info: Donaudy can be more difficult than it looks

Total: 37

	Beginning		Intermediate		Advanced
	1	2	3	4	5
Registration					X
Accompaniment support			X		
Articulation				X	
Text interpretation		X			
Phrase Length				X	
Range				X	
Tempo		X			
Rhythm			X		
Diction/Language			X		
Lyrical Flow				X	
Melismas			X		

Breathing

Song Title: **Drink to me only with thine eyes**
Composer: English Melody, 18th Century, Arranged by Roger Quilter
Key: D Major
Tessitura: D4 to D5
Publisher/Edition: 15 Recital Songs in English, Low Voice, Boosey & Hawkes, Hal Leonard
Typically Sung By: Various
Challenges: Legato, *p* to *mf* singing
Other info: Transposable, good vowel sequences

Total: 33

	Beginning		Intermediate		Advanced
	1	2	3	4	5
Registration				X	
Accompaniment support				X	
Articulation			X		
Text interpretation			X		
Phrase Length				X	
Range			X		
Tempo			X		
Rhythm		X			
Diction/Language			X		
Lyrical Flow			X		
Melismas	X				

Breathing

Song Title:	**From the Land of the Sky Blue Water**
Composer:	Charles Wakefield Cadman
Key:	A-flat Major
Tessitura:	A-flat3 to E-flat4
Publisher/Edition:	GIA Publications, IMSLP.org
Typically Sung By:	Tenor, Baritone
Challenges:	Harmonic language is tricky
Other info:	Good transition piece for Baritone to Tenor

Total: 26

	Beginning		Intermediate		Advanced
	1	2	3	4	5
Registration			X		
Accompaniment support		X			
Articulation			X		
Text interpretation		X			
Phrase Length			X		
Range		X			
Tempo		X			
Rhythm			X		
Diction/Language		X			
Lyrical Flow			X		
Melismas	X				

Breathing

Song Title:	*Grablied für die Mutter*
Composer:	Franz Schubert
Key:	B minor
Tessitura:	F-sharp4 to E5
Publisher/Edition:	Bärenreiter
Typically Sung By:	Various
Challenges:	Heavy subject matter
Other info:	Deceptively difficult

Total: 39

	Beginning		Intermediate		Advanced
	1	2	3	4	5
Registration				X	
Accompaniment support			X		
Articulation				X	
Text interpretation				X	
Phrase Length				X	
Range				X	
Tempo				X	
Rhythm			X		
Diction/Language			X		
Lyrical Flow					X
Melismas	X				

Breathing

Song Title: **Hands, Eyes, and Heart**
Composer: Ralph Vaughan Williams
Key: E-flat Major
Tessitura: E-flat4 to C5
Publisher/Edition: Vaughan Williams Collected Songs in 3 Volumes, Vol. 1, Oxford Univ. Press
Typically Sung By: Mezzo
Challenges: Mixed meters
Other info: Much easier than "Silent Noon"

Total: 27

	Beginning		Intermediate		Advanced
	1	2	3	4	5
Registration		X			
Accompaniment support			X		
Articulation			X		
Text interpretation			X		
Phrase Length			X		
Range			X		
Tempo		X			
Rhythm		X			
Diction/Language			X		
Lyrical Flow		X			
Melismas	X				

Breathing

Song Title: **I Like It Here**
Composer: Alec Wilder
Key: F Major
Tessitura: D4 to A5
Publisher/Edition: Hal Leonard
Typically Sung By: Soprano
Challenges: Harmonically challenging
Other info: Jazz influence

Total: 25

	Beginning		Intermediate		Advanced
	1	2	3	4	5
Registration			X		
Accompaniment support				X	
Articulation		X			
Text interpretation		X			
Phrase Length		X			
Range		X			
Tempo		X			
Rhythm			X		
Diction/Language		X			
Lyrical Flow		X			
Melismas	X				

Breathing

Song Title:	*Lieblingsplätzchen*
Composer:	Felix Mendelssohn
Key:	G Major
Tessitura:	G4 to D5
Publisher/Edition:	Felix Mendelssohn Songs for Voice and Piano, Dover Publications
Typically Sung By:	Various
Challenges:	Chromatic pitches, ascending lines
Other info:	Accessible phrase lengths

Total: 27

	Beginning		Intermediate		Advanced
	1	2	3	4	5
Registration			X		
Accompaniment support		X			
Articulation			X		
Text interpretation			X		
Phrase Length			X		
Range		X			
Tempo		X			
Rhythm		X			
Diction/Language			X		
Lyrical Flow			X		
Melismas	X				

Breathing

Song Title:	*Ma rendi pur contento*
Composer:	Vincezo Bellini
Key:	E-flat Major
Tessitura:	E-flat3 to D-flat4
Publisher/Edition:	Ricordi
Typically Sung By:	Tenor, Baritone
Challenges:	Some chromaticism, leap up to E-flat
Other info:	Intermediate Italian diction

Total: 42

	Beginning		Intermediate		Advanced
	1	2	3	4	5
Registration				X	
Accompaniment support		X			
Articulation				X	
Text interpretation		X			
Phrase Length				X	
Range				X	
Tempo				X	
Rhythm					X
Diction/Language				X	
Lyrical Flow				X	
Melismas					X

Breathing

Song Title:	*Parla più piano*	
Composer:	Nino Rota	
Key:	C-sharp minor	Total: 38
Tessitura:	C-sharp3 to E4	
Publisher/Edition:	Theme song from *The Godfather*	
Typically Sung By:	Baritone, Tenor	
Challenges:	Hook song but difficult	
Other info:	Ideal vowels through passaggio	

	Beginning		Intermediate		Advanced
	1	2	3	4	5
Registration				X	
Accompaniment support				X	
Articulation				X	
Text interpretation		X			
Phrase Length			X		
Range				X	
Tempo			X		
Rhythm				X	
Diction/Language				X	
Lyrical Flow				X	
Melismas		X			

Breathing

Song Title:	**Places to Live**	
Composer:	William Bolcom	
Key:	D Major	Total: 39
Tessitura:	C4 to C5	
Publisher/Edition:	Cabaret Songs, Edward B. Marks Music Company	
Typically Sung By:	Mezzo Soprano, Soprano	
Challenges:	Tricky rhythms	
Other info:	20th Century Cabaret Song	

	Beginning		Intermediate		Advanced
	1	2	3	4	5
Registration		X			
Accompaniment support					X
Articulation				X	
Text interpretation				X	
Phrase Length				X	
Range			X		
Tempo		X			
Rhythm					X
Diction/Language				X	
Lyrical Flow					X
Melismas	X				

Breathing

Song Title:	*Se bel rio*	
Composer:	Raffaello Rontani	
Key:	F Major	Total: 27
Tessitura:	E4 to F5	
Publisher/Edition:	30 Arie Antiche, Vol 2, Ed. Parisotti, Ricordi	
Typically Sung By:	Mezzo Soprano, Soprano	
Challenges:	Ascending lines, long phrases	
Other info:	Middle Voice	

	Beginning		Intermediate		Advanced
	1	2	3	4	5
Registration		X			
Accompaniment support		X			
Articulation			X		
Text interpretation		X			
Phrase Length			X		
Range		X			
Tempo		X			
Rhythm				X	
Diction/Language			X		
Lyrical Flow			X		
Melismas	X				

Breathing

Song Title:	**Sea-Shell**	
Composer:	Carl Engel	
Key:	G-flat Major	Total: 33
Tessitura:	G-flat4 to Cb5	
Publisher/Edition:	50 Art Songs from the Modern Repertoire, G. Schirmer, Inc.	
Typically Sung By:	Mezzo Soprano, Soprano	
Challenges:	Chromatic pitches, difficult harmonic accompaniment	
Other info:	Long phrases	

	Beginning		Intermediate		Advanced
	1	2	3	4	5
Registration			X		
Accompaniment support			X		
Articulation			X		
Text interpretation		X			
Phrase Length				X	
Range				X	
Tempo				X	
Rhythm			X		
Diction/Language			X		
Lyrical Flow			X		
Melismas	X				

Breathing

Song Title:	**Serenade**
Composer:	Franz Joseph Haydn
Key:	B-flat Major
Tessitura:	C3 to A3
Publisher/Edition:	The Young Singer, Book 1, Bass, R.D. Row Music Company
Typically Sung By:	Bass-Baritone, Bass
Challenges:	Ear training, flexibility
Other info:	Also good for beginning bass

Total: 25

	Beginning		Intermediate		Advanced
	1	2	3	4	5
Registration			X		
Accompaniment support		X			
Articulation			X		
Text interpretation		X			
Phrase Length			X		
Range		X			
Tempo		X			
Rhythm	X				
Diction/Language			X		
Lyrical Flow			X		
Melismas	X				

Breathing

Song Title:	**Shall I Compare Thee?**
Composer:	Stephen Paulus
Key:	C Major
Tessitura:	G4 to E5
Publisher/Edition:	American Art Song for the Sacred Service, Classical Vocal Reprints
Typically Sung By:	Soprano, Tenor
Challenges:	Unconventional harmony, long phrases
Other info:	Popular flavor

Total: 38

	Beginning		Intermediate		Advanced
	1	2	3	4	5
Registration				X	
Accompaniment support				X	
Articulation			X		
Text interpretation				X	
Phrase Length				X	
Range				X	
Tempo			X		
Rhythm				X	
Diction/Language			X		
Lyrical Flow				X	
Melismas	X				

Breathing

Song Title:	**The Lass From Low Countree**
Composer:	John Jacob Niles
Key:	B minor
Tessitura:	E2 to B2
Publisher/Edition:	G. Schirmer, Inc.
Typically Sung By:	Mezzo Soprano, Baritone
Challenges:	Middle voice
Other info:	Sounds harder than it is

Total: 26

	Beginning		Intermediate		Advanced
	1	2	3	4	5
Registration			X		
Accompaniment support		X			
Articulation		X			
Text interpretation			X		
Phrase Length		X			
Range			X		
Tempo			X		
Rhythm		X			
Diction/Language		X			
Lyrical Flow			X		
Melismas	X				

Breathing

Song Title:	*Vezzosette e care pupillette*
Composer:	Andrea Falconieri
Key:	F Major
Tessitura:	E4 to F5
Publisher/Edition:	30 Arie Antiche, vol. 2, Ed. Parisotti, Ricordi
Typically Sung By:	Various
Challenges:	Irregular phrases, catch breaths
Other info:	Lower registration, double consonants

Total: 37

	Beginning		Intermediate		Advanced
	1	2	3	4	5
Registration			X		
Accompaniment support				X	
Articulation					X
Text interpretation		X			
Phrase Length			X		
Range			X		
Tempo			X		
Rhythm				X	
Diction/Language					X
Lyrical Flow				X	
Melismas	X				

Registration

Song Title:	**At Sea**			
Composer:	Charles Ives			
Key:	___			
Tessitura:	C-sharp3 to D4			
Publisher/Edition:	Redding			
Typically Sung By:	Baritone, Middle Voice			
Challenges:	Strong musician required			
Other info:	Lyric line			

Total: 35

	Beginning		Intermediate		Advanced
	1	2	3	4	5
Registration			X		
Accompaniment support					X
Articulation			X		
Text interpretation				X	
Phrase Length				X	
Range		X			
Tempo			X		
Rhythm			X		
Diction/Language			X		
Lyrical Flow				X	
Melismas	X				

Registration

Song Title:	***Belle Hermione, hèlas!***
Composer:	Jean-Baptiste Lully
Key:	E minor
Tessitura:	E3 to E4
Publisher/Edition:	Cadmus et Hermione, Broude Brothers
Typically Sung By:	Baritone
Challenges:	Ascends to top, language
Other info:	Dotted rhythms, nasal resonance

Total: 44

	Beginning		Intermediate		Advanced
	1	2	3	4	5
Registration				X	
Accompaniment support				X	
Articulation				X	
Text interpretation			X		
Phrase Length					X
Range				X	
Tempo					X
Rhythm				X	
Diction/Language					X
Lyrical Flow				X	
Melismas		X			

Registration

Song Title:	**Blessing of the Boats**	
Composer:	Ricky Ian Gordon	
Key:	F Major	Total: 43
Tessitura:	F4 to G5	
Publisher/Edition:	Finding Home, The Songs of Ricky Ian Gordon, Hal Leonard	
Typically Sung By:	Soprano	
Challenges:	Sustained higher tessitura, changing harmonies	
Other info:	Crossover piece	

	Beginning		Intermediate		Advanced
	1	2	3	4	5
Registration					X
Accompaniment support				X	
Articulation					X
Text interpretation				X	
Phrase Length				X	
Range					X
Tempo				X	
Rhythm			X		
Diction/Language				X	
Lyrical Flow				X	
Melismas	X				

Registration

Song Title:	***Dem Schutzengel***	
Composer:	Johannes Brahms	
Key:	G Major	Total: 24
Tessitura:	D4 to D5	
Publisher/Edition:	Complete Songs for Solo Voice and Piano, Series IV, Dover	
Typically Sung By:	Various	
Challenges:	Consonant heavy	
Other info:	Useful for breath support	

	Beginning		Intermediate		Advanced
	1	2	3	4	5
Registration		X			
Accompaniment support		X			
Articulation			X		
Text interpretation		X			
Phrase Length		X			
Range		X			
Tempo			X		
Rhythm		X			
Diction/Language			X		
Lyrical Flow		X			
Melismas	X				

Registration

Song Title:	***Der König in Thule***	
Composer:	Carl Friedrich Zelter	
Key:	A minor	**Total: 21**
Tessitura:	A4 to C5	
Publisher/Edition:	Anthology of Music: The German Solo Song and The Ballad, Edited by Hans Joachim Moser, Arno Volk Verlag	
Typically Sung By:	Various	
Challenges:	Many verses to memorize	
Other info:	Strophic, utilitarian accompaniment	

	Beginning		Intermediate		Advanced
	1	2	3	4	5
Registration		X			
Accompaniment support	X				
Articulation		X			
Text interpretation		X			
Phrase Length		X			
Range		X			
Tempo		X			
Rhythm		X			
Diction/Language			X		
Lyrical Flow		X			
Melismas	X				

Registration

Song Title:	**Diaphenia**	
Composer:	Francis Pilkington	
Key:	B-flat Major	**Total: 28**
Tessitura:	C5 to F5	
Publisher/Edition:	English Songs: Renaissance to Baroque, High Voice, Hal Leonard	
Typically Sung By:	Soprano, Tenor	
Challenges:	High key sits in passaggio	
Other info:	Small range, strophic	

	Beginning		Intermediate		Advanced
	1	2	3	4	5
Registration			X		
Accompaniment support		X			
Articulation			X		
Text interpretation			X		
Phrase Length		X			
Range			X		
Tempo			X		
Rhythm		X			
Diction/Language			X		
Lyrical Flow			X		
Melismas	X				

Registration

Song Title:	***Dolce Scherza***
Composer:	G. A. Perti
Key:	A-flat Major
Tessitura:	G4 to E-flat5
Publisher/Edition:	Italian Songs of the 18th Century, Ed. by Albert Fuchs
Typically Sung By:	Various
Challenges:	Melismatic phrases, leaps
Other info:	Small range, accessible for young singers

Total: 28

	Beginning		Intermediate		Advanced
	1	2	3	4	5
Registration		X			
Accompaniment support			X		
Articulation			X		
Text interpretation		X			
Phrase Length		X			
Range			X		
Tempo		X			
Rhythm			X		
Diction/Language			X		
Lyrical Flow			X		
Melismas		X			

Registration

Song Title:	***Douce dame jolie***
Composer:	Guillaume de Machaut
Key:	G minor
Tessitura:	G4 to D5
Publisher/Edition:	German, French and Italian Song Classics, Ed. Horatio Parker
Typically Sung By:	Various
Challenges:	Long lyric lines
Other info:	Good beginning French piece, useful for teaching breath

Total: 23

	Beginning		Intermediate		Advanced
	1	2	3	4	5
Registration		X			
Accompaniment support		X			
Articulation			X		
Text interpretation		X			
Phrase Length		X			
Range		X			
Tempo		X			
Rhythm		X			
Diction/Language			X		
Lyrical Flow		X			
Melismas	X				

Registration

Song Title:	***En las montañas de Asturias***
Composer:	Joaquin Rodrigo
Key:	E Major
Tessitura:	E to C-sharp
Publisher/Edition:	35 Songs of Joaquin Rodrigo, Schott
Typically Sung By:	Soprano
Challenges:	Middle voice registration
Other info:	Can be accompanied by guitar

Total: 29

	Beginning		Intermediate		Advanced
	1	2	3	4	5
Registration			X		
Accompaniment support			X		
Articulation				X	
Text interpretation		X			
Phrase Length		X			
Range			X		
Tempo		X			
Rhythm			X		
Diction/Language			X		
Lyrical Flow			X		
Melismas	X				

Registration

Song Title:	***Fleurs***
Composer:	Francis Poulenc
Key:	D-flat Major
Tessitura:	D-flat4 to F5
Publisher/Edition:	Poulenc Mélodies et Chansons, Salabert
Typically Sung By:	Female
Challenges:	Tricky harmony, chromaticism
Other info:	Sustained, legato

Total: 44

	Beginning		Intermediate		Advanced
	1	2	3	4	5
Registration					X
Accompaniment support				X	
Articulation				X	
Text interpretation				X	
Phrase Length					X
Range					X
Tempo				X	
Rhythm			X		
Diction/Language				X	
Lyrical Flow					X
Melismas	X				

Registration

Song Title:	***Jeg elsker Dig***	
Composer:	Edvard Grieg	
Key:	C Major	
Tessitura:	E3 to C4	**Total: 42**
Publisher/Edition:	A Grieg Song Anthology, Leyerle Publications	
Typically Sung By:	Various	
Challenges:	Norwegian, difficult dynamic markings	
Other info:	Middle voice	

	Beginning		Intermediate		Advanced
	1	2	3	4	5
Registration					X
Accompaniment support				X	
Articulation					X
Text interpretation			X		
Phrase Length				X	
Range				X	
Tempo				X	
Rhythm			X		
Diction/Language					X
Lyrical Flow				X	
Melismas	X				

Registration

Song Title:	***La Diva de L'Empire***	
Composer:	Erik Satie	
Key:	G Major	
Tessitura:	F-sharp4 to E5	**Total: 40**
Publisher/Edition:	Erik Satie Mélodies et Chansons, Salabert Editions	
Typically Sung By:	High Voice	
Challenges:	Fast articulation	
Other info:	Cabaret style, humorous	

	Beginning		Intermediate		Advanced
	1	2	3	4	5
Registration				X	
Accompaniment support					X
Articulation					X
Text interpretation				X	
Phrase Length			X		
Range		X		X	
Tempo					
Rhythm				X	
Diction/Language				X	
Lyrical Flow				X	
Melismas	X				

Registration

Song Title:	***La Maison Grise***
Composer:	André Messager
Key:	D-flat Major
Tessitura:	D-flat3 to G-flat4
Publisher/Edition:	The First Book of Baritone/Bass Solos, Part III, edited by Joan Boytim, Hal Leonard
Typically Sung By:	Various
Challenges:	Breath support, legato line
Other info:	Beautiful melody

Total: 30

	Beginning		Intermediate		Advanced
	1	2	3	4	5
Registration		X			
Accompaniment support			X		
Articulation			X		
Text interpretation			X		
Phrase Length				X	
Range			X		
Tempo				X	
Rhythm		X			
Diction/Language			X		
Lyrical Flow		X			
Melismas	X				

Registration

Song Title:	***L'esule***
Composer:	Giuseppe Verdi
Key:	A-flat Major
Tessitura:	F3 to C4
Publisher/Edition:	Ricordi
Typically Sung By:	Soprano, Tenor
Challenges:	Extensive vocalism in passaggio
Other info:	Scalar passages, long prelude

Total: 44

	Beginning		Intermediate		Advanced
	1	2	3	4	5
Registration				X	
Accompaniment support				X	
Articulation				X	
Text interpretation			X		
Phrase Length					X
Range					X
Tempo					X
Rhythm				X	
Diction/Language				X	
Lyrical Flow					X
Melismas	X				

Registration

Song Title:	***Marmotte***
Composer:	Ludwig van Beethoven
Key:	A minor
Tessitura:	A3 to C4
Publisher/Edition:	Beethoven, Songs (complete), Kalmus
Typically Sung By:	Baritone, Tenor
Challenges:	Various languages used in song
Other info:	Strophic

Total: 25

	Beginning		Intermediate		Advanced
	1	2	3	4	5
Registration		X			
Accompaniment support			X		
Articulation			X		
Text interpretation		X			
Phrase Length		X			
Range		X			
Tempo		X			
Rhythm		X			
Diction/Language			X		
Lyrical Flow			X		
Melismas	X				

Registration

Song Title:	**My German Boyfriend**
Composer:	Richard Pearson Thomas
Key:	D Major
Tessitura:	D4 to E5
Publisher/Edition:	Portage Press
Typically Sung By:	Mezzo Soprano, Soprano
Challenges:	Leaps in the melody, chromatic
Other info:	Humorous, for an advanced singer

Total: 45

	Beginning		Intermediate		Advanced
	1	2	3	4	5
Registration					X
Accompaniment support					X
Articulation					X
Text interpretation				X	
Phrase Length				X	
Range				X	
Tempo			X		
Rhythm				X	
Diction/Language					X
Lyrical Flow					X
Melismas	X				

Registration

Song Title:	*Per pianto la mia carne si distilla*	
Composer:	Eleonora Orsini	
Key:	G minor	
Tessitura:	G4 to C5	Total: 38
Publisher/Edition:	The Solo Song: 1580-1730, Ed. Carol MacClintock, Norton	
Typically Sung By:	Various	
Challenges:	Specific and controlled style of singing	
Other info:	Simple ornamentation, strophic, middle voice registration	

	Beginning		Intermediate		Advanced
	1	2	3	4	5
Registration			X		
Accompaniment support				X	
Articulation			X		
Text interpretation			X		
Phrase Length				X	
Range			X		
Tempo			X		
Rhythm				X	
Diction/Language			X		
Lyrical Flow			X		
Melismas					X

Registration

Song Title:	**There is a lady sweet and kind**	
Composer:	Peter Warlock	
Key:	B-flat Major	
Tessitura:	B-flat2 to F4	Total: 28
Publisher/Edition:	Warlock Songs, Boosey & Hawkes	
Typically Sung By:	Tenor, Baritone, Bass	
Challenges:	Intervallic leaps to higher pitches	
Other info:	Speech range, text driven	

	Beginning		Intermediate		Advanced
	1	2	3	4	5
Registration				X	
Accompaniment support			X		
Articulation				X	
Text interpretation		X			
Phrase Length		X			
Range			X		
Tempo		X			
Rhythm		X			
Diction/Language		X			
Lyrical Flow			X		
Melismas	X				

Registration

Song Title: ***Utro* (Morning)**
Composer: Sergei Rachmaninoff
Key: G Major
Tessitura: F-sharp3 to B3
Publisher/Edition: A Century of Russian Song; G. Schirmer, Inc.
Typically Sung By: Bass
Challenges: Language, for an advanced male singer
Other info: Useful for passaggio work

Total: 39

	Beginning		Intermediate		Advanced
	1	2	3	4	5
Registration				X	
Accompaniment support				X	
Articulation					X
Text interpretation				X	
Phrase Length				X	
Range				X	
Tempo				X	
Rhythm				X	
Diction/Language					X
Lyrical Flow					
Melismas	X				

Registration

Song Title: ***Weihnachtlisches Wiegenlied***
Composer: Avro Pärt
Key: F Major
Tessitura: C4 to C5
Publisher/Edition: Zwei Wiegenlied für Gesang und Klavier, Avro Pärt
Typically Sung By: Various
Challenges: Long, legato line
Other info: Useful for support and registration in middle voice

Total: 33

	Beginning		Intermediate		Advanced
	1	2	3	4	5
Registration			X		
Accompaniment support			X		
Articulation			X		
Text interpretation			X		
Phrase Length				X	
Range			X		
Tempo				X	
Rhythm			X		
Diction/Language			X		
Lyrical Flow			X		
Melismas	X				

Resonance

Song Title:	***Almen se non poss'io***
Composer:	Vincenzo Bellini
Key:	A Major
Tessitura:	E3 to D4
Publisher/Edition:	15 Composizioni da Camera for Low Voice & Piano, Ricordi, Hal Leonard
Typically Sung By:	Various
Challenges:	Melismatic phrases, largo tempo
Other info:	For an advanced student

Total: 42

	Beginning		Intermediate		Advanced
	1	2	3	4	5
Registration				X	
Accompaniment support			X		
Articulation			X		
Text interpretation			X		
Phrase Length				X	
Range				X	
Tempo					X
Rhythm				X	
Diction/Language			X		
Lyrical Flow					X
Melismas				X	

Resonance

Song Title:	***Ave Maria (su due note)***
Composer:	Gioacchino Rossini
Key:	E-flat Major
Tessitura:	G4 to A4
Publisher/Edition:	Melodies Italiani, Belwin Mills
Typically Sung By:	Medium Voice
Challenges:	Intonation, fatigue
Other info:	Focus on articulation rather than pitch

Total: 22

	Beginning		Intermediate		Advanced
	1	2	3	4	5
Registration	X				
Accompaniment support		X			
Articulation			X		
Text interpretation		X			
Phrase Length		X			
Range	X				
Tempo		X			
Rhythm			X		
Diction/Language		X			
Lyrical Flow			X		
Melismas	X				

Resonance

Song Title: **_Bois Epais_**
Composer: Jean-Baptiste Lully
Key: F Major
Tessitura: E4 to C5
Publisher/Edition: The Language of Song, Elementary, High, Faber Music
Typically Sung By: Mezzo Soprano, Bass
Challenges: Range, registration
Other info: Strengthens and extends range

Total: 29

	Beginning		Intermediate		Advanced
	1	2	3	4	5
Registration			X		
Accompaniment support		X			
Articulation			X		
Text interpretation			X		
Phrase Length			X		
Range			X		
Tempo			X		
Rhythm		X			
Diction/Language			X		
Lyrical Flow			X		
Melismas	X				

Resonance

Song Title: **_Chant Breton_**
Composer: Edouard Lalo
Key: E minor
Tessitura: F4 to C-sharp5
Publisher/Edition: Edition Peters
Typically Sung By: Soprano, Mezzo Soprano
Challenges: Difficult rhythms
Other info: Melody subservient to text

Total: 27

	Beginning		Intermediate		Advanced
	1	2	3	4	5
Registration	X				
Accompaniment support			X		
Articulation			X		
Text interpretation		X			
Phrase Length		X			
Range			X		
Tempo			X		
Rhythm			X		
Diction/Language			X		
Lyrical Flow			X		
Melismas	X				

Resonance

Song Title:	**Declaration of Independence**
Composer:	Celius Dougherty
Key:	F Major
Tessitura:	C4 to A4
Publisher/Edition:	Celius Dougherty: 30 Art Songs in the original keys for medium/high voice and piano, G. Schirmer, Inc.
Typically Sung By:	Various
Challenges:	Voice independent of accompaniment
Other info:	Speech-driven text

Total: 28

	Beginning		Intermediate		Advanced
	1	2	3	4	5
Registration		X			
Accompaniment support				X	
Articulation			X		
Text interpretation			X		
Phrase Length		X			
Range		X			
Tempo			X		
Rhythm		X			
Diction/Language			X		
Lyrical Flow			X		
Melismas	X				

Resonance

Song Title:	*Envoi de Fleurs*
Composer:	Charles Gounod
Key:	E-flat Major
Tessitura:	F4 to B-flat4
Publisher/Edition:	Songs, Vol. 11, Kalmus Scores
Typically Sung By:	Medium Voice
Challenges:	Expression
Other info:	Lesser known song by important composer

Total: 29

	Beginning		Intermediate		Advanced
	1	2	3	4	5
Registration			X		
Accompaniment support			X		
Articulation			X		
Text interpretation		X			
Phrase Length			X		
Range			X		
Tempo		X			
Rhythm			X		
Diction/Language			X		
Lyrical Flow			X		
Melismas	X				

Resonance

Song Title:	**Grandma**
Composer:	Theodore Chanler
Key:	A minor
Tessitura:	E4 to E5
Publisher/Edition:	The First Book of Soprano Solos, Part II, edited by Joan Boytim, Hal Leonard
Typically Sung By:	Soprano
Challenges:	Sequentially moves up to the second passaggio
Other info:	Humorous

Total: 24

	Beginning		Intermediate		Advanced
	1	2	3	4	5
Registration			X		
Accompaniment support			X		
Articulation		X			
Text interpretation	X				
Phrase Length		X			
Range			X		
Tempo			X		
Rhythm		X			
Diction/Language		X			
Lyrical Flow		X			
Melismas	X				

Resonance

Song Title:	**Gute Nacht**
Composer:	Robert Franz
Key:	D minor
Tessitura:	G4 to C5
Publisher/Edition:	60 Ausgewälte Lieder von Robert Franz, C. F. Peters
Typically Sung By:	Various
Challenges:	Accompaniment can hinder vocal line
Other info:	Narrow range

Total: 29

	Beginning		Intermediate		Advanced
	1	2	3	4	5
Registration		X			
Accompaniment support			X		
Articulation			X		
Text interpretation			X		
Phrase Length			X		
Range			X		
Tempo			X		
Rhythm		X			
Diction/Language			X		
Lyrical Flow			X		
Melismas	X				

Resonance

Song Title:	**I Could Have Danced All Night**
Composer:	Lerner & Loewe
Key:	C Major
Tessitura:	E4 to C5
Publisher/Edition:	Hal Leonard
Typically Sung By:	Soprano, Mezzo Soprano
Challenges:	Wide Range, dialect
Other info:	Middle voice registration

Total: 35

	Beginning		Intermediate		Advanced
	1	2	3	4	5
Registration				X	
Accompaniment support			X		
Articulation				X	
Text interpretation	X				
Phrase Length			X		
Range				X	
Tempo			X		
Rhythm			X		
Diction/Language				X	
Lyrical Flow					X
Melismas	X				

Resonance

Song Title:	*Immer leiser wird mein Schlummer*
Composer:	Johannes Brahms
Key:	F minor
Tessitura:	F4 to F5
Publisher/Edition:	Johannes Brahms 75 Songs, High Voice, Hal Leonard
Typically Sung By:	Female
Challenges:	Passaggio work, wide range, controlled singing, difficult to Interpret
Other info:	Mature text

Total: 43

	Beginning		Intermediate		Advanced
	1	2	3	4	5
Registration				X	
Accompaniment support			X		
Articulation			X		
Text interpretation					X
Phrase Length					X
Range					X
Tempo					X
Rhythm			X		
Diction/Language				X	
Lyrical Flow					X
Melismas	X				

Resonance

Song Title:	***La Brise***
Composer:	Camille Saint-Saëns
Key:	E minor
Tessitura:	E4 to D5
Publisher/Edition:	John Church Co., Theodore Presser Distributors
Typically Sung By:	Mezzo Soprano, Baritone
Challenges:	French language - quickly moving text
Other info:	Rhythmic momentum assists breath energy

Total: 41

	Beginning		Intermediate		Advanced
	1	2	3	4	5
Registration				X	
Accompaniment support				X	
Articulation					X
Text interpretation				X	
Phrase Length				X	
Range				X	
Tempo				X	
Rhythm			X		
Diction/Language			X		
Lyrical Flow				X	
Melismas		X			

Resonance

Song Title:	***La Sauterelle***
Composer:	Francis Poulenc
Key:	A minor
Tessitura:	E4 to E5
Publisher/Edition:	The French Song Anthology, High Voice, Hal Leonard
Typically Sung By:	Various
Challenges:	Long Phrases, chromaticism
Other info:	Registration is difficult

Total: 34

	Beginning		Intermediate		Advanced
	1	2	3	4	5
Registration				X	
Accompaniment support			X		
Articulation				X	
Text interpretation				X	
Phrase Length			X		
Range			X		
Tempo			X		
Rhythm			X		
Diction/Language			X		
Lyrical Flow			X		
Melismas	X				

Resonance

Song Title:	*Le Soir*
Composer:	Charles Gounod
Key:	E-flat Major
Tessitura:	E3 to G4
Publisher/Edition:	Charles Gounod, Songs, Volume I, for High Voice, Kalmus
Typically Sung By:	Various
Challenges:	Long phrases, long postlude
Other info:	Transposable

Total: 39

	Beginning		Intermediate		Advanced
	1	2	3	4	5
Registration				X	
Accompaniment support				X	
Articulation				X	
Text interpretation				X	
Phrase Length				X	
Range				X	
Tempo			X		
Rhythm			X		
Diction/Language				X	
Lyrical Flow				X	
Melismas	X				

Resonance

Song Title:	**O do not Love too Long**
Composer:	Ned Rorem
Key:	C minor
Tessitura:	D3 to D5
Publisher/Edition:	Ned Rorem Song Album, High Voice, Boosey and Hawkes, Hal Leonard
Typically Sung By:	Various
Challenges:	Tuning, syllabic
Other info:	Useful in breath work, transposable

Total: 36

	Beginning		Intermediate		Advanced
	1	2	3	4	5
Registration			X		
Accompaniment support				X	
Articulation				X	
Text interpretation		X			
Phrase Length				X	
Range			X		
Tempo				X	
Rhythm			X		
Diction/Language				X	
Lyrical Flow				X	
Melismas	X				

Resonance

Song Title:	***Posate, dormite***
Composer:	Giovanni Battista Bassani
Key:	A-flat Major
Tessitura:	B-flat4 to E-flat5
Publisher/Edition:	Arie antiche, Vol. 3, Ricordi
Typically Sung By:	Various
Challenges:	Sits in passaggio
Other info:	Useful for balancing registration, recitative to help with speech-quality resonance

Total: 34

	Beginning		Intermediate		Advanced
	1	2	3	4	5
Registration			X		
Accompaniment support			X		
Articulation			X		
Text interpretation		X			
Phrase Length				X	
Range				X	
Tempo				X	
Rhythm		X			
Diction/Language				X	
Lyrical Flow				X	
Melismas	X				

Resonance

Song Title:	***Prison***
Composer:	Gabriel Fauré
Key:	E minor
Tessitura:	E4 to E5
Publisher/Edition:	Fauré, 30 Songs for Voice and Piano, High, International Music Company
Typically Sung By:	Various
Challenges:	Upper passaggio, onset on high notes
Other info:	Mature subject

Total: 45

	Beginning		Intermediate		Advanced
	1	2	3	4	5
Registration					X
Accompaniment support					X
Articulation					X
Text interpretation					X
Phrase Length			X		
Range				X	
Tempo				X	
Rhythm					X
Diction/Language				X	
Lyrical Flow				X	
Melismas	X				

Resonance

Song Title: *Seit ich ihn gesehen*
Composer: Robert Schumann
Key: B-flat Major
Tessitura: F4 to E-flat5
Publisher/Edition: Frauenliebe und Leben, Op. 42, High, International Music Company
Typically Sung By: Soprano, Mezzo Soprano
Challenges: Middle Voice, legato, sustained
Other info: Part of a cycle, mature subject matter

Total: 29

	Beginning		Intermediate		Advanced
	1	2	3	4	5
Registration		X			
Accompaniment support			X		
Articulation				X	
Text interpretation			X		
Phrase Length			X		
Range		X			
Tempo			X		
Rhythm			X		
Diction/Language			X		
Lyrical Flow		X			
Melismas	X				

Resonance

Song Title: **September Song**
Composer: Kurt Weill
Key: C Major
Tessitura: E3 to C4
Publisher/Edition: The Singer's Musical Theatre Anthology, Rev Ed, Bar/Bass, V. 1, Hal Leonard
Typically Sung By: Baritone
Challenges: Brief sections of high tessitura
Other info: Crossover piece for baritones

Total: 31

	Beginning		Intermediate		Advanced
	1	2	3	4	5
Registration			X		
Accompaniment support			X		
Articulation			X		
Text interpretation				X	
Phrase Length				X	
Range			X		
Tempo			X		
Rhythm		X			
Diction/Language			X		
Lyrical Flow		X			
Melismas	X				

Resonance

Song Title:	**Sometimes a day goes by**	
Composer:	John Kander	
Key:	B-flat Major	Total: 22
Tessitura:	D3 to B-flat3	
Publisher/Edition:	The Singer's Musical Theatre Anthology, Baritone/Bass, Vol. 4, Hal Leonard	
Typically Sung By:	Baritone, Bass	
Challenges:	Tricky rhythms	
Other info:	Ballad, expression	

	Beginning		Intermediate		Advanced
	1	2	3	4	5
Registration		X			
Accompaniment support			X		
Articulation		X			
Text interpretation		X			
Phrase Length		X			
Range		X			
Tempo			X		
Rhythm		X			
Diction/Language		X			
Lyrical Flow	X				
Melismas	X				

Resonance

Song Title:	**The Lamb**	
Composer:	Theodore Chanler	
Key:	F minor	Total: 21
Tessitura:	F4 to C5	
Publisher/Edition:	G. Schirmer, Inc.	
Typically Sung By:	Mezzo Soprano	
Challenges:	Ascending skips	
Other info:	Small range, short in length, repetitive phrases	

	Beginning		Intermediate		Advanced
	1	2	3	4	5
Registration		X			
Accompaniment support		X			
Articulation		X			
Text interpretation		X			
Phrase Length		X			
Range		X			
Tempo			X		
Rhythm		X			
Diction/Language		X			
Lyrical Flow	X				
Melismas	X				

Support

Song Title:	**A Brisk Young Sailor**	
Composer:	George Butterworth	
Key:	E Major	Total: 18
Tessitura:	G-sharp4 to E5	
Publisher/Edition:	Folk Songs from Sussex and other songs by George Butterworth, Galliard Stainer & Bell Ltd., Galazy Music Corp.	
Typically Sung By:	Soprano, Mezzo Soprano	
Challenges:	6/4 meter	
Other info:	Transition piece for alto to soprano	

	Beginning		Intermediate		Advanced
	1	2	3	4	5
Registration		X			
Accompaniment support		X			
Articulation		X			
Text interpretation	X				
Phrase Length		X			
Range		X			
Tempo		X			
Rhythm		X			
Diction/Language	X				
Lyrical Flow	X				
Melismas	X				

Support

Song Title:	**Beautiful Dreamer**	
Composer:	Stephen Foster	
Key:	D Major	Total: 25
Tessitura:	D4 to D5	
Publisher/Edition:	University of Pittsburgh Edition	
Typically Sung By:	Various	
Challenges:	Sustained, ascending leaps	
Other info:	Descending lines assist with registration	

	Beginning		Intermediate		Advanced
	1	2	3	4	5
Registration		X			
Accompaniment support		X			
Articulation		X			
Text interpretation			X		
Phrase Length			X		
Range		X			
Tempo		X			
Rhythm		X			
Diction/Language			X		
Lyrical Flow			X		
Melismas	X				

Support

Song Title:	***Berglied***	
Composer:	Carl Friederich Zelter	
Key:	E minor	
Tessitura:	G4 to C5	**Total: 31**
Publisher/Edition:	IMSLP.org	
Typically Sung By:	Various	
Challenges:	Long phrases, articulation	
Other info:	Written in the bass clef, for bass voice	

	Beginning		Intermediate		Advanced
	1	2	3	4	5
Registration			X		
Accompaniment support		X			
Articulation			X		
Text interpretation			X		
Phrase Length			X		
Range				X	
Tempo			X		
Rhythm			X		
Diction/Language			X		
Lyrical Flow			X		
Melismas	X				

Support

Song Title:	**Compensation**	
Composer:	Charles Lloyd, Jr.	
Key:	---	**Total: 27**
Tessitura:	E-flat4 to B-flat5	
Publisher/Edition:	Anthology of Art Songs by Black American Composers, Edward B. Marks Music Co.	
Typically Sung By:	Low male voice	
Challenges:	No tonal center	
Other info:	Long, lyric line	

	Beginning		Intermediate		Advanced
	1	2	3	4	5
Registration		X			
Accompaniment support				X	
Articulation		X			
Text interpretation			X		
Phrase Length			X		
Range		X			
Tempo			X		
Rhythm		X			
Diction/Language		X			
Lyrical Flow			X		
Melismas	X				

Support

Song Title:	***Der Frühling***	
Composer:	Johannes Brahms	
Key:	E Major	
Tessitura:	E-flat4 to D-flat5	**Total: 28**
Publisher/Edition:	Edition Peters	
Typically Sung By:	Various	
Challenges:	Sustained upper tessitura	
Other info:	Strophic, 6/8 meter	

	Beginning		Intermediate		Advanced
	1	2	3	4	5
Registration			X		
Accompaniment support			X		
Articulation			X		
Text interpretation				X	
Phrase Length		X			
Range		X			
Tempo		X			
Rhythm			X		
Diction/Language			X		
Lyrical Flow		X			
Melismas	X				

Support

Song Title:	***Es hat die Rose sich beklagt***	
Composer:	Robert Franz	
Key:	D-flat Major	
Tessitura:	E-flat3 to D-flat4	**Total: 28**
Publisher/Edition:	Pathways of Song, Vol. 3, High Voice, Arranged by Frank LaForge and Will Earhart, Witmark Educational Publications	
Typically Sung By:	Various	
Challenges:	Articulation, sits in middle register	
Other info:	Legato, vocal freedom	

	Beginning		Intermediate		Advanced
	1	2	3	4	5
Registration			X		
Accompaniment support		X			
Articulation			X		
Text interpretation		X			
Phrase Length		X			
Range			X		
Tempo			X		
Rhythm			X		
Diction/Language			X		
Lyrical Flow			X		
Melismas	X				

Support

Song Title:	**Ev'ry Time We Say Goodbye**	
Composer:	Cole Porter	
Key:	B-flat Major	Total: 34
Tessitura:	D4 to B-flat5	
Publisher/Edition:	Ella Fitzgerald: Original keys for Singers, Hal Leonard	
Typically Sung By:	Medium and low voice	
Challenges:	Low registration	
Other info:	Jazz standard, legato	

	Beginning		Intermediate		Advanced
	1	2	3	4	5
Registration			X		
Accompaniment support				X	
Articulation			X		
Text interpretation		X			
Phrase Length				X	
Range			X		
Tempo				X	
Rhythm				X	
Diction/Language			X		
Lyrical Flow			X		
Melismas	X				

Support

Song Title:	**Fain Would I, Chloris**	
Composer:	John Blow	
Key:	D minor	Total: 33
Tessitura:	G4 to D5	
Publisher/Edition:	John Blow 10 Songs for High Voice, Stainer & Bell	
Typically Sung By:	Soprano	
Challenges:	Soprano range but male text, intonation	
Other info:	Ornamentation	

	Beginning		Intermediate		Advanced
	1	2	3	4	5
Registration				X	
Accompaniment support			X		
Articulation				X	
Text interpretation				X	
Phrase Length			X		
Range				X	
Tempo		X			
Rhythm		X			
Diction/Language			X		
Lyrical Flow			X		
Melismas	X				

Support

Song Title:	***Gottes Macht und Vorsehung***	
Composer:	Ludwig van Beethoven	
Key:	C Major	**Total: 28**
Tessitura:	G4 to F5	
Publisher/Edition:	Beethoven: 30 Selected Songs, Edition Peters	
Typically Sung By:	Various	
Challenges:	Ascending lines, passaggio work	
Other info:	Sustained, legato	

	Beginning		Intermediate		Advanced
	1	2	3	4	5
Registration			X		
Accompaniment support	X				
Articulation			X		
Text interpretation			X		
Phrase Length			X		
Range			X		
Tempo			X		
Rhythm		X			
Diction/Language			X		
Lyrical Flow			X		
Melismas	X				

Support

Song Title:	**If he really knew me**	
Composer:	Carole Bayer Sager & Marvin Hamlisch	
Key:	G Major	**Total: 30**
Tessitura:	G3 to A4	
Publisher/Edition:	Hal Leonard	
Typically Sung By:	Mezzo Soprano, Alto	
Challenges:	Upward leaps, tricky rhythms	
Other info:	Belt, low tessitura	

	Beginning		Intermediate		Advanced
	1	2	3	4	5
Registration				X	
Accompaniment support			X		
Articulation		X			
Text interpretation		X			
Phrase Length		X			
Range				X	
Tempo		X			
Rhythm				X	
Diction/Language		X			
Lyrical Flow				X	
Melismas	X				

Support

Song Title:	*La Fortuna*	
Composer:	Alessandro Scarlatti	Total: 28
Key:	D Major	
Tessitura:	F4 to D5	
Publisher/Edition:	Seven Centuries of Solo-Song, Vol. 2, Low Voice, James Woodside, Published by Boston Music Company	
Typically Sung By:	Various	
Challenges:	Agility, tempo	
Other info:	Opera aria	

	Beginning		Intermediate		Advanced
	1	2	3	4	5
Registration		X			
Accompaniment support			X		
Articulation			X		
Text interpretation		X			
Phrase Length			X		
Range		X			
Tempo			X		
Rhythm			X		
Diction/Language		X			
Lyrical Flow				X	
Melismas	X				

Support

Song Title:	*Lasst mich ruhen*	
Composer:	Franz Liszt	
Key:	F-sharp minor	Total: 43
Tessitura:	F-sharp4 to C-sharp5	
Publisher/Edition:	IMSLP.org	
Typically Sung By:	Mezzo Soprano	
Challenges:	Sustained, frequent modulations, chromasticism	
Other info:	Text suitable for mature singer	

	Beginning		Intermediate		Advanced
	1	2	3	4	5
Registration					X
Accompaniment support					X
Articulation				X	
Text interpretation				X	
Phrase Length					X
Range			X		
Tempo					X
Rhythm			X		
Diction/Language				X	
Lyrical Flow				X	
Melismas	X				

Support

Song Title:	***Madrigal***
Composer:	Vincent d'Indy
Key:	A minor
Tessitura:	E3 to E4
Publisher/Edition:	The French Song Anthology, High Voice, Hal Leonard
Typically Sung By:	Various
Challenges:	Long phrases
Other info:	Masculine text, sounds more difficult than it is

Total: 26

	Beginning		Intermediate		Advanced
	1	2	3	4	5
Registration		X			
Accompaniment support			X		
Articulation				X	
Text interpretation		X			
Phrase Length			X		
Range		X			
Tempo		X			
Rhythm		X			
Diction/Language			X		
Lyrical Flow		X			
Melismas	X				

Support

Song Title:	***O tu ch'innanzi morte***
Composer:	Claudio Monteverdi
Key:	F Major
Tessitura:	B-flat2 to F3
Publisher/Edition:	Anthology of Italian Opera, Bass, Ed. Paolo Toscano, Ricordi, Hal Leonard
Typically Sung By:	Bass
Challenges:	Vocal independence
Other info:	Beginner bass piece

Total: 28

	Beginning		Intermediate		Advanced
	1	2	3	4	5
Registration		X			
Accompaniment support			X		
Articulation			X		
Text interpretation			X		
Phrase Length			X		
Range		X			
Tempo			X		
Rhythm		X			
Diction/Language			X		
Lyrical Flow			X		
Melismas	X				

Support

Song Title:	*Plaisir d'amour*
Composer:	Jean-Paul Martini
Key:	G Major
Tessitura:	D4 to E5
Publisher/Edition:	The French Song Anthology, High Voice, Hal Leonard
Typically Sung By:	Various
Challenges:	Syllabic nature as the melody passes through the passaggio
Other info:	6/8 meter, also great for registration

Total: 27

	Beginning		Intermediate		Advanced
	1	2	3	4	5
Registration			X		
Accompaniment support			X		
Articulation			X		
Text interpretation		X			
Phrase Length			X		
Range			X		
Tempo		X			
Rhythm		X			
Diction/Language			X		
Lyrical Flow		X			
Melismas	X				

Support

Song Title:	*Si dolce è'l tormento*
Composer:	Claudio Monteverdi
Key:	D minor
Tessitura:	G4 to D5
Publisher/Edition:	Five Songs by Claudio Monteverdi, Ed. George Hunter and Claude Palisca, Theodore Presser Co.
Typically Sung By:	Soprano, Tenor
Challenges:	Phrasing, Upper Passagio
Other info:	Useful for Intonation, 17th Century Composition

Total: 27

	Beginning		Intermediate		Advanced
	1	2	3	4	5
Registration			X		
Accompaniment support			X		
Articulation			X		
Text interpretation		X			
Phrase Length		X			
Range			X		
Tempo			X		
Rhythm		X			
Diction/Language			X		
Lyrical Flow		X			
Melismas	X				

Support

Song Title:	**The Water Mill**	
Composer:	Ralph Vaughan Williams	
Key:	C Major	Total: 39
Tessitura:	E4 to C5	
Publisher/Edition:	Vaughan Williams Collected Songs in Three Volumes, Vol. 2, Oxford University Press	
Typically Sung By:	Mezzo Soprano, Baritone	
Challenges:	Lots of text, chromaticism, endless lines	
Other info:	Characterization piece, storyteller	

	Beginning		Intermediate		Advanced
	1	2	3	4	5
Registration		X			
Accompaniment support				X	
Articulation					X
Text interpretation				X	
Phrase Length					X
Range		X			
Tempo			X		
Rhythm				X	
Diction/Language					X
Lyrical Flow				X	
Melismas	X				

Support

Song Title:	***Tout Gai!***	
Composer:	Maurice Ravel	
Key:	G-flat Major	Total: 23
Tessitura:	G-flat4 to E-flat5	
Publisher/Edition:	Maurice Ravel, Collected Songs, Medium/Low Voice, Durand, Hal Leonard	
Typically Sung By:	Various	
Challenges:	Repetitive text, folk influence	
Other info:	Good introduction to French repertoire	

	Beginning		Intermediate		Advanced
	1	2	3	4	5
Registration		X			
Accompaniment support			X		
Articulation		X			
Text interpretation	X				
Phrase Length		X			
Range		X			
Tempo			X		
Rhythm		X			
Diction/Language		X			
Lyrical Flow			X		
Melismas	X				

Support

Song Title:	***Tu mancavi a tormentarmi***
Composer:	Antonio Cesti
Key:	C minor
Tessitura:	F4 to E-flat5
Publisher/Edition:	Arie Antiche, Vol. 2, Ricordi, Hal Leonard
Typically Sung By:	Soprano, Tenor
Challenges:	Upward leap of 7th, sits in passaggio, slow tempo
Other info:	Descending phrases

Total: 34

	Beginning		Intermediate		Advanced
	1	2	3	4	5
Registration				X	
Accompaniment support			X		
Articulation			X		
Text interpretation		X			
Phrase Length				X	
Range			X		
Tempo				X	
Rhythm			X		
Diction/Language			X		
Lyrical Flow				X	
Melismas	X				

Support

Song Title:	***Wo die schönen Trompeten blasen***
Composer:	Gustav Mahler
Key:	D minor
Tessitura:	D4 to D5
Publisher/Edition:	CD Sheet Music, Late Romatic German Lieder (Version 2.0), The Ultimate Collection
Typically Sung By:	Various
Challenges:	Piano reduction, sustained, difficult dynamic markings
Other info:	Advanced repertoire, from *Des Knaben Wunderhorn*

Total: 36

	Beginning		Intermediate		Advanced
	1	2	3	4	5
Registration				X	
Accompaniment support				X	
Articulation			X		
Text interpretation			X		
Phrase Length				X	
Range				X	
Tempo				X	
Rhythm		X			
Diction/Language			X		
Lyrical Flow				X	
Melismas	X				

Transition from Alto to Soprano

Song Title:	***Canzonetta (Tu fai la superbetta)***
Composer:	Willem de Fesch
Key:	F Major
Tessitura:	F3 to F4
Publisher/Edition:	The Solo Song outside German speaking countries, by Fritz Noske; Tesori Antichi complied by Mart Roeder
Typically Sung By:	Soprano, Mezzo Soprano
Challenges:	Wide ranging intervals, registration
Other info:	Useful for resonance

Total: 24

	Beginning		Intermediate		Advanced
	1	2	3	4	5
Registration			X		
Accompaniment support		X			
Articulation		X			
Text interpretation		X			
Phrase Length		X			
Range			X		
Tempo		X			
Rhythm		X			
Diction/Language		X			
Lyrical Flow			X		
Melismas	X				

Transition from Alto to Soprano

Song Title:	**Come Down From the Tree**
Composer:	Stephen Flaherty
Key:	F Major
Tessitura:	C3 to C4
Publisher/Edition:	Audra McDonald, How Glory Goes, Hal Leonard
Typically Sung By:	Soprano
Challenges:	Easy vocalises that approach piece
Other info:	Gentleness of song invokes lighter vocalism, crossover piece from *Once on the Island*

Total: 23

	Beginning		Intermediate		Advanced
	1	2	3	4	5
Registration			X		
Accompaniment support		X			
Articulation		X			
Text interpretation	X				
Phrase Length		X			
Range			X		
Tempo		X			
Rhythm			X		
Diction/Language		X			
Lyrical Flow		X			
Melismas	X				

Transition from Alto to Soprano

Song Title:	***Die Spröde***	
Composer:	Carl Friedrich Zelter	
Key:	D Major	
Tessitura:	E4 to F-sharp5	Total: 31
Publisher/Edition:	Karl Friedrich Zelter Lieder, G. Henle	
Typically Sung By:	Soprano, Mezzo Soprano	
Challenges:	Registration	
Other info:	Good intro to German	

	Beginning		Intermediate		Advanced
	1	2	3	4	5
Registration			X		
Accompaniment support		X			
Articulation			X		
Text interpretation		X			
Phrase Length			X		
Range				X	
Tempo			X		
Rhythm			X		
Diction/Language			X		
Lyrical Flow				X	
Melismas	X				

Transition from Alto to Soprano

Song Title:	**Dream Valley**	
Composer:	Roger Quilter	
Key:	G-flat Major	
Tessitura:	E-flat4 to E-flat5	Total: 30
Publisher/Edition:	Roger Quilter 55 Songs, High Voice, Hal Leonard	
Typically Sung By:	Various	
Challenges:	Develops passaggio, many dynamic indications	
Other info:	Frequent meter changes	

	Beginning		Intermediate		Advanced
	1	2	3	4	5
Registration			X		
Accompaniment support			X		
Articulation			X		
Text interpretation				X	
Phrase Length		X			
Range			X		
Tempo		X			
Rhythm			X		
Diction/Language			X		
Lyrical Flow			X		
Melismas	X				

Transition from Alto to Soprano

Song Title:	*E l'uccellino*	
Composer:	Giacomo Puccini	
Key:	D Major	**Total: 29**
Tessitura:	F4 to F5	
Publisher/Edition:	Oxford Press	
Typically Sung By:	Mezzo Soprano, Soprano	
Challenges:	Syncopated entrances, lower passaggio	
Other info:	Buoyant accompaniment, good for aria preparation	

	Beginning		Intermediate		Advanced
	1	2	3	4	5
Registration			X		
Accompaniment support			X		
Articulation			X		
Text interpretation		X			
Phrase Length			X		
Range			X		
Tempo		X			
Rhythm			X		
Diction/Language			X		
Lyrical Flow			X		
Melismas	X				

Transition from Alto to Soprano

Song Title:	**I Love All Graceful Things**	
Composer:	Eric Thiman	
Key:	A-flat Major	**Total: 25**
Tessitura:	F4 to F5	
Publisher/Edition:	The First Book of Soprano Solos, edited by Joan Boytim, Hal Leonard	
Typically Sung By:	Soprano	
Challenges:	Develops passaggio	
Other info:	Beautiful melody	

	Beginning		Intermediate		Advanced
	1	2	3	4	5
Registration			X		
Accompaniment support		X			
Articulation			X		
Text interpretation		X			
Phrase Length		X			
Range			X		
Tempo		X			
Rhythm		X			
Diction/Language		X			
Lyrical Flow			X		
Melismas	X				

Transition from Alto to Soprano

Song Title: *Je te veux*
Composer: Erik Satie
Key: C Major
Tessitura: E4 to D5
Publisher/Edition: Salabert ed.
Typically Sung By: Mezzo Soprano, Soprano
Challenges: Cabaret style, romantic text
Other info: Upward moving melodic sequences help support and registration

Total: 36

	Beginning		Intermediate		Advanced
	1	2	3	4	5
Registration				X	
Accompaniment support				X	
Articulation			X		
Text interpretation				X	
Phrase Length				X	
Range				X	
Tempo		X			
Rhythm			X		
Diction/Language			X		
Lyrical Flow				X	
Melismas	X				

Transition from Alto to Soprano

Song Title: **June on Castle Hill**
Composer: Gerald Finzi
Key: B-flat minor
Tessitura: G-flat4 to D-flat5
Publisher/Edition: Boosey & Hawkes
Typically Sung By: Mezzo Soprano, baritone
Challenges: Minor/major modulation
Other info: Registration through descending leaps

Total: 30

	Beginning		Intermediate		Advanced
	1	2	3	4	5
Registration		X			
Accompaniment support			X		
Articulation			X		
Text interpretation				X	
Phrase Length			X		
Range			X		
Tempo			X		
Rhythm		X			
Diction/Language				X	
Lyrical Flow		X			
Melismas	X				

Transition from Alto to Soprano

Song Title: *Le charme*
Composer: Ernest Chausson
Key: G Major
Tessitura: G4 to D5
Publisher/Edition: Chausson, 20 Songs for voice and piano, High, International Music Company
Typically Sung By: Soprano, Mezzo Soprano
Challenges: Wide range, typical challenges of French language
Other info: Many dynamic and musical directions

Total: 33

	Beginning		Intermediate		Advanced
	1	2	3	4	5
Registration			X		
Accompaniment support			X		
Articulation				X	
Text interpretation			X		
Phrase Length			X		
Range				X	
Tempo			X		
Rhythm			X		
Diction/Language				X	
Lyrical Flow			X		
Melismas	X				

Transition from Alto to Soprano

Song Title: *Le Mariage des Roses*
Composer: César Franck
Key: B Major
Tessitura: F-sharp4 to D5
Publisher/Edition: Anthology of French Song, Ed. Max Spicker, G. Schirmer, Hal Leonard
Typically Sung By: Soprano, Mezzo Soprano
Challenges: Few tricky leaps and chromatic alterations
Other info: vowels bring down head voice, 6/8 meter

Total: 28

	Beginning		Intermediate		Advanced
	1	2	3	4	5
Registration			X		
Accompaniment support			X		
Articulation			X		
Text interpretation			X		
Phrase Length			X		
Range		X			
Tempo		X			
Rhythm		X			
Diction/Language			X		
Lyrical Flow			X		
Melismas	X				

Transition from Alto to Soprano

Song Title:	**Loveliest of Trees**
Composer:	John Duke
Key:	A-flat Major
Tessitura:	A4 to E5
Publisher/Edition:	The First Book of Mezzo Soprano/Alto Solos, Part I, edited by Joan Boytim, Hal Leonard
Typically Sung By:	Various
Challenges:	Independent accompaniment
Other info:	Descending intervals

Total: 26

	Beginning		Intermediate		Advanced
	1	2	3	4	5
Registration			X		
Accompaniment support			X		
Articulation			X		
Text interpretation			X		
Phrase Length			X		
Range		X			
Tempo		X			
Rhythm		X			
Diction/Language		X			
Lyrical Flow		X			
Melismas	X				

Transition from Alto to Soprano

Song Title:	*Malurous qu'o uno fenno*
Composer:	Joseph Canteloube
Key:	F Major
Tessitura:	F4 to F5
Publisher/Edition:	Chants d'Auvergne, Paris, Heugel
Typically Sung By:	Soprano, Mezzo Soprano
Challenges:	Dialect
Other info:	Folksong, humorous

Total: 37

	Beginning		Intermediate		Advanced
	1	2	3	4	5
Registration			X		
Accompaniment support				X	
Articulation					X
Text interpretation		X			
Phrase Length		X			
Range			X		
Tempo				X	
Rhythm				X	
Diction/Language					X
Lyrical Flow				X	
Melismas	X				

Transition from Alto to Soprano

Song Title:	***Ogni, amatore***
Composer:	Niccolo Piccinni
Key:	A Major
Tessitura:	A4 to D5
Publisher/Edition:	Italian Arias of the Baroque and Classical Eras, Alfred
Typically Sung By:	Soprano
Challenges:	Flexibility, melismas
Other info:	Ideal first aria

Total: 31

	Beginning		Intermediate		Advanced
	1	2	3	4	5
Registration			X		
Accompaniment support			X		
Articulation			X		
Text interpretation		X			
Phrase Length			X		
Range				X	
Tempo			X		
Rhythm			X		
Diction/Language		X			
Lyrical Flow			X		
Melismas		X			

Transition from Alto to Soprano

Song Title:	**On the Seashore of Endless Words**
Composer:	John Alden Carpenter
Key:	A-flat Major
Tessitura:	E-flat4 to E-flat5
Publisher/Edition:	Collection of American Art Song - 50 Songs by 29 Composers, G. Schirmer, Hal Leonard
Typically Sung By:	Various
Challenges:	Meter, tempo and key changes, *ff* in passaggio, chromaticism
Other info:	Useful for working on recitativo and support

Total: 35

	Beginning		Intermediate		Advanced
	1	2	3	4	5
Registration				X	
Accompaniment support				X	
Articulation			X		
Text interpretation			X		
Phrase Length				X	
Range				X	
Tempo			X		
Rhythm			X		
Diction/Language			X		
Lyrical Flow			X		
Melismas	X				

Transition from Alto to Soprano

Song Title: ***Padre, addio***
Composer: Antonio Lotti
Key: E-flat Major
Tessitura: E-flat4 to E-flat5
Publisher/Edition: 30 Italian Songs and Arias of the 17th and 18th Centuries, Ed. Roger Nichols, Edition Peters
Typically Sung By: Soprano, Mezzo Soprano
Challenges: Long melismas may be divided with an added catch breath, adagio tempo
Other info: Trills and dotted rhythms assist with flexibility

Total: 34

	Beginning		Intermediate		Advanced
	1	2	3	4	5
Registration			X		
Accompaniment support			X		
Articulation		X			
Text interpretation		X			
Phrase Length					X
Range		X			
Tempo					X
Rhythm			X		
Diction/Language		X			
Lyrical Flow			X		
Melismas				X	

Transition from Alto to Soprano

Song Title: ***Santa Lucia***
Composer: Popular Neapolitan Song
Key: E-flat Major
Tessitura: F4 to F5
Publisher/Edition: Neapolitan Songs, Amsco Publications
Typically Sung By: Various
Challenges: No introduction, *ff* dynamics on G5
Other info: Descending arpeggi, dotted rhythms

Total: 26

	Beginning		Intermediate		Advanced
	1	2	3	4	5
Registration				X	
Accompaniment support			X		
Articulation			X		
Text interpretation	X				
Phrase Length		X			
Range			X		
Tempo		X			
Rhythm		X			
Diction/Language		X			
Lyrical Flow		X			
Melismas	X				

Transition from Alto to Soprano

Song Title: ***Suo-gan***
Composer: Welsh Folk Song
Key: F Major
Tessitura: F3 to C4
Publisher/Edition: Royal Conservatory, Resonance: A Comprehensive Voice Series, Voice Level 3 Repertoire, Frederick Harris Music Co.
Typically Sung By: Mezzo Soprano, Soprano
Challenges: Slow tempo, long phrases
Other info: Simple melody

Total: 19

	Beginning		Intermediate		Advanced
	1	2	3	4	5
Registration		X			
Accompaniment support		X			
Articulation		X			
Text interpretation	X				
Phrase Length		X			
Range		X			
Tempo			X		
Rhythm		X			
Diction/Language		X			
Lyrical Flow					
Melismas	X				

Transition from Alto to Soprano

Song Title: **The Trees They Grow So High**
Composer: Benjamin Britten (arr.)
Key: G minor
Tessitura: B-flat3 to D5
Publisher/Edition: Boosey & Hawkes
Typically Sung By: Various
Challenges: Opening section without accompaniment
Other info: Comfortable tessitura, text driven

Total: 31

	Beginning		Intermediate		Advanced
	1	2	3	4	5
Registration		X			
Accompaniment support			X		
Articulation				X	
Text interpretation				X	
Phrase Length			X		
Range		X			
Tempo		X			
Rhythm			X		
Diction/Language				X	
Lyrical Flow			X		
Melismas	X				

Transition from Alto to Soprano

Song Title: ***Tirana del Tripili***
Composer: Paolo Esteve
Key: D Major
Tessitura: D4 to D5
Publisher/Edition: Spanish Theater Songs of the Baroque and Classical Era (Medium High)
Typically Sung By: Alto or Mezzo Soprano to Soprano, Baritone to Tenor
Challenges: Chromaticism, pianissimo singing
Other info: Spanish text

Total: 35

	Beginning		Intermediate		Advanced
	1	2	3	4	5
Registration		X			
Accompaniment support			X		
Articulation				X	
Text interpretation				X	
Phrase Length			X		
Range		X			
Tempo			X		
Rhythm			X		
Diction/Language				X	
Lyrical Flow				X	
Melismas			X		

Transition from Alto to Soprano

Song Title: ***Vanne, segu'il mio desio***
Composer: G. F. Handel
Key: D-flat Major
Tessitura: D-flat4 to E-flat5
Publisher/Edition: G. Schirmer, Inc.
Typically Sung By: Mezzo to soprano
Challenges: Melismatic, long phrases
Other info: Trills assist with flexibility

Total: 35

	Beginning		Intermediate		Advanced
	1	2	3	4	5
Registration				X	
Accompaniment support			X		
Articulation			X		
Text interpretation		X			
Phrase Length			X		
Range				X	
Tempo		X			
Rhythm			X		
Diction/Language			X		
Lyrical Flow				X	
Melismas				X	

Transition from Baritone to Tenor

Song Title:	***A...***				Total: 37
Composer:	Felipe Pedrell Sabaté				
Key:	F Major				
Tessitura:	A3 to F4				
Publisher/Edition:	Canciones de España, Vol. 3: High Voice, Scarecrow Press, Inc.				
Typically Sung By:	Men				
Challenges:	Declamatory at E/F break				
Other info:	Feels grandiose, but accessible				

	Beginning		Intermediate		Advanced
	1	2	3	4	5
Registration				X	
Accompaniment support				X	
Articulation				X	
Text interpretation		X			
Phrase Length			X		
Range				X	
Tempo				X	
Rhythm				X	
Diction/Language		X			
Lyrical Flow				X	
Melismas		X			

Transition from Baritone to Tenor

Song Title:	***Amor mi tiene in pugno***				Total: 38
Composer:	Stefano Donaudy				
Key:	E-flat Major				
Tessitura:	E-flat3 to E-flat4				
Publisher/Edition:	Donaudy 36 Arie, Ricordi				
Typically Sung By:	Men				
Challenges:	Text heavy, detailed tempo and dynamic markings				
Other info:	Ideal vowels in passaggio				

	Beginning		Intermediate		Advanced
	1	2	3	4	5
Registration				X	
Accompaniment support				X	
Articulation				X	
Text interpretation			X		
Phrase Length				X	
Range				X	
Tempo				X	
Rhythm			X		
Diction/Language			X		
Lyrical Flow				X	
Melismas	X				

Transition from Baritone to Tenor

Song Title: ***Amour d'antan***
Composer: Ernest Chausson
Key: E minor
Tessitura: D3 to F-sharp4
Publisher/Edition: Chausson, 20 Songs for Voice and Piano, High, International Music Company
Typically Sung By: Various
Challenges: Chromaticism, syncopation, tonality
Other info: An easier French piece

Total: 27

	Beginning		Intermediate		Advanced
	1	2	3	4	5
Registration			X		
Accompaniment support			X		
Articulation			X		
Text interpretation		X			
Phrase Length		X			
Range			X		
Tempo		X			
Rhythm			X		
Diction/Language			X		
Lyrical Flow		X			
Melismas	X				

Transition from Baritone to Tenor

Song Title: ***Auf geheimem Waldespfade***
Composer: Robert Franz
Key: E Major
Tessitura: E3 to C4
Publisher/Edition: 40 Songs for Voice and Piano, High Key, Ed. Sergius Kagen, International
Typically Sung By: Various
Challenges: Rhythm, syncopation
Other info: Easier song by a famous composer

Total: 28

	Beginning		Intermediate		Advanced
	1	2	3	4	5
Registration		X			
Accompaniment support			X		
Articulation			X		
Text interpretation			X		
Phrase Length			X		
Range		X			
Tempo		X			
Rhythm			X		
Diction/Language			X		
Lyrical Flow			X		
Melismas	X				

Transition from Baritone to Tenor

Song Title: **Come Away, Come Away, Death**
Composer: Gerald Finzi
Key: D minor
Tessitura: D3 to D4
Publisher/Edition: Gerald Finzi Collected Songs, High Voice, Boosey & Hawkes
Typically Sung By: Baritone, Tenor
Challenges: Independent vocal line, ascending vocal line
Other info: Rhythmically interesting

Total: 32

	Beginning		Intermediate		Advanced
	1	2	3	4	5
Registration			X		
Accompaniment support				X	
Articulation			X		
Text interpretation		X			
Phrase Length			X		
Range			X		
Tempo			X		
Rhythm				X	
Diction/Language			X		
Lyrical Flow			X		
Melismas	X				

Transition from Baritone to Tenor

Song Title: ***Dein Angesicht***
Composer: Robert Schumann
Key: E-flat Major
Tessitura: G3 to E4
Publisher/Edition: Schumann, 85 Songs for Voice and Piano, International Music Company
Typically Sung By: Various
Challenges: Difficult vowel sequences through passaggio
Other info: Controlled *p* dynamic

Total: 34

	Beginning		Intermediate		Advanced
	1	2	3	4	5
Registration			X		
Accompaniment support			X		
Articulation			X		
Text interpretation			X		
Phrase Length				X	
Range			X		
Tempo				X	
Rhythm			X		
Diction/Language				X	
Lyrical Flow			X		
Melismas	X				

Transition from Baritone to Tenor

Song Title: ***Figlia mia***
Composer: G.F. Handel
Key: F minor
Tessitura: F3 to D-flat4
Publisher/Edition: A Selection of Italian Arias c. 1600-1800, Vol.1, High Voice, Ed. Anthony Lewis, ABRSM
Typically Sung By: Tenor
Challenges: Melancholy and mature text
Other info: From *Tamerlano*, intro to ornamentation, useful consonants for resonance

Total: 23

	Beginning		Intermediate		Advanced
	1	2	3	4	5
Registration		X			
Accompaniment support		X			
Articulation		X			
Text interpretation		X			
Phrase Length			X		
Range		X			
Tempo			X		
Rhythm		X			
Diction/Language		X			
Lyrical Flow		X			
Melismas	X				

Transition from Baritone to Tenor

Song Title: ***In der Fremde***
Composer: Johannes Brahms
Key: A Major
Tessitura: A3 to G4
Publisher/Edition: Johannes Brahms Complete Songs for Solo Voice and Piano, Series I, Dover
Typically Sung By: Various
Challenges: Expression
Other info: Modified strophic

Total: 33

	Beginning		Intermediate		Advanced
	1	2	3	4	5
Registration			X		
Accompaniment support			X		
Articulation				X	
Text interpretation			X		
Phrase Length				X	
Range				X	
Tempo			X		
Rhythm		X			
Diction/Language				X	
Lyrical Flow		X			
Melismas	X				

Transition from Baritone to Tenor

Song Title: **Jeanie With the Light Brown Hair**
Composer: Stephen Foster
Key: F Major
Tessitura: F3 to C4
Publisher/Edition: Songs of Stephen Foster, University of Pittsburgh Edition
Typically Sung By: Men
Challenges: Ascending leaps, more difficult than it looks
Other info: Descending leaps, dotted rhythms

Total: 29

	Beginning		Intermediate		Advanced
	1	2	3	4	5
Registration				X	
Accompaniment support		X			
Articulation			X		
Text interpretation			X		
Phrase Length			X		
Range			X		
Tempo		X			
Rhythm		X			
Diction/Language			X		
Lyrical Flow			X		
Melismas	X				

Transition from Baritone to Tenor

Song Title: ***Komm, Jesu, komm zu deiner Kirche***
Composer: J.S. Bach
Key: C Major
Tessitura: D3 to E4
Publisher/Edition: available on IMSLP.org
Typically Sung By: Tenor, Baritone
Challenges: Stamina required
Other info: Ideal vowels in passaggio

Total: 34

	Beginning		Intermediate		Advanced
	1	2	3	4	5
Registration			X		
Accompaniment support			X		
Articulation				X	
Text interpretation		X			
Phrase Length				X	
Range				X	
Tempo		X			
Rhythm			X		
Diction/Language			X		
Lyrical Flow			X		
Melismas			X		

Transition from Baritone to Tenor

Song Title: ***La Rose (Ode anacréontique)***
Composer: Gabriel Fauré
Key: E-flat Major
Tessitura: G3 to E-flat4
Publisher/Edition: IMSLP.org
Typically Sung By: Tenor, Baritone
Challenges: Long phrases, frequent use of *mf* to *f*
Other info: Advanced piece

Total: 43

	Beginning		Intermediate		Advanced
	1	2	3	4	5
Registration					X
Accompaniment support				X	
Articulation					X
Text interpretation				X	
Phrase Length				X	
Range					X
Tempo			X		
Rhythm			X		
Diction/Language					X
Lyrical Flow				X	
Melismas	X				

Transition from Baritone to Tenor

Song Title: **Margot**
Composer: Sigmund Romberg
Key: A Major
Tessitura: E3 to C4
Publisher/Edition: The Singer's Musical Theatre Anthology, Tenor, Vol. 2, Hal Leonard
Typically Sung By: Baritone, Tenor
Challenges: Ascending leaps into upper register
Other info: Downward leaps, operetta

Total: 28

	Beginning		Intermediate		Advanced
	1	2	3	4	5
Registration				X	
Accompaniment support			X		
Articulation			X		
Text interpretation		X			
Phrase Length				X	
Range			X		
Tempo		X			
Rhythm		X			
Diction/Language		X			
Lyrical Flow		X			
Melismas	X				

Transition from Baritone to Tenor

Song Title: ***Marie***
Composer: Robert Franz
Key: F Major
Tessitura: F3 to C4
Publisher/Edition: German, French, and Italian Song Classics, Ed. Horatio Parker
Typically Sung By: Various
Challenges: Rhythmic patterns are tricky
Other info: Sounds more difficult than it is

Total: 28

	Beginning		Intermediate		Advanced
	1	2	3	4	5
Registration			X		
Accompaniment support			X		
Articulation			X		
Text interpretation		X			
Phrase Length		X			
Range		X			
Tempo		X			
Rhythm			X		
Diction/Language			X		
Lyrical Flow			X		
Melismas		X			

Transition from Baritone to Tenor

Song Title: **Passing By**
Composer: Edward Purcell
Key: G Major
Tessitura: G3 to D4
Publisher/Edition: 56 Songs You Like To Sing, G. Schirmer, Hal Leonard
Typically Sung By: Baritone to Tenor
Challenges: Sectionalized by tempo variations
Other info: Antiquated text

Total: 23

	Beginning		Intermediate		Advanced
	1	2	3	4	5
Registration		X			
Accompaniment support		X			
Articulation			X		
Text interpretation		X			
Phrase Length			X		
Range		X			
Tempo		X			
Rhythm		X			
Diction/Language		X			
Lyrical Flow		X			
Melismas	X				

Transition from Baritone to Tenor

Song Title: **Phillis Has Such Charming Graces**
Composer: Anthony Young
Key: B-flat minor
Tessitura: E4 to G-flat5
Publisher/Edition: The First Book of Tenor Solos, Part II, edited by Joan Boytim, Hal Leonard
Typically Sung By: Tenor, Baritone
Challenges: Song weaves in and out of the upper passaggio
Other info: Lesser-known song from the British Isles

Total: 21

	Beginning		Intermediate		Advanced
	1	2	3	4	5
Registration		X			
Accompaniment support		X			
Articulation		X			
Text interpretation	X				
Phrase Length		X			
Range			X		
Tempo		X			
Rhythm		X			
Diction/Language		X			
Lyrical Flow		X			
Melismas	X				

Transition from Baritone to Tenor

Song Title: *Pria che spunti in ciel l'aurora*
Composer: Andrea Falconieri
Key: E-flat Major
Tessitura: B-flat3 to G4
Publisher/Edition: Il Matrimonio Segreto, Ricordi
Typically Sung By: Baritone, Tenor
Challenges: Stamina is required
Other info: Competition aria

Total: 42

	Beginning		Intermediate		Advanced
	1	2	3	4	5
Registration				X	
Accompaniment support			X		
Articulation				X	
Text interpretation			X		
Phrase Length				X	
Range				X	
Tempo			X		
Rhythm				X	
Diction/Language				X	
Lyrical Flow				X	
Melismas					X

Transition from Baritone to Tenor

Song Title: ***Segui, segui dolente core***
Composer: Andrea Falconieri
Key: D Major
Tessitura: F3 to E4
Publisher/Edition: Arie antiche, Vol. 4, Ricordi, Hal Leonard
Typically Sung By: Baritone to Tenor
Challenges: Vowels in passaggio
Other info: Flexibility, narrow range

Total: 28

	Beginning		Intermediate		Advanced
	1	2	3	4	5
Registration		X			
Accompaniment support			X		
Articulation			X		
Text interpretation		X			
Phrase Length			X		
Range		X			
Tempo			X		
Rhythm			X		
Diction/Language			X		
Lyrical Flow			X		
Melismas	X				

Transition from Baritone to Tenor

Song Title: ***Sérénade Florentine***
Composer: Henri Duparc
Key: F Major
Tessitura: A3 to F4
Publisher/Edition: Henri Duparc, Complete songs for Voice and Piano, Dover
Typically Sung By: Various
Challenges: Sits in upper passaggio, controlled singing, difficult dynamic indications
Other info: Lyric line

Total: 29

	Beginning		Intermediate		Advanced
	1	2	3	4	5
Registration		X			
Accompaniment support			X		
Articulation			X		
Text interpretation			X		
Phrase Length			X		
Range		X			
Tempo			X		
Rhythm			X		
Diction/Language			X		
Lyrical Flow			X		
Melismas	X				

Transition from Baritone to Tenor

Song Title:	**The last rose of summer**
Composer:	Benjamin Britten (arr.)
Key:	E-flat Major
Tessitura:	E-flat3 to E-flat4
Publisher/Edition:	Benjamin Britten Complete Folksong Arrangements, High Voice, Boosey & Hawkes, Hal Leonard
Typically Sung By:	Various
Challenges:	Head voice, melismatic phrases
Other info:	Many descending phrases

Total: 38

	Beginning		Intermediate		Advanced
	1	2	3	4	5
Registration				X	
Accompaniment support				X	
Articulation			X		
Text interpretation			X		
Phrase Length				X	
Range				X	
Tempo			X		
Rhythm			X		
Diction/Language			X		
Lyrical Flow				X	
Melismas			X		

Transition from Baritone to Tenor

Song Title:	**Water Parted from the Sea**
Composer:	T. A. Arne
Key:	F Major
Tessitura:	F3 to D4
Publisher/Edition:	Bayley and Ferguson: English Songs of the Georgian Period
Typically Sung By:	Various
Challenges:	Flexibility needed
Other info:	Dotted rhythms are helpful, antiquated text, suitable for young singer

Total: 28

	Beginning		Intermediate		Advanced
	1	2	3	4	5
Registration			X		
Accompaniment support		X			
Articulation			X		
Text interpretation		X			
Phrase Length		X			
Range			X		
Tempo			X		
Rhythm			X		
Diction/Language		X			
Lyrical Flow		X			
Melismas			X		

Suggested Repertoire by Genre

Baroque Arias

Song Title:	*Air de Thésée: Ah! Qu'on daigne du moins*
Composer:	Jean-Phillippe Rameau
Key:	C minor
Tessitura:	C3 to C4
Publisher/Edition:	Recueil D'airs de Rameau
Typically Sung By:	Baritone
Challenges:	Higher tessitura, French style
Other info:	Includes recitative

Total: 35

	Beginning		Intermediate		Advanced
	1	2	3	4	5
Registration				X	
Accompaniment support			X		
Articulation				X	
Text interpretation		X			
Phrase Length				X	
Range				X	
Tempo				X	
Rhythm		X			
Diction/Language				X	
Lyrical Flow			X		
Melismas	X				

Baroque Arias

Song Title:	**As when the dove (Recit: Oh, didst thou know)**
Composer:	G.F. Handel
Key:	F Major
Tessitura:	G4 to F5
Publisher/Edition:	45 ARIAS from Operas and Oratorios for Voice and Piano, High Voice, Volume II, Ed. Kagen, Internation Music Co.
Typically Sung By:	Soprano
Challenges:	Large intervallic leaps, long vocal lines
Other info:	Good introduction to recitative, ABA form: ornamentation is required

Total: 32

	Beginning		Intermediate		Advanced
	1	2	3	4	5
Registration			X		
Accompaniment support			X		
Articulation			X		
Text interpretation		X			
Phrase Length				X	
Range			X		
Tempo				X	
Rhythm			X		
Diction/Language		X			
Lyrical Flow			X		
Melismas		X			

Baroque Arias

Song Title:	**Come Sorrow, Come**	
Composer:	Thomas Morley	
Key:	A minor	Total: 31
Tessitura:	B4 to E4	
Publisher/Edition:	The First Book of Ayres, The English Lute-Songs, Series I, Stainer & Bell	
Typically Sung By:	High soprano	
Challenges:	Long, sustained line	
Other info:	Lute song	

	Beginning		Intermediate		Advanced
	1	2	3	4	5
Registration			X		
Accompaniment support				X	
Articulation		X			
Text interpretation			X		
Phrase Length			X		
Range			X		
Tempo				X	
Rhythm		X			
Diction/Language			X		
Lyrical Flow			X		
Melismas	X				

Baroque Arias

Song Title:	***Der wahren Tugend Gegenstreit ruhrt von der Erden Eirelkeit***	
Composer:	Constantin Christian Dedekind	
Key:	D minor	Total: 26
Tessitura:	F4 to C5	
Publisher/Edition:	Anthology of Music: The German Solo Song and The Ballad, Arno Volk Verlag	
Typically Sung By:	Various	
Challenges:	Four verses	
Other info:	Stylistic training, piano part for figured bass	

	Beginning		Intermediate		Advanced
	1	2	3	4	5
Registration		X			
Accompaniment support		X			
Articulation				X	
Text interpretation		X			
Phrase Length		X			
Range		X			
Tempo		X			
Rhythm		X			
Diction/Language			X		
Lyrical Flow			X		
Melismas		X			

Baroque Arias

Song Title: ***Amante disprezzato sopra, l'Aria di Ruggiero***
Composer: Gabriello Puliti
Key: F Major
Tessitura: F3 to C4
Publisher/Edition: Anthology of Music, The Monody, Ed. K.G. Fellerer, Arno Volk Verlag Köln
Typically Sung By: Various
Challenges: Many verses
Other info: 5-note range, intro to baroque style

Total: 20

	Beginning		Intermediate		Advanced
	1	2	3	4	5
Registration	X				
Accompaniment support		X			
Articulation			X		
Text interpretation			X		
Phrase Length		X			
Range	X				
Tempo		X			
Rhythm	X				
Diction/Language		X			
Lyrical Flow		X			
Melismas	X				

Baroque Arias

Song Title: ***Dieu Tout Puissant***
Composer: André Destouches
Key: A minor
Tessitura: F3 to D4
Publisher/Edition: French Airs of the Early 18th Century, Ed. by Nell Tangeman, Boosey & Hawkes
Typically Sung By: Tenor
Challenges: Some difficult French
Other info: Moderately easy aria

Total: 29

	Beginning		Intermediate		Advanced
	1	2	3	4	5
Registration			X		
Accompaniment support			X		
Articulation			X		
Text interpretation		X			
Phrase Length			X		
Range			X		
Tempo			X		
Rhythm			X		
Diction/Language			X		
Lyrical Flow		X			
Melismas	X				

Baroque Arias

Song Title: ***Ecco, che pur baciate***
Composer: Domenico Obizzi
Key: B-flat Major
Tessitura: G4 to E-flat3
Publisher/Edition: L'Aria Barocca, Ed. John Glenn Paton, Leyerle Publications
Typically Sung By: Various
Challenges: Requires ornamentation
Other info: From *Madrigali et Arie*, 1627

Total: 25

	Beginning		Intermediate		Advanced
	1	2	3	4	5
Registration		X			
Accompaniment support		X			
Articulation			X		
Text interpretation		X			
Phrase Length		X			
Range		X			
Tempo		X			
Rhythm		X			
Diction/Language		X			
Lyrical Flow			X		
Melismas			X		

Baroque Arias

Song Title: ***Himmelstochter, Ruh der Seelen***
Composer: C.P.E. Bach
Key: G Major
Tessitura: B3 to F4
Publisher/Edition: C. P. E. Bach Arias and Chamber Cantatas, Ed. Bertil van Boer
Typically Sung By: Tenor
Challenges: Repeated notes in high range
Other info: Challenging dynamic level

Total: 37

	Beginning		Intermediate		Advanced
	1	2	3	4	5
Registration				X	
Accompaniment support				X	
Articulation				X	
Text interpretation		X			
Phrase Length			X		
Range			X		
Tempo			X		
Rhythm				X	
Diction/Language				X	
Lyrical Flow				X	
Melismas		X			

Baroque Arias

Song Title:	**Hush, no more, be silent**
Composer:	Henry Purcell
Key:	G minor
Tessitura:	D3 to B3
Publisher/Edition:	The Fairy Queen Vocal Score, Faber Music
Typically Sung By:	Bass, low voices
Challenges:	Sustained vocal line
Other info:	Many rests, useful for breathing

Total: 29

	Beginning		Intermediate		Advanced
	1	2	3	4	5
Registration				X	
Accompaniment support				X	
Articulation		X			
Text interpretation		X			
Phrase Length			X		
Range				X	
Tempo				X	
Rhythm		X			
Diction/Language		X			
Lyrical Flow	X				
Melismas	X				

Baroque Arias

Song Title:	***Komm, süßer Schlaf***
Composer:	Georg Philipp Telemann
Key:	F Major
Tessitura:	F4 to E5
Publisher/Edition:	Hortus Musicus 12: Lieder und Arien für Gesang und Basso continuo (Klavier), Bärenreiter
Typically Sung By:	Various
Challenges:	Chromaticism
Other info:	Figured bass

Total: 30

	Beginning		Intermediate		Advanced
	1	2	3	4	5
Registration		X			
Accompaniment support		X			
Articulation				X	
Text interpretation		X			
Phrase Length			X		
Range			X		
Tempo		X			
Rhythm				X	
Diction/Language			X		
Lyrical Flow			X		
Melismas		X			

Baroque Arias

Song Title:	***Le Carpillon***	
Composer:	André Campra	
Key:	G minor	**Total: 32**
Tessitura:	F-sharp4 to E-flat5	
Publisher/Edition:	French Airs of the Early 18th Century, Ed. by Nell Tangeman, Boosey & Hawkes	
Typically Sung By:	Soprano, Mezzo, Tenor	
Challenges:	Melismatic, trills	
Other info:	Da capo form, moderately easy aria	

	Beginning		Intermediate		Advanced
	1	2	3	4	5
Registration		X			
Accompaniment support			X		
Articulation			X		
Text interpretation			X		
Phrase Length				X	
Range		X			
Tempo		X			
Rhythm			X		
Diction/Language			X		
Lyrical Flow			X		
Melismas				X	

Baroque Arias

Song Title:	***Mortels, Que Vous Sert-il***	
Composer:	André Campra	
Key:	F Major	**Total: 25**
Tessitura:	G4 to E5	
Publisher/Edition:	The Baroque Operatic Arias II, André Campra, Oxford University Press	
Typically Sung By:	Soprano	
Challenges:	French performance practice	
Other info:	Scored for continuo	

	Beginning		Intermediate		Advanced
	1	2	3	4	5
Registration		X			
Accompaniment support			X		
Articulation		X			
Text interpretation		X			
Phrase Length		X			
Range		X			
Tempo		X			
Rhythm			X		
Diction/Language		X			
Lyrical Flow			X		
Melismas		X			

Baroque Arias

Song Title:	***Nun scheint in vollem Glanze der Himmel***	
Composer:	Joseph Haydn	
Key:	D Major	**Total: 38**
Tessitura:	A3 to C3	
Publisher/Edition:	Die Schöpfung, Bärenreiter	
Typically Sung By:	Bass	
Challenges:	Wide range	
Other info:	Can be sung in English	

	Beginning		Intermediate		Advanced
	1	2	3	4	5
Registration				X	
Accompaniment support			X		
Articulation			X		
Text interpretation		X			
Phrase Length				X	
Range				X	
Tempo				X	
Rhythm			X		
Diction/Language				X	
Lyrical Flow				X	
Melismas			X		

Baroque Arias

Song Title:	***O Del Ben***	
Composer:	Antonio Cesti	
Key:	C minor	**Total: 20**
Tessitura:	G4 to D5	
Publisher/Edition:	L'Aria Barocca, Ed. John Glenn Paton, Leyerle Publications	
Typically Sung By:	Various	
Challenges:		
Other info:	From *Il Pomo D'oro*	

	Beginning		Intermediate		Advanced
	1	2	3	4	5
Registration		X			
Accompaniment support					
Articulation		X			
Text interpretation					
Phrase Length		X			
Range		X			
Tempo			X		
Rhythm			X		
Diction/Language		X			
Lyrical Flow		X			
Melismas		X			

Baroque Arias

Song Title:	***Pupille Amate***
Composer:	Giovanni Bononcini
Key:	D Major
Tessitura:	F4 to E5
Publisher/Edition:	The Baroque Opera Arias I, Giovanni Bononcini, Oxford University Press
Typically Sung By:	Tenor
Challenges:	Requires agility
Other info:	Piano reduction included

Total: 42

	Beginning		Intermediate		Advanced
	1	2	3	4	5
Registration				X	
Accompaniment support				X	
Articulation			X		
Text interpretation		X			
Phrase Length				X	
Range				X	
Tempo				X	
Rhythm				X	
Diction/Language			X		
Lyrical Flow					X
Melismas					X

Baroque Arias

Song Title:	***Se pietade in te non trovi***
Composer:	Domenico Manzolo
Key:	D minor
Tessitura:	G4 to D5
Publisher/Edition:	L'Aria Barocca, Ed. John Glenn Paton, Leyerle Publications
Typically Sung By:	Various
Challenges:	Some chromaticism
Other info:	From *Conzonette*, 1623

Total: 20

	Beginning		Intermediate		Advanced
	1	2	3	4	5
Registration		X			
Accompaniment support		X			
Articulation		X			
Text interpretation		X			
Phrase Length		X			
Range		X			
Tempo		X			
Rhythm	X				
Diction/Language		X			
Lyrical Flow		X			
Melismas	X				

Baroque Arias

Song Title: ***Sen corre l'agnelletta***
Composer: Domenico Sarri
Key: F minor
Tessitura: F4 to E5
Publisher/Edition: Arie Antiche, vol. 3, Ricordi, Hal Leonard
Typically Sung By: Mezzo Soprano, Soprano
Challenges: Difficult harmonies, ascending diminished 7ths
Other info: Rhythmic accompaniment assists with breath energy

Total: 28

	Beginning		Intermediate		Advanced
	1	2	3	4	5
Registration		X			
Accompaniment support			X		
Articulation			X		
Text interpretation		X			
Phrase Length			X		
Range		X			
Tempo		X			
Rhythm			X		
Diction/Language			X		
Lyrical Flow			X		
Melismas		X			

Baroque Arias

Song Title: ***Tout cede à vos doux appas***
Composer: Pascal Collasse
Key: F Major
Tessitura: F3 to C4
Publisher/Edition: Pathways of Song, Warner Brothers Publications
Typically Sung By: Various
Challenges: Messa di voce
Other info: Middle voice, trills for flexibility

Total: 19

	Beginning		Intermediate		Advanced
	1	2	3	4	5
Registration		X			
Accompaniment support		X			
Articulation		X			
Text interpretation	X				
Phrase Length		X			
Range		X			
Tempo		X			
Rhythm		X			
Diction/Language		X			
Lyrical Flow	X				
Melismas	X				

Baroque Arias

Song Title:	***Vergiß dich selbst, mein schönster Engel!***
Composer:	Georg Philipp Telemann
Key:	F Major
Tessitura:	E4 to D5
Publisher/Edition:	Hortus Musicus 12: Lieder und Arien für Gesang und Basso continuo (Klavier), Bärenreiter
Typically Sung By:	Various
Challenges:	Tricky leaps and harmonies
Other info:	No introduction

Total: 25

	Beginning		Intermediate		Advanced
	1	2	3	4	5
Registration		X			
Accompaniment support		X			
Articulation			X		
Text interpretation		X			
Phrase Length		X			
Range			X		
Tempo		X			
Rhythm		X			
Diction/Language			X		
Lyrical Flow			X		
Melismas	X				

Baroque Arias

Song Title:	**Weep No More**
Composer:	G.F. Handel
Key:	B-flat Major
Tessitura:	B-flat3 to B-flat4
Publisher/Edition:	The First Book of Mezzo Soprano/Alto Solos, Part II, edited by Joan Boytim, Hal Leonard
Typically Sung By:	Mezzo Soprano, Alto
Challenges:	Sustained and legato vocal line, very low, *p*
Other info:	Also useful for support

Total: 23

	Beginning		Intermediate		Advanced
	1	2	3	4	5
Registration			X		
Accompaniment support		X			
Articulation		X			
Text interpretation		X			
Phrase Length			X		
Range			X		
Tempo		X			
Rhythm		X			
Diction/Language		X			
Lyrical Flow	X				
Melismas	X				

Beginning Bass

Song Title: *Adieu!*
Composer: August Heinrich von Weyrauch (Attributed to Schubert)
Key: C Major
Tessitura: C3 to G3
Publisher/Edition: Pathways of Song, Vol. 1, Ed. Frank LaForge and Will Earhart, Witmark Educational Publications
Typically Sung By: Various
Challenges: Language, intonation of repeated pitches
Other info: Reinforcing resonance on repeated pitches

Total: 25

	Beginning		Intermediate		Advanced
	1	2	3	4	5
Registration			X		
Accompaniment support			X		
Articulation			X		
Text interpretation		X			
Phrase Length		X			
Range		X			
Tempo		X			
Rhythm		X			
Diction/Language			X		
Lyrical Flow		X			
Melismas	X				

Beginning Bass

Song Title: *Aria da cantar stanza*
Composer: Cosimo Bottegari
Key: F minor
Tessitura: B-flat2 to F3
Publisher/Edition: The Solo Song: 1580-1730, Ed. Carol MacClintock, Norton
Typically Sung By: Various
Challenges: Often accompanied by lute, sparse, many verses
Other info: Originally SATB, transposable

Total: 27

	Beginning		Intermediate		Advanced
	1	2	3	4	5
Registration			X		
Accompaniment support			X		
Articulation			X		
Text interpretation		X			
Phrase Length			X		
Range			X		
Tempo		X			
Rhythm		X			
Diction/Language			X		
Lyrical Flow		X			
Melismas	X				

Beginning Bass

Song Title: ***Bois épais***
Composer: Jean Baptiste Lully
Key: D Major
Tessitura: C-sharp2 to B3
Publisher/Edition: The First Book of Baritone/Bass Solos, Part II, edited by Joan Boytim, Hal Leonard
Typically Sung By: Various
Challenges: Dramatic sections, language
Other info: Varied dynamics, supported vocal line

Total: 26

	Beginning		Intermediate		Advanced
	1	2	3	4	5
Registration			X		
Accompaniment support		X			
Articulation			X		
Text interpretation			X		
Phrase Length			X		
Range			X		
Tempo			X		
Rhythm	X				
Diction/Language			X		
Lyrical Flow	X				
Melismas	X				

Beginning Bass

Song Title: ***Chevaliers de la table***
Composer: Traditional, Arranged by Jay Althouse
Key: E-flat Major
Tessitura: E-flat3 to B-flat3
Publisher/Edition: International Folk Songs for Solo Singers, Medium Low, Alfred
Typically Sung By: Various
Challenges: Language, lots of text
Other info: Hook piece, strophic, folksong, alternate pitches written in

Total: 24

	Beginning		Intermediate		Advanced
	1	2	3	4	5
Registration			X		
Accompaniment support		X			
Articulation			X		
Text interpretation	X				
Phrase Length			X		
Range			X		
Tempo		X			
Rhythm	X				
Diction/Language			X		
Lyrical Flow		X			
Melismas	X				

Beginning Bass

Song Title:	**Deep River**
Composer:	Traditional Spiritual, Arranged by Moses Hogan
Key:	C Major
Tessitura:	C2 to C3
Publisher/Edition:	The Deep River Collection, Low Voice, Ten Spirituals for Low Voice and Piano, Arr. by Moses Hogan, Hal Leonard
Typically Sung By:	Various
Challenges:	Lento
Other info:	Ideal vowels for C3, useful for breath support

Total: 31

	Beginning		Intermediate		Advanced
	1	2	3	4	5
Registration				X	
Accompaniment support			X		
Articulation		X			
Text interpretation		X			
Phrase Length				X	
Range			X		
Tempo				X	
Rhythm			X		
Diction/Language		X			
Lyrical Flow			X		
Melismas	X				

Beginning Bass

Song Title:	**Down Among the Dead Men**
Composer:	Traditional, 1715
Key:	B minor
Tessitura:	D3 to B3
Publisher/Edition:	Bass Songs, Imperial Edition
Typically Sung By:	Bass
Challenges:	Lots of text, large intervallic leaps
Other info:	Antiquated text

Total: 33

	Beginning		Intermediate		Advanced
	1	2	3	4	5
Registration				X	
Accompaniment support			X		
Articulation				X	
Text interpretation			X		
Phrase Length			X		
Range				X	
Tempo		X			
Rhythm		X			
Diction/Language			X		
Lyrical Flow				X	
Melismas	X				

Beginning Bass

Song Title: **Eldorado**
Composer: Richard H. Walthew
Key: C Major
Tessitura: E-flat3 to B-flat4
Publisher/Edition: The First Book of Baritone/Bass Solos, Book II, edited by Joan Boytim, Hal Leonard
Typically Sung By: Bass, Bass-Baritone
Challenges: Chromatic line, tempo/harmonic change
Other info: Small turns assist with flexibility

Total: 31

	Beginning		Intermediate		Advanced
	1	2	3	4	5
Registration			X		
Accompaniment support			X		
Articulation			X		
Text interpretation		X			
Phrase Length			X		
Range			X		
Tempo			X		
Rhythm			X		
Diction/Language			X		
Lyrical Flow			X		
Melismas		X			

Beginning Bass

Song Title: *Gioite al canto mio*
Composer: Jacopo Peri
Key: E Major
Tessitura: E3 to B3
Publisher/Edition: Italian Songs of the 17th and 18th Centuries, Vol. 2, Low, International Music Company
Typically Sung By: Various
Challenges: Lots of text at upbeat tempo
Other info: Invocazione di Orfeo from *Euridice*, small range

Total: 31

	Beginning		Intermediate		Advanced
	1	2	3	4	5
Registration			X		
Accompaniment support			X		
Articulation				X	
Text interpretation		X			
Phrase Length		X			
Range			X		
Tempo			X		
Rhythm			X		
Diction/Language				X	
Lyrical Flow			X		
Melismas	X				

Beginning Bass

Song Title:	*Gleich Merlin, dem eitlen Weisen*
Composer:	Fanny Mendelssohn Hensel
Key:	E-flat Major
Tessitura:	D3 to C4
Publisher/Edition:	Alfred Publishing
Typically Sung By:	Baritone, Bass
Challenges:	Some chromaticism
Other info:	Short to moderate phrasing with consistent breaths

Total: 24

	Beginning		Intermediate		Advanced
	1	2	3	4	5
Registration			X		
Accompaniment support			X		
Articulation			X		
Text interpretation		X			
Phrase Length			X		
Range		X			
Tempo		X			
Rhythm	X				
Diction/Language			X		
Lyrical Flow	X				
Melismas	X				

Beginning Bass

Song Title:	*Hör' ich das Liedchen klingen*
Composer:	Robert Schumann
Key:	E minor
Tessitura:	D3 to A3
Publisher/Edition:	The First Book of Baritone/Bass Solos, Book I, edited by Joan Boytim, Hal Leonard
Typically Sung By:	Bass, Bass-Baritone
Challenges:	Controlled line, independent vocal line
Other info:	Legato, long line

Total: 28

	Beginning		Intermediate		Advanced
	1	2	3	4	5
Registration		X			
Accompaniment support				X	
Articulation			X		
Text interpretation		X			
Phrase Length			X		
Range		X			
Tempo				X	
Rhythm		X			
Diction/Language			X		
Lyrical Flow		X			
Melismas	X				

Beginning Bass

Song Title:	**Leave Me, Loathsome Light**
Composer:	G.F. Handel
Key:	D Major
Tessitura:	D2 to B2
Publisher/Edition:	The First Book of Baritone/Bass Solos, Book I, edited by Joan Boytim, Hal Leonard
Typically Sung By:	Bass
Challenges:	Ascending leaps in B section
Other info:	Consonants useful for resonance work, from *Semele*

Total: 25

	Beginning		Intermediate		Advanced
	1	2	3	4	5
Registration				X	
Accompaniment support		X			
Articulation		X			
Text interpretation		X			
Phrase Length			X		
Range			X		
Tempo			X		
Rhythm	X				
Diction/Language		X			
Lyrical Flow		X			
Melismas	X				

Beginning Bass

Song Title:	***Les Poissons***
Composer:	Alan Menken
Key:	G Major
Tessitura:	B2 to G3
Publisher/Edition:	The Teen's Musical Theatre Collection, Young Men's Edition, Hal Leonard
Typically Sung By:	Bass, Baritone
Challenges:	Sung with a French accent, lots of text
Other info:	Intro to French text, small range, characterization, from *The Little Mermaid*

Total: 23

	Beginning		Intermediate		Advanced
	1	2	3	4	5
Registration	X				
Accompaniment support		X			
Articulation				X	
Text interpretation	X				
Phrase Length		X			
Range	X				
Tempo		X			
Rhythm		X			
Diction/Language				X	
Lyrical Flow			X		
Melismas	X				

Beginning Bass

Song Title: ***Maledetto sia l'aspetto***
Composer: Claudio Monteverdi
Key: B-flat Major
Tessitura: B-flat2 to B-flat3
Publisher/Edition: Songs for Beginning Bass Voice, Alan Ord
Typically Sung By: Bass
Challenges: Ascending line, lots of text
Other info: Strophic, baroque style

Total: 26

	Beginning		Intermediate		Advanced
	1	2	3	4	5
Registration			X		
Accompaniment support		X			
Articulation			X		
Text interpretation		X			
Phrase Length		X			
Range			X		
Tempo		X			
Rhythm		X			
Diction/Language			X		
Lyrical Flow			X		
Melismas	X				

Beginning Bass

Song Title: ***Meeresleuchten***
Composer: Carl Loewe
Key: E Major
Tessitura: E2 to B4
Publisher/Edition: Carl Loewes Werke Gesamtausgabe der Balladen, Legenden, Lieder und Gesänge für eine Singstimme, Breitkopf & Härtel
Typically Sung By: Bass
Challenges: Legato line over repeated chordal accompaniment, wide leaps
Other info: Ideal for teaching consistant resonance and flexibility

Total: 30

	Beginning		Intermediate		Advanced
	1	2	3	4	5
Registration			X		
Accompaniment support			X		
Articulation			X		
Text interpretation			X		
Phrase Length			X		
Range				X	
Tempo		X			
Rhythm		X			
Diction/Language			X		
Lyrical Flow			X		
Melismas	X				

Beginning Bass

	Song Title:	***Qui veut chaser une migraine***			
	Composer:	Gabriel Bataille			
	Key:	A minor (modal)			Total: 23
	Tessitura:	C3 to E3			
	Publisher/Edition:	The Solo Song: 1580-1730, Ed. Carol MacClintock, Norton			
	Typically Sung By:	All male voices			
	Challenges:	Drinking song with gross humor			
	Other info:	Transposable, small range			

	Beginning		Intermediate		Advanced
	1	2	3	4	5
Registration		X			
Accompaniment support		X			
Articulation			X		
Text interpretation		X			
Phrase Length		X			
Range		X			
Tempo		X			
Rhythm		X			
Diction/Language			X		
Lyrical Flow		X			
Melismas	X				

Beginning Bass

	Song Title:	***Reiterlied***			
	Composer:	Carl Loewe			
	Key:	A Major			Total: 31
	Tessitura:	C3 to A4			
	Publisher/Edition:	Songs for Beginning Bass Voice, Alan Ord			
	Typically Sung By:	Bass			
	Challenges:	Lots of text			
	Other info:	Useful English translation			

	Beginning		Intermediate		Advanced
	1	2	3	4	5
Registration			X		
Accompaniment support		X			
Articulation				X	
Text interpretation			X		
Phrase Length		X			
Range			X		
Tempo			X		
Rhythm		X			
Diction/Language				X	
Lyrical Flow				X	
Melismas	X				

Beginning Bass

Song Title:	*Se nel ben sempre incostante*	
Composer:	Alessandro Stradella	Total: 29
Key:	E Major	
Tessitura:	E3 to B3	
Publisher/Edition:	Italian Songs of the 17th and 18th Centuries, Vol. 2, Low, International Music Company	
Typically Sung By:	Various	
Challenges:	Some melismatic phrases	
Other info:	Useful for flexibility, lots of stepwise motion	

	Beginning		Intermediate		Advanced
	1	2	3	4	5
Registration			X		
Accompaniment support			X		
Articulation			X		
Text interpretation		X			
Phrase Length			X		
Range			X		
Tempo			X		
Rhythm		X			
Diction/Language			X		
Lyrical Flow		X			
Melismas		X			

Beginning Bass

Song Title:	**Soldier, Soldier, Will You Marry Me?**	
Composer:	American Folksong, Arranged by Brian Dean	Total: 19
Key:	E-flat Major	
Tessitura:	E-flat3 to B-flat3	
Publisher/Edition:	15 Easy Folksong Arrangements, Low Voice, Hal Leonard	
Typically Sung By:	Various	
Challenges:	Many verses, lots of text	
Other info:	Ideal vowels in upper range, storytelling, two characters, alternate pitches given	

	Beginning		Intermediate		Advanced
	1	2	3	4	5
Registration		X			
Accompaniment support	X				
Articulation			X		
Text interpretation	X				
Phrase Length		X			
Range			X		
Tempo	X				
Rhythm	X				
Diction/Language		X			
Lyrical Flow		X			
Melismas	X				

Beginning Bass

Song Title:	**Strike the Viol**	
Composer:	Henry Purcell	Total: 38
Key:	E minor	
Tessitura:	E3 to B3	
Publisher/Edition:	Purcell 40 Songs for Voice and Piano, Low, International Music Company	
Typically Sung By:	Bass	
Challenges:	Melismatic passages	
Other info:	Buoyancy employs lighter mechanism, flexibility	

	Beginning		Intermediate		Advanced
	1	2	3	4	5
Registration			X		
Accompaniment support				X	
Articulation			X		
Text interpretation		X			
Phrase Length				X	
Range		X			
Tempo				X	
Rhythm				X	
Diction/Language			X		
Lyrical Flow				X	
Melismas					X

Beginning Bass

Song Title:	**Waitin' for the Light to Shine**	
Composer:	Roger Miller	Total: 22
Key:	E Major	
Tessitura:	B2 to B3	
Publisher/Edition:	The Singer's Musical Theatre Anthology, Baritone/Bass, Vol. 4, Hal Leonard	
Typically Sung By:	Low Male	
Challenges:	Dialect, voice is somewhat independent	
Other info:	Accessible piece, simple and straightforward, from *Big River*	

	Beginning		Intermediate		Advanced
	1	2	3	4	5
Registration			X		
Accompaniment support		X			
Articulation		X			
Text interpretation		X			
Phrase Length		X			
Range			X		
Tempo	X				
Rhythm		X			
Diction/Language		X			
Lyrical Flow		X			
Melismas	X				

Easier Songs by Important Composers

Song Title:	***An mein Klavier***	
Composer:	Franz Schubert	
Key:	F Major	**Total: 24**
Tessitura:	G4 to C5	
Publisher/Edition:	Schubert 200 Songs, International Music Company	
Typically Sung By:	Various	
Challenges:	Consonant-heavy language	
Other info:	Stepwise motion, breaths after every phrase	

	Beginning		Intermediate		Advanced
	1	2	3	4	5
Registration		X			
Accompaniment support			X		
Articulation			X		
Text interpretation		X			
Phrase Length		X			
Range		X			
Tempo		X			
Rhythm		X			
Diction/Language			X		
Lyrical Flow		X			
Melismas	X				

Easier Songs by Important Composers

Song Title:	***Da unten im Tale***	
Composer:	Johannes Brahms	
Key:	F Major	**Total: 26**
Tessitura:	F4 to D5	
Publisher/Edition:	CD Sheet Music Mid-Romantic German Lieder (Version 2.0)	
Typically Sung By:	Various	
Challenges:	Lyric and long vocal lines, four verses	
Other info:	Strophic, beautiful melody	

	Beginning		Intermediate		Advanced
	1	2	3	4	5
Registration	X				
Accompaniment support			X		
Articulation			X		
Text interpretation		X			
Phrase Length				X	
Range	X				
Tempo				X	
Rhythm		X			
Diction/Language			X		
Lyrical Flow		X			
Melismas	X				

Easier Songs by Important Composers

Song Title:	***Das Kinderspiel***
Composer:	W.A. Mozart
Key:	G Major
Tessitura:	G4 to C5
Publisher/Edition:	Mozart Complete Songs for Medium Voice, Bärenreiter
Typically Sung By:	Various
Challenges:	Catch breaths, lots of text
Other info:	Florid writing promotes lighter mechanism, strophic

Total: 23

	Beginning		Intermediate		Advanced
	1	2	3	4	5
Registration	X				
Accompaniment support	X				
Articulation				X	
Text interpretation		X			
Phrase Length			X		
Range	X				
Tempo		X			
Rhythm		X			
Diction/Language				X	
Lyrical Flow		X			
Melismas	X				

Easier Songs by Important Composers

Song Title:	***Der Gleichsinn***
Composer:	Joseph Haydn
Key:	A Major
Tessitura:	G-sharp4 to E5
Publisher/Edition:	Pathways of Song, Vol. 4, High Voice, Witmark Educational Publications
Typically Sung By:	Soprano
Challenges:	Climax in area of passaggio, lots of text
Other info:	Good for characterization: varied emotions in strophes

Total: 26

	Beginning		Intermediate		Advanced
	1	2	3	4	5
Registration			X		
Accompaniment support	X				
Articulation				X	
Text interpretation		X			
Phrase Length		X			
Range			X		
Tempo		X			
Rhythm	X				
Diction/Language				X	
Lyrical Flow			X		
Melismas	X				

Easier Songs by Important Composers

Song Title: ***Der Mond***
Composer: Felix Mendelssohn
Key: E Major
Tessitura: G-sharp4 to E5
Publisher/Edition: Mendelssohn 79 Songs, Kalmus
Typically Sung By: Various
Challenges: Syllabic text on 8th notes, ascending leaps into passaggio
Other info: Beautiful melody

Total: 33

	Beginning		Intermediate		Advanced
	1	2	3	4	5
Registration			X		
Accompaniment support				X	
Articulation				X	
Text interpretation		X			
Phrase Length			X		
Range			X		
Tempo		X			
Rhythm				X	
Diction/Language				X	
Lyrical Flow			X		
Melismas	X				

Easier Songs by Important Composers

Song Title: ***Des Sennen Abschied***
Composer: Robert Schumann
Key: C Major
Tessitura: E4 to E5
Publisher/Edition: Robert Schumann Lieder, Vol. 2, Edition Peters
Typically Sung By: Various
Challenges: Difficult range, large intervallic leaps
Other info: Beautiful melody

Total: 30

	Beginning		Intermediate		Advanced
	1	2	3	4	5
Registration				X	
Accompaniment support			X		
Articulation			X		
Text interpretation		X			
Phrase Length		X			
Range				X	
Tempo		X			
Rhythm			X		
Diction/Language			X		
Lyrical Flow			X		
Melismas	X				

Easier Songs by Important Composers

Song Title:	***Die Landlust***
Composer:	Joseph Haydn
Key:	C Major
Tessitura:	G4 to C5
Publisher/Edition:	Haydn Canzonettas and Songs, Edition Peters
Typically Sung By:	Various
Challenges:	Many verses
Other info:	Accessible phrase lengths, strophic

Total: 27

	Beginning		Intermediate		Advanced
	1	2	3	4	5
Registration		X			
Accompaniment support		X			
Articulation				X	
Text interpretation		X			
Phrase Length		X			
Range		X			
Tempo		X			
Rhythm		X			
Diction/Language				X	
Lyrical Flow				X	
Melismas	X				

Easier Songs by Important Composers

Song Title:	***Diggi, daggi, shurry, murry***
Composer:	W.A. Mozart
Key:	C minor
Tessitura:	C3 to A3
Publisher/Edition:	Kalmus
Typically Sung By:	Low voice male
Challenges:	Fast articulation
Other info:	Nonsense syllables, simpler aria, from *Bastien und Bastienne*

Total: 30

	Beginning		Intermediate		Advanced
	1	2	3	4	5
Registration				X	
Accompaniment support			X		
Articulation				X	
Text interpretation	X				
Phrase Length			X		
Range				X	
Tempo	X				
Rhythm			X		
Diction/Language				X	
Lyrical Flow		X			
Melismas	X				

Easier Songs by Important Composers

Song Title:	***Ei, wie schmeckt der Coffee süße***
Composer:	J.S. Bach
Key:	D Major
Tessitura:	D4 to A5
Publisher/Edition:	Bach Arias From Secular Cantatas, Vol. II, Kalmus Edition
Typically Sung By:	Soprano
Challenges:	Florid writing
Other info:	Fun character piece from a cantata about coffee

Total: 37

	Beginning		Intermediate		Advanced
	1	2	3	4	5
Registration				X	
Accompaniment support				X	
Articulation				X	
Text interpretation		X			
Phrase Length			X		
Range				X	
Tempo		X			
Rhythm				X	
Diction/Language				X	
Lyrical Flow				X	
Melismas		X			

Easier Songs by Important Composers

Song Title:	***Gruß***
Composer:	Felix Mendelssohn
Key:	D Major
Tessitura:	F-sharp4 to C-sharp5
Publisher/Edition:	Felix Mendelssohn Songs for Voice and Piano, Dover
Typically Sung By:	Various
Challenges:	Ascending arpeggios, chromaticism
Other info:	Legato line, moving piano part helps breath energy

Total: 19

	Beginning		Intermediate		Advanced
	1	2	3	4	5
Registration			X		
Accompaniment support					
Articulation		X			
Text interpretation		X			
Phrase Length		X			
Range		X			
Tempo	X				
Rhythm	X				
Diction/Language			X		
Lyrical Flow		X			
Melismas	X				

Easier Songs by Important Composers

Song Title:	***Hat man nicht auch Gold beineben***
Composer:	Ludwig van Beethoven
Key:	B-flat Major
Tessitura:	E-flat3 to C4
Publisher/Edition:	Bass-Lieder Arien, Edition Peters
Typically Sung By:	Bass
Challenges:	Lots of text, rhythmically tricky
Other info:	Accessible for a graduate student, from *Fidelio*

Total: 39

	Beginning		Intermediate		Advanced
	1	2	3	4	5
Registration				X	
Accompaniment support				X	
Articulation					X
Text interpretation		X			
Phrase Length		X			
Range					X
Tempo			X		
Rhythm					X
Diction/Language				X	
Lyrical Flow				X	
Melismas	X				

Easier Songs by Important Composers

Song Title:	**A Legend**
Composer:	Pyotr Ilyich Tchaikovsky
Key:	E minor
Tessitura:	E4 to B4
Publisher/Edition:	The First Book of Mezzo Soprano/Alto Solos, Part II, edited by Joan Boytim, Hal Leonard
Typically Sung By:	Soprano, Mezzo Soprano
Challenges:	Onsets in passaggio, tricky leaps
Other info:	Often sung in English

Total: 25

	Beginning		Intermediate		Advanced
	1	2	3	4	5
Registration			X		
Accompaniment support		X			
Articulation			X		
Text interpretation		X			
Phrase Length		X			
Range		X			
Tempo		X			
Rhythm		X			
Diction/Language			X		
Lyrical Flow			X		
Melismas	X				

Easier Songs by Important Composers

Song Title: *Litanei*
Composer: Franz Schubert
Key: E-flat Major
Tessitura: E-flat4 to C5
Publisher/Edition: Breitkopf & Hartel
Typically Sung By: Various
Challenges: Langsam tempo, long lines, many verses
Other info: Lullaby, strophic, transposable, useful for support

Total: 34

	Beginning		Intermediate		Advanced
	1	2	3	4	5
Registration			X		
Accompaniment support			X		
Articulation				X	
Text interpretation		X			
Phrase Length				X	
Range			X		
Tempo				X	
Rhythm			X		
Diction/Language				X	
Lyrical Flow			X		
Melismas	X				

Easier Songs by Important Composers

Song Title: *Mein Garten*
Composer: Robert Schumann
Key: A minor
Tessitura: A4 to E5
Publisher/Edition: Schumann Complete Songs Vol.2: 87 Songs by Robert Schumann, Edition Peters
Typically Sung By: Various
Challenges: *p* and *pp* dynamics, sits in passaggio
Other info: Melancholy text

Total: 28

	Beginning		Intermediate		Advanced
	1	2	3	4	5
Registration			X		
Accompaniment support			X		
Articulation			X		
Text interpretation			X		
Phrase Length		X			
Range		X			
Tempo		X			
Rhythm		X			
Diction/Language			X		
Lyrical Flow				X	
Melismas	X				

Easier Songs by Important Composers

Song Title:	**More Love or More Disdain**	
Composer:	Henry Purcell	
Key:	G Major	Total: 26
Tessitura:	G4 to C5	
Publisher/Edition:	Henry Purcell 40 Songs, High Voice, Vol. 2, International Music Company	
Typically Sung By:	Various	
Challenges:	Tessitura and range	
Other info:	Character piece	

	Beginning		Intermediate		Advanced
	1	2	3	4	5
Registration		X			
Accompaniment support			X		
Articulation			X		
Text interpretation			X		
Phrase Length		X			
Range			X		
Tempo		X			
Rhythm		X			
Diction/Language			X		
Lyrical Flow		X			
Melismas	X				

Easier Songs by Important Composers

Song Title:	***Non, je n'irai plus au bois***	
Composer:	Bergerettes, Arranged by J.B. Weckerlin	Total: 31
Key:	A minor	
Tessitura:	E4 to E5	
Publisher/Edition:	Bergerettes, Twenty Romances and Songs of the Eighteenth Century, G. Schirmer, Hal Leonard	
Typically Sung By:	Soprano	
Challenges:	Lots of text, tempo changes	
Other info:	Well supported, good storytelling piece	

	Beginning		Intermediate		Advanced
	1	2	3	4	5
Registration			X		
Accompaniment support		X			
Articulation				X	
Text interpretation		X			
Phrase Length		X			
Range			X		
Tempo			X		
Rhythm			X		
Diction/Language				X	
Lyrical Flow				X	
Melismas	X				

Easier Songs by Important Composers

Song Title: ***Oiseaux si tous les ans***
Composer: W.A. Mozart
Key: C Major
Tessitura: A3 to F4
Publisher/Edition: Mozart Complete Songs for High Voice, Bärenreiter
Typically Sung By: Various
Challenges: Modulation in middle of song
Other info: Accessible phrase lengths, dotted rhythms, invokes lighter mechanism

Total: 31

	Beginning		Intermediate		Advanced
	1	2	3	4	5
Registration			X		
Accompaniment support			X		
Articulation			X		
Text interpretation		X			
Phrase Length			X		
Range			X		
Tempo		X			
Rhythm		X	X		
Diction/Language			X		
Lyrical Flow			X		
Melismas	X				

Easier Songs by Important Composers

Song Title: ***Sehnsucht nach dem frühlinge***
Composer: W.A. Mozart
Key: F Major
Tessitura: F3 to F5
Publisher/Edition: Mozart Complete Songs for High Voice, Bärenreiter
Typically Sung By: Various
Challenges: Ascending arpeggios, 10 verses
Other info: Strophic, invokes lighter mechanism

Total: 27

	Beginning		Intermediate		Advanced
	1	2	3	4	5
Registration			X		
Accompaniment support		X			
Articulation				X	
Text interpretation		X			
Phrase Length		X			
Range		X			
Tempo		X			
Rhythm		X			
Diction/Language				X	
Lyrical Flow			X		
Melismas	X				

Easier Songs by Important Composers

Song Title: ***Sonntag***
Composer: Johannes Brahms
Key: F Major
Tessitura: C3 to C4
Publisher/Edition: Johannes Brahms 75 Songs, High Voice, Hal Leonard
Typically Sung By: Various
Challenges: Large ascending leap, lots of text
Other info: Supported vocal line, beautiful melody

Total: 26

	Beginning		Intermediate		Advanced
	1	2	3	4	5
Registration			X		
Accompaniment support			X		
Articulation			X		
Text interpretation		X			
Phrase Length			X		
Range		X			
Tempo		X			
Rhythm	X				
Diction/Language			X		
Lyrical Flow			X		
Melismas	X				

Easier Songs by Important Composers

Song Title: ***Wanderers Nachtlied***
Composer: Franz Schubert
Key: B-flat Major
Tessitura: B-flat3 to B-flat4
Publisher/Edition: The First Book of Tenor Solos, Part II, edited by Joan Boytim, Hal Leonard
Typically Sung By: Various
Challenges: Sustained, lento
Other info: Useful for support

Total: 32

	Beginning		Intermediate		Advanced
	1	2	3	4	5
Registration			X		
Accompaniment support			X		
Articulation			X		
Text interpretation			X		
Phrase Length				X	
Range			X		
Tempo				X	
Rhythm			X		
Diction/Language			X		
Lyrical Flow		X			
Melismas	X				

Song and Aria Index for a Variety of Technical Goals and Genres

The following index will help you get started in making appropriate repertoire choices. The songs and arias are organized by the particular area of vocal production that needs to be developed or by genre (i.e. articulation, breath, resonance, characterization, humorous).

SUGGESTED REPERTOIRE FOR TECHNICAL ISSUES		
What is the PRIMARY technical issue to be addressed with repertoire?	Title of the piece	Composer of the piece
Agility	*Agita de' venti dall'onte*	Antonio Vivaldi
Agility	*Aria di romanesca*	Giulio Caccini
Agility	*Aufträge*	Robert Schumann
Agility	*Batti, batti*	W.A. Mozart
Agility	*Beggar's Song*	Samuel Barber
Agility	*Ch'io mai vi possa*	G. Handel
Agility	*Charmant Papillon*	André Campra
Agility	*Chi mi confort'ahime!*	Giulio Caccini
Agility	Come and Trip It	G.F. Handel
Agility	Come Live With Me	G.F. Handel
Agility	*Die Post*	Franz Schubert
Agility	*Die Forelle*	Franz Schubert
Agility	*Gia il sole dal Gange*	Alessandro Scarlatti
Agility	I Heard a Blackbird in a Tree	Albert Arlen
Agility	*Ich folge dir gleichfalls*	J.S. Bach
Agility	*Il Bacio*	Luigi Arditi
Agility	*La Pastorella delle Alpi*	Gioacchino Rossini
Agility	*La Solitundine (2nd aria)*	G.F. Handel
Agility	*Lagrimetta alle pupille*	Antonio Vivaldi
Agility	*Mandoline*	Gabriel Fauré
Agility	*O servi, volate*	Antonio Vivaldi
Agility	*Par min dirti*	Antonio Vivaldi
Agility	*Passepied*	Léo Delibes
Agility	*Pur dicesti, o bocca bella*	Antonio Lotti
Agility	*Saper bramate*	Giovanni Paisiello
Agility	*Se parto, se resto*	Antonio Vivaldi
Agility	Should He Upbraid	Henry Rowley Bishop
Agility	*Spesso vibra per suo gioco*	Alessandro Scarlatti
Agility	The cuckoo	Madeleine Dring
Agility	The Lass With the Delicate Air	Michael Arne
Agility	There the Brisk, Sparkling Nectar	G.F. Handel
Agility	Shepherd! Thy Demeanour Vary	Thomas Brown
Agility	So Shall the Lute and Harp	G.F. Handel
Agility	*Spriate pur, spirate*	Stefano Donaudy
Agility	Think No More Lad	George Butterworth
Agility	*Ti sento*	Antonio Vivaldi
Agility	*Um Mitternacht*	Carl Friderich Zelter
Agility	*Un Momento di Contento*	G.F. Handel
Agility	*Un moto di gioia*	W.A. Mozart
Agility	*Vittoria, Vittoria*	Giacomo Carissimi
Agility	*Wer hat dies Liedlein erdacht*	Gustav Mahler

Articulation	Anthem	Anderson & Ulvaeus, Rice
Articulation	*Arie aus dem Spiegel von Arcadien*	Arnold Schoenberg
Articulation	Away to Twiver	Peter Warlock
Articulation	*Bei der Wiege*	Felix Mendelssohn
Articulation	Bread and Cherries	Ivor Gurney
Articulation	*Cantique*	Nadia Boulanger
Articulation	*Che fiero costume*	Giovanni Legrenzi
Articulation	Ching-a-ring chaw	Aaron Copland (arr.)
Articulation	*Christbaum*	Peter Cornelius
Articulation	Come Away Death	Rodger Quilter
Articulation	*Danza, danza, fanciulla*	Francesco Durante
Articulation	*Deh, rendetemi*	Francesco Provenzale
Articulation	Diaphenia	Dominick Argento
Articulation	*Die beiden Grenadiere*	Robert Schumann
Articulation	Dirge	Dominick Argento
Articulation	Early in the Morning	Ned Rorem
Articulation	*Ein goldenes Kettlein*	Joseph Marx
Articulation	*El Caballito*	Silvestra Revueltas
Articulation	*El tra la la y el punteado*	Enrique Granados
Articulation	*Fußreise*	Hugo Wolf
Articulation	Green Finch and Linnet Bird	Stephen Sondheim
Articulation	Hymn	Dominick Argento
Articulation	I bought me a cat	Aaron Copland (arr.)
Articulation	I Feel Pretty	Leonard Bernstein & Stephen Sondheim
Articulation	I Whistle a Happy Tune	Richard Rodgers
Articulation	*Il Giglio e la Rosa*	Gaetano Donizetti
Articulation	*Im Sturme*	Johann Karl Gottfried Loewe
Articulation	*Kommen und Scheiden*	Fanny Mendelssohn Hensel
Articulation	*Liebst du um Schönheit*	Clara Wieck Schumann
Articulation	Lion Tamer	Stephen Schwartz
Articulation	Love is a plaintive song	Gilbert & Sullivan
Articulation	Love's Philosophy	Roger Quilter
Articulation	*Mai*	Gabriel Fauré
Articulation	*Mandoline*	Claude Debussy
Articulation	*Meine Liebe is grün*	Johannes Brahms
Articulation	Mirth Admit Me	G.F. Handel
Articulation	Mr. Snow	Rodgers & Hammerstein
Articulation	Nine of the Clock	Ivor Gurney
Articulation	*Nun lass uns Frieden Schliessen*	Hugo Wolf
Articulation	Oh Fair to See	Gerald Finzi
Articulation	Oliver Cromwell	Benjamin Britten (arr.)
Articulation	*Per pietà*	Alessandro Stradella
Articulation	*Per pieta bell'idol mio*	Vincenzo Bellini
Articulation	*Persin le bimbe vengono da be*	W.A. Mozart
Articulation	*Petit Oiseau*	Hector Berlioz
Articulation	*Petite Abeille*	Bertrand de Bacilly
Articulation	Sailor's Song	Franz Joseph Haydn
Articulation	*Se cerca, se dice*	Antonio Vivaldi
Articulation	Sea Fever	John Ireland
Articulation	Simple Gifts	Traditional

Articulation	Sleep	Dominick Argento
Articulation	Spick and Span	Theodore Chanler
Articulation	Spring	Dominick Argento
Articulation	The Lads in Their Hundreds	George Butterworth
Articulation	They All Laughed	George Gershwin
Articulation	*Toglietemi la vita ancor*	Alessandro Scarlatti
Articulation	Tonight at Eight	Jerry Bock and Sheldon Harnick
Articulation	Vanilla Ice Cream	Jerry Bock
Articulation	*Widmung*	Robert Schumann
Articulation	Winter	Dominick Argento
Articulation	*Wohin?*	Franz Schubert
Articulation	*Zéphyr*	Claude Debussy
Breathing	A Minor Bird	Celius Dougherty
Breathing	*Adieu*	Gabriel Fauré
Breathing	All At Once	Kurt Weill
Breathing	*An Chloe*	W.A. Mozart
Breathing	*An den Mond*	Franz Schubert
Breathing	*Aria di Agratina*	Franz Joseph Haydn
Breathing	*Aria di Rosina*	Franz Joseph Haydn
Breathing	*Auf Flüglen des Gesanges*	Felix Mendelssohn Bartholdy
Breathing	*Ballade des gros dindons*	Emmanuel Chabrier
Breathing	*Bist du bei mir*	J.S. Bach
Breathing	*Blind*	John Ireland
Breathing	*Caro Mio Ben*	Giuseppe Giordani
Breathing	*Cavatina di Alcina*	Franz Joseph Haydn
Breathing	*Che cangi tempra*	Gaetano Donizetti
Breathing	*Che t'ho fatt'io*	Francesca Caccini
Breathing	Come Again, Sweet Love	John Dowland
Breathing	Comedy Tonight	Stephen Sondheim
Breathing	*Da unten im Tale*	Johannes Brahms
Breathing	*Das Veilchen*	Franz Liszt
Breathing	*Date abbiento al mio dolore*	Stefano Donaudy
Breathing	*Dein Angesicht*	Robert Schumann
Breathing	*Der Zauberer*	W.A. Mozart
Breathing	*Die Lotosblume*	Robert Schumann
Breathing	Down by the Sally Gardens	Richard Donovan
Breathing	Drink to Me Only with Thine Eyes	Colonel Mellish, arr. Quilter
Breathing	*Elégie*	Jules Massenet
Breathing	*Es muss ein wunderbares sein*	Franz Liszt
Breathing	*Fa così lodoletta che fuggi*	Leonardo Vinci
Breathing	For Your Delight	Richard Hundley
Breathing	From the Land of the Sky-Blue Water	Charles Wakefield Cadman
Breathing	*Grablied für die Mutter*	Franz Schubert
Breathing	Hands, Eyes and Heart	Ralph Vaughan Williams
Breathing	*Heidenröslein*	Franz Schubert
Breathing	Hope	John Ireland
Breathing	I Like It Here	Alec Wilder
Breathing	*Im Wunderschönen Monat Mai*	Robert Schumann
Breathing	In a Myrtle Shade	Charles Griffes
Breathing	*In stiller Nacht*	Johannes Brahms

Breathing	Johanna	Stephen Sondheim
Breathing	*La Serenata*	Francesco Paolo Tosti
Breathing	*Lachen und Weinen*	Franz Schubert
Breathing	*Les matelots*	Gabriel Fauré
Breathing	*Lieblingsplätzchen*	Felix Mendelssohn
Breathing	Linden Lea	Ralph Vaughan Williams
Breathing	*Ma rendi pur contento*	Vincenzo Bellini
Breathing	Newborn	John Ireland
Breathing	*Nocturne*	Gabriel Fauré
Breathing	*Non piango e non sospiro*	Giulio Caccini
Breathing	*O Leggiadri Occhi Belli*	Anonymous
Breathing	*O Luna lucente*	Joseph Haydn
Breathing	O Mistress Mine	Roger Quilter
Breathing	*O pargoletto arciero*	Bernardo Pasquini
Breathing	O Waly, Waly	Benjamin Britten (arr.)
Breathing	*Ouvre tes yeux bleus*	Jules Massenet
Breathing	*Parla piu piano*	Nino Rota
Breathing	Passing By	Peter Warlock
Breathing	Places to Live	William Bolcom
Breathing	*Pur Ritorno*	G.F. Handel
Breathing	*Questa mano e questo cuore*	Joseph Haydn
Breathing	*S'il est un charmant gazon*	Franz Liszt
Breathing	*Se bel rio*	Raffaello Rontani
Breathing	Sea Fever	John Ireland
Breathing	Sea-Shell	Carl Engel
Breathing	Serenade	Franz Josef Haydn
Breathing	Shall I compare thee?	Stephen Paulus
Breathing	Shall We Gather by the River	Aaron Copland (arr.)
Breathing	Silvia, now your scorn	Henry Purcell
Breathing	Sometimes I Feel Like a Motherless Child	Anonymous
Breathing	*Stringhe e ferri*	Gioacchino Rossini
Breathing	The Ashgrove	Benjamin Britten (arr.)
Breathing	The Black Dress	John Jacob Niles (arr.)
Breathing	The Daisies	Samuel Barber
Breathing	The English Songs	Franz Joseph Haydn
Breathing	The Lass From Low Countree	John Jacob Niles (arr.)
Breathing	The Only Child	John Ireland
Breathing	The Salley Gardens	Benjamin Britten (arr.)
Breathing	The Water is Wide	Mark Hayes (arr.)
Breathing	The Year's at the Spring	Amy Beach
Breathing	They Call the Wind Maria	Lerner and Loewe
Breathing	Tired	Ralph Vaughan Williams
Breathing	*Verborgenheit*	Hugo Wolf
Breathing	*Vezzosette e care pupillette*	Andrea Falconieri
Breathing	When I Have Sung My Songs	Ernest Charles
Breathing	When one has a Sweetheart	Clara Kathleen Rogers
Breathing	Wher'er You Walk	G.F. Handel
Breathing	With Rue My Heart is Laden	George Butterworth
Legato	*An Sylvia*	Franz Schubert
Legato	*Chanson d'Automne*	Jean Berger

Legato	De Gospel Train	Harry Burleigh
Legato	*Der Neurigiere*	Franz Schubert
Legato	*Der Nussbaum*	Robert Schumann
Legato	*Die Lotosblume*	Robert Schumann
Legato	*Die Mainacht*	Johannes Brahms
Legato	For Your Delight	Richard Hundley
Legato	*Frülingsglaube*	Franz Schubert
Legato	Go Down in the Lonesome Valley	Harry Burleigh
Legato	Leave Me	G.F. Handel
Legato	Linden Lea	Ralph Vaughan Williams
Legato	Maiden Snow	Richard Hundley
Legato	Music for a While	Henry Purcell
Legato	My Heart is Like a Singing Bird	C.H.H. Parry
Legato	Now Sleeps the Crimson Petal	Roger Quilter
Legato	*O del mio amato ben*	Stefano Donaudy
Legato	*O di tua man*	Antonio Vivaldi
Legato	*O Isis und Osiris*	W.A. Mozart
Legato	O Mistress Mine	Roger Quilter
Legato	Peace Crowned with Roses	G.F. Handel
Legato	*Piango, gemo, sospiro*	Antonio Vivaldi
Legato	*Romance*	Claude Debussy
Legato	*Sapphische Ode*	Johannes Brahms
Legato	The Lord's Prayer	Albert Hay Malotte
Legato	*Widmung*	Robert Franz
Registration	A Birthday	Sharon Davis
Registration	A-tisket A-tasket	Ella Fitzgerald and Van Alexander
Registration	*Almen se non poss'io*	Vincenzo Bellini
Registration	Arm, Arm Ye Brave	G.F. Handel
Registration	At Sea	Charles Ives
Registration	*Auf Flügeln des Gesanges*	Felix Mendelssohn
Registration	*Bei der Wiege*	Felix Mendelssohn
Registration	*Belle Hermione, Hèlas!*	Jean-Baptiste Lully
Registration	Black Coffee	Burke and Webster
Registration	Blackberry Winter	Alec Wilder
Registration	Blessing of the Boats	Ricky Ian Gordon
Registration	Blow, Blow Thou Winter Wind	Madeleine Dring
Registration	Blow, Blow Thou Winter Wind	Roger Quilter
Registration	*Ch'io mai vi possa*	G. F. Handel
Registration	*Che cangi tempra*	Gaetano Donizetti
Registration	*Che faro senza Euridice?*	Christoph Willibald Gluck
Registration	Come Away Death	Madeleine Dring
Registration	Come Away Death	Gerald Finzi
Registration	Come in Morning	Kurt Weill
Registration	Come Ready and See Me	Richard Hundley
Registration	*Dem Schutzengel*	Johannes Brahms
Registration	*Der Jager im Walde*	Johannes Brahms
Registration	*Der kleine Sandman bin ich*	Englebert Humperdinck
Registration	*Der König in Thule*	Carl Friedrich Zelter
Registration	*Der Mond*	Felix Mendelssohn
Registration	*Der Tod und das Madchen*	Franz Schubert

Registration	Diaphenia	Francis Pilkington
Registration	*Die Sonne scheint nicht mehr*	Johannes Brahms
Registration	*Dolce Scherza*	Giacomo Antonio Perti
Registration	Don't put your daughter on the Stage, Mrs. Worthington	Sir Noël Coward
Registration	*Douce dame jolie*	Guillaume de Machaut
Registration	Dream a Little Dream	Wilbur Schwandt & Andre
Registration	*Du bist wie eine blume*	Robert Schumann
Registration	*En las montañas de Asturias*	Joaqin Rodrigo
Registration	*Erlaube mir feins Mädchen*	Johannes Brahms
Registration	*Erstes Grün*	Robert Schumann
Registration	*Esser mesto il mio cor*	Friedrich von Flotow
Registration	*Estribillo*	Joaquin Rodrigo
Registration	Faithfu'Johnnie	Ludwig Beethoven
Registration	*Figlia mia*	G.F. Handel
Registration	*Filli, Non T'amo Piu*	Giacomo Carissimi
Registration	*Fleurs*	Francis Poulenc
Registration	Four Nights	Ralph Vaughan Williams
Registration	Happy Working Song	Alan Menken
Registration	Have you seen but a white lily grow	Unknown
Registration	*Hochlandisches Wiegenlied*	Robert Schumann
Registration	Hush, Be Silent	Henry Purcell
Registration	I Remember	Stephen Sondheim
Registration	In a simple way I love you	Nancy Ford
Registration	*In einem Kühlen Grunde*	Traditional
Registration	In the dark pinewood	Samuel Barber
Registration	In the Springtime	Betty Jackson King
Registration	Is it Really Me?	Harvey Schmidt
Registration	It Was a Lover and His Lass	Madeleine Dring
Registration	*Jeg elsker Dig*	Edvard Grieg
Registration	Karen	Charles Ives
Registration	*La belle table est mise*	arr. William Arms Fischer
Registration	*La Diva de L'Empire*	Erik Satie
Registration	*La Maison Grise*	André Messager
Registration	*La Mañana*	Alberto Ginastera
Registration	The last rose of summer	Benjamin Britten (arr.)
Registration	*Le Fils de la Femme Poisson*	Charles Trenet
Registration	*L'esule*	Giuseppe Verdi
Registration	*L'Ora è tarda*	Paolo Tosti
Registration	*Le Charme*	Ernest Chausson
Registration	Love Has Eyes	Henry Bishop
Registration	Love Look Away	Rodgers & Hammerstein
Registration	Loveliest of Trees	George Butterworth
Registration	Loveliest of Trees	John Duke
Registration	*Lydia*	Gabriel Fauré
Registration	*Marmotte*	Ludwig Beethoven
Registration	Menelaus	Ralph Vaughan Williams
Registration	Much More	Harvey Schmidt
Registration	My German Boyfriend	Richard Pearson Thomas
Registration	*Nel pur ardor*	Jacopo Peri
Registration	*Non, je ne crois pas*	Unknown
Registration	*O chiome belle*	Francesca Caccini

Rcegistration	*O crudel che il mio pianto non vedi*	Vincenzo Bellini
Registration	*O servi, volate*	Antonio Vivaldi
Registration	Once Upon a Dream	Sammy Fain and Jack Lawrence
Registration	Parting	Thomas Pasatieri
Registration	*Per pianto la mia carne*	Eleonora Orsini
Registration	*Phantasie*	Gustav Mahler
Registration	*Quien amores ten*	Luis de Milan
Registration	*Romance*	Claude Debussy
Registration	*Selve, voi che le speranze*	Salvator Rosa
Registration	*Sérénade Italienne*	Ernest Chausson
Registration	Smile	Charles (Charlie) Chaplan
Registration	*Sogno d'infanzia*	Vincenzo Bellini
Registration	Sometimes I feel like a motherless child	Traditional
Registration	*Sorge il sol! Che fait tu?*	Stefano Donaudy
Registration	Spring Day	Edwin McArthur
Registration	Strings in the Earth and Air	Richard Hundley
Registration	*Suleika*	Felix Mendelssohn
Registration	Take, O take those lips away	Madeleine Dring
Registration	That's him	Kurt Weill
Registration	The Aureole	George Whitefield Chadwick
Registration	The Boy Next Door	Martin and Blane
Registration	The Cloak, the Boat and the Shoes	Ben Moore
Registration	The Cuckoo	Madeleine Dring
Registration	The Lost chord	Arthur Sullivan
Registration	The Nightingale, Charm'd by the Rose	Nicolai Rimsky-Korsakov
Registration	The Slitheree-Dee	Shel Silverstein
Registration	The Sound of Music	Rodgers & Hammerstein
Registration	The Virgin's Cradle-Hymn	Herbert Fryer
Registration	There is a lady sweet and kind	Peter Warlock
Registration	They Can't Take That Away From Me	George Gershwin
Registration	Those Evening Bells	Charles Ives
Registration	Under the Greenwood Tree	Madeleine Dring
Registration	*Utro* (Morning)	Sergei Rachmaninoff
Registration	*Vieni, o mio diletto*	Antonio Vivaldi
Registration	Wayfaring Stranger	John Jacob Niles (arr.)
Registration	*Weihnachtliches Wiegenlied*	Arvo Pärt
Registration	When a felon's not engaged in his employment	Gilbert & Sullivan
Registration	When I was One and Twenty	George Butterworth
Registration	Wind of the Western Sea	Graham Peel
Registration	You don't know this man	Jason Robert Brown
Registration	Young And Foolish	Arnold B. Horwitt & Albert Hague
Registration	*Życzenie*	Fryderyk Chopin
Resonance	*Almen se non poss'io*	Vincenzo Bellini
Resonance	*Ave Maria (su due note)*	Gioacchino Rossini
Resonance	*Bois Epais*	Jean-Baptiste Lully
Resonance	*Chant Breton*	Edouard Lalo
Resonance	Create In Me A Clean Heart	Carl F. Mueller
Resonance	Declaration of Independence	Celius Dougherty
Resonance	*Der Nussbaum*	Robert Schumann

Resonance	*Dimmi, ben mio*	Ludwig van Beethoven
Resonance	*Du Ring an meinem Finger*	Robert Schumann
Resonance	Eileen Aroon	Traditional
Resonance	Envoi de Fleurs	Charles Gounod
Resonance	Grandma	Theodore Chanler
Resonance	*Gute Nacht*	Robert Franz
Resonance	I Am in Need of Music	Ben Moore
Resonance	I Could Have Danced All Night	Frederick Loewe
Resonance	I Know that My Redeemer Liveth	G.F. Handel
Resonance	I Wish it so	Marc Blitzstein
Resonance	*Ich liebe dich*	Ludwig van Beethoven
Resonance	*Ich liebe dich*	Edvard Grieg
Resonance	*Il bacio*	Luigi Arditi
Resonance	*Immer leiser wird mein Schlummer*	Johannes Brahms
Resonance	*La Brise*	Camille Saint-Saëns
Resonance	*La sauterelle*	Francis Poulenc
Resonance	*Le Chanson du Tambourine*	Unknown
Resonance	*Le Soir*	Charles Gounod
Resonance	*Le Violette*	Alessandro Scarlatti
Resonance	*Ma rendi pur contento*	Vincenzo Bellini
Resonance	Man is for the Woman Made	Henry Purcell
Resonance	Moonlight's Watermelon	Richard Hundley
Resonance	Music for a while	Henry Purcell
Resonance	*Non posso disperar*	Giovanni Battista Bononcini
Resonance	*Nos plaisirs seront peu durables*	G. F. Handel
Resonance	Nymphs and Shepherds	Henry Purcell
Resonance	*O Cessate di Piagarmi*	Alessandro Scarlatti
Resonance	*O che odor di buono*	Stefano Donaudy
Resonance	*O del mio dolce ardor*	Christoph Willibald Gluck
Resonance	*O do not love too long*	Ned Rorem
Resonance	Ol' Man River	Jerome Kern
Resonance	Old Sir Faulk	William Walton
Resonance	*Posate, dormite*	Giovanni Battista Bassani
Resonance	*Prison*	Gabriel Fauré
Resonance	*Rosefrail*	Ernest John Moeran
Resonance	*Sebben crudele*	Antonio Caldara
Resonance	*Seit ich ihn gesehen*	Schumann
Resonance	September Song	Kurt Weill
Resonance	Shall We Gather at the River	Aaron Copland (arr.)
Resonance	*Si mes vers avaient des ailes*	Reynaldo Hahn
Resonance	Silent Noon	Ralph Vaughan Williams
Resonance	*Sogno d'infanzia*	Vincenzo Bellini
Resonance	Sometimes a day goes by	John Kander
Resonance	Song at Night	Trevor Hold
Resonance	Tea for Two	Vincent Youmans & Irving Caesar
Resonance	The Lamb	Theodore Chanler
Resonance	The Metropolitan Tower	Lori Laitman
Resonance	The Pilgrim's Home	G. F. Handel
Resonance	*Un certo non so che*	Antonio Vivaldi
Resonance	*Vaga luna*	Vincenzo Bellini
Resonance	*Verdi prati*	G. F. Handel

Resonance	*Vittoria, Vittoria*	Giacomo Carissimi
Resonance	When I Was a Lad	Arthur Sullivan
Resonance	Where'er You Walk	G.F. Handel
Resonance	Windy Nights	Seymour Barab
Support	A Brisk Young Sailor	George Butterworth
Support	Amazing Grace	Jay Althouse (arr.)
Support	Asleep	Elizabeth Sprague Coolidge
Support	Beautiful Dreamer	Stephen Foster
Support	*Berglied*	Carl Friederich Zelter
Support	Compensation	Charles Lloyd, Jr.
Support	Dedication	Robert Franz
Support	*Der Frühling*	Johannes Brahms
Support	*Die Forelle*	Franz Schubert
Support	*Es hat die Rose sich beklagt*	Robert Franz
Support	Everything Else	Tom Kitt
Support	Ev'ry time We Say Goodbye	Cole Porter
Support	Fain Would I, Chloris	John Blow
Support	Give me your hand	John Duke
Support	Gottes Macht und Vorsehung	Ludwig van Beethoven
Support	Hawk and Buckle	Ivor Gurney
Support	How Sweet the Moonlight Sleeps	Michael Head
Support	If he really knew me	Carole Bayer Sager & Marvin Hamlisch
Support	Joshua fit the Battle of Jericho	Anonymous
Support	*La Fortuna*	Alessandro Scarlatti
Support	*Lasst mich ruhen*	Franz Liszt
Support	*Liebes Mädchen hör' mir zu*	Joseph Haydn
Support	*Liebhaber in allen Gestalten*	Franz Schubert
Support	Look for the Silver Lining	Jerome Kern
Support	Luck	Ricky Ian Gordon
Support	*Madrigal*	Vincent d'Indy
Support	My Romance	Richard Rodgers
Support	*O tu ch'innanzi morte*	Claudio Monteverdi
Support	*Plaisir d'amour*	Jean-Paul Martini
Support	*Printemps qui commence*	Camille Saint-Saëns
Support	*Selve amiche, ombrose piante*	Antonio Caldara
Support	Shenandoah	Jay Althouse (arr.)
Support	*Si dolce è'l tormento*	Claudio Monteverdi
Support	Smile	Charles (Charlie) Chaplan
Support	The Ash Grove	Roger Quilter
Support	The Best Things Happen While You're Dancing	Irving Berlin
Support	The Daisies	Samuel Barber
Support	The Mock Turtle's Song	John Duke
Support	The Water Mill	Ralph Vaughan Williams
Support	The Way to Your Heart	Mandy Geller
Support	*Tout Gai!*	Maurice Ravel
Support	*Tu mancavi a tormentarmi*	Antonio Cesti
Support	*Vilia*	Franz Lehar
Support	Where e'er you walk	G. F. Handel
Support	*Wo die schönen Trompeten blasen*	Gustav Mahler

Transition from Alto to Soprano	As Joseph Was A-walking	Eric Thiman
Transition from Alto to Soprano	Behold, a Virgin Shall Be with Child	John LaMontaine
Transition from Alto to Soprano	*Canzonetta (Tu fai la superbetta)*	Willlem de Fesch
Transition from Alto to Soprano	*C'est à ce joli mois de May*	Anonymous
Transition from Alto to Soprano	Come Down from the Tree	Stephen Flaherty
Transition from Alto to Soprano	Come, Cheerful Day	Thomas Campion
Transition from Alto to Soprano	*Das Veilchen*	W.A. Mozart
Transition from Alto to Soprano	*Des Liebsten Schwur*	Johannes Brahms
Transition from Alto to Soprano	*Die Männer sind méchant*	Franz Schubert
Transition from Alto to Soprano	*Die Spröde*	Carl Friderich Zelter
Transition from Alto to Soprano	*Dolce Amor, Bendato Dio*	Francesco Bruni
Transition from Alto to Soprano	Dream Valley	Roger Quilter
Transition from Alto to Soprano	*E l'uccellino*	Giacomo Puccini
Transition from Alto to Soprano	*Fere Selvaggie*	Giulio Caccini
Transition from Alto to Soprano	Go 'way from my Window	John Jacob Niles (arr.)
Transition from Alto to Soprano	I Have a Fawn	Katherine K. Davis
Transition from Alto to Soprano	I Heard the Voice of Jesus Say	Charles Harriss
Transition from Alto to Soprano	I Love all graceful things	Eric Thiman
Transition from Alto to Soprano	How unhappy's the nymph	William Boyce
Transition from Alto to Soprano	*Je te veux*	Erik Satie
Transition from Alto to Soprano	Jesus, the Very Thought of Thee	Eric Thiman
Transition from Alto to Soprano	June on Castle Hill	Gerald Finzi
Transition from Alto to Soprano	*L'Amour s'envole*	Arranged by J.B. Weckerlin
Transition from Alto to Soprano	*Le charme*	Ernest Chausson
Transition from Alto to Soprano	*Le Mariage des Roses*	César Franck
Transition from Alto to Soprano	Loveliest of Trees	John Duke
Transition from Alto to Soprano	Make Someone Happy	Jule Styne, Betty Comden and Adolph Green
Transition from Alto to Soprano	*Malurous qu'o uno fenno*	Joseph Canteloube
Transition from Alto to Soprano	Music When Soft Voices Die	Roger Quilter
Transition from Alto to Soprano	My Love Rode By	Mary Evelene Calbreath
Transition from Alto to Soprano	*Ogni, amatore*	Niccolo Piccinni
Transition from Alto to Soprano	On the Seashore of Endless Worlds	John Alden Carpenter
Transition from Alto to Soprano	*Or che il cielo a me ti rende*	Vincenzo Righini
Transition from Alto to Soprano	*Padre, addio*	Antonio Lotti
Transition from Alto to Soprano	Path to the Moon	Eric Thiman
Transition from Alto to Soprano	Piercing Eyes	Joseph Haydn
Transition from Alto to Soprano	*Santa Lucia*	Traditional Neapolitan Song
Transition from Alto to Soprano	*Schlummerlied*	Robert Franz
Transition from Alto to Soprano	*Se nel ben sempre incostante*	Alessandro Stradella
Transition from Alto to Soprano	Spring is Singing in the Garden	W.A. Anderson
Transition from Alto to Soprano	*Suo-gan*	Welsh folk song
Transition from Alto to Soprano	The Birds No More Shall Sing	G.F. Handel
Transition from Alto to Soprano	The Sleep That Flits on Baby's Eyes	John Alden Carpenter
Transition from Alto to Soprano	The Trees They Grow So High	Benjamin Britten (arr.)
Transition from Alto to Soprano	The Water is Wide	Mark Hayes (arr.)
Transition from Alto to Soprano	The Water of Tyne (Ma Bonny Lad)	Atkinson (arr.)
Transition from Alto to Soprano	This Little Rose	William Roy
Transition from Alto to Soprano	Thoroughly Modern Millie	James "Jimmy" Van Heusen
Transition from Alto to Soprano	Till There was You	Meredith Willson
Transition from Alto to Soprano	*Tirana del Tripili*	Attributed to Blas de Lasema

Transition from Alto to Soprano	*Vanne, segu'il mio desio*	G. F. Handel
Transition from Alto to Soprano	When I Bring to Your Colour'd Toys	John Alden Carpenter
Transition from Alto to Soprano	*Widmung*	Robert Franz
Transition from Baritone to Tenor	100 Years	J. Ondrasik/ 5 for Fighting
Transition from Baritone to Tenor	*A...*	Felipe Pedrell Sabaté
Transition from Baritone to Tenor	*Amor mi tiene in pugno*	Stefano Donaudy
Transition from Baritone to Tenor	*Amour d'antan*	Ernest Chausson
Transition from Baritone to Tenor	*Auf geheimem Waldespfade*	Robert Franz
Transition from Baritone to Tenor	*Bergere legere*	Anonymous
Transition from Baritone to Tenor	*Bitte*	Robert Franz
Transition from Baritone to Tenor	Charming Chloë	Unknown
Transition from Baritone to Tenor	Come away, come away, death	Gerald Finzi
Transition from Baritone to Tenor	*Das Fischermädchen*	Franz Schubert
Transition from Baritone to Tenor	Dear Prudence	John Lennon and Paul McCartney
Transition from Baritone to Tenor	*Dein Angesicht*	Robert Schumann
Transition from Baritone to Tenor	*Dein Blaues Auge*	Johannes Brahms
Transition from Baritone to Tenor	*Der Lindenbaum (Winterreise)*	Franz Schubert
Transition from Baritone to Tenor	Don't get around much anymore	Duke Ellington
Transition from Baritone to Tenor	Down By the Sally Gardens	Richard Donovan (arr.)
Transition from Baritone to Tenor	*Figlia mia*	G.F. Handel
Transition from Baritone to Tenor	*Gott ist gerecht*	J.S. Bach
Transition from Baritone to Tenor	Imagine	John Lennon
Transition from Baritone to Tenor	*In der Fremde*	Johannes Brahms
Transition from Baritone to Tenor	It must be so	Leonard Bernstein
Transition from Baritone to Tenor	Jeanie With the Light Brown Hair	Stephen Foster
Transition from Baritone to Tenor	Jesse James	Arr. Elie Siegmeister
Transition from Baritone to Tenor	*Komm, Jesu, komm zu deiner Kirche*	J.S. Bach
Transition from Baritone to Tenor	*La Rose (Ode anacréontique)*	Gabriel Fauré
Transition from Baritone to Tenor	*La statue de bronze*	Erik Satie
Transition from Baritone to Tenor	Last Rose of Summer	Benjamin Britten (arr.)
Transition from Baritone to Tenor	*Margot*	Sigmund Romberg
Transition from Baritone to Tenor	*Marie*	Robert Franz
Transition from Baritone to Tenor	On The Street Where You Live	Lerner & Loewe
Transition from Baritone to Tenor	Passing By	Edward Purcell
Transition from Baritone to Tenor	Phillis Has Such Charming Graces	Anthony Young
Transition from Baritone to Tenor	*Pria che spunti in ciel l'aurora*	Domenico Cimarosa
Transition from Baritone to Tenor	*Rugiadose, Odorose*	Alessandro Scarlatti
Transition from Baritone to Tenor	*Segui, segui dolente core*	Andrea Falconieri
Transition from Baritone to Tenor	*Sérénade Florentine*	Henri Duparc
Transition from Baritone to Tenor	*Sonntag*	Johannes Brahms
Transition from Baritone to Tenor	Water Parted from the Sea	T.A. Arne
Transition from Baritone to Tenor	*Wohin*	Franz Schubert

SUGGESTED REPERTOIRE BY GENRE		
Songs from Tricky Categories	**Title of the piece**	**Composer of the piece**
Baroque Aria	*Ach, dass ich Wassers gnug hatte*	Johann Christoph Bach
Baroque Aria	*Ach, reiner Geist!*	Georg Philipp Telemann
Baroque Aria	*Ah! Qu'on daigne du moins*	Jean-Phillippe Rameau
Baroque Aria	*As when the dove* (Recit: Oh, didst thou know)	G.F. Handel
Baroque Aria	*Bäche von gesalznen Zähren*	J.S. Bach
Baroque Aria	*Bekennen will ich seinen Namen*	J.S. Bach
Baroque Aria	*Bellezza che s'ama*	Alessandro Scarlatti
Baroque Aria	*Bist du Bei Mir*	J.S. Bach
Baroque Aria	Canary Cantata	Georg Philipp Telemann
Baroque Aria	Come and Trip It	G. F. Handel
Baroque Aria	Come Sorrow Come	Thomas Morley
Baroque Aria	*Der fünfundzwanzigste Psalm*	C.P.E. Bach
Baroque Aria	*Der wahren Tugend Gegenstreit ruhrt von der Erden Eitelkeit*	Constantin Christian Dedekind
Baroque Aria	*Des Reichtums Glanz auf weiter Erden* (BWV 204)	J.S. Bach
Baroque Aria	*Die Armen will der Herr umarmen* (BWV 191)	J.S. Bach
Baroque Aria	*Die Elenden sollen essen*	J.S. Bach
Baroque Aria	*Dieu Tout Puissant*	André Destouches
Baroque Aria	*Donna haser senza amore*	Gabriello Puliti
Baroque Aria	*Ecco, che pur baciate*	Domenico Obizzi
Baroque Aria	*Eile, mich, Gott, zu erretten*	Heinrich Schütz
Baroque Aria	*Erfreue dich Seele*	J.S. Bach
Baroque Aria	*Es ist ein' Ros'entsprungen*	Traditional
Baroque Aria	*Fürchte dich nicht* (BWV 228)	J.S. Bach
Baroque Aria	*Fürchtet euch nicht*	Heinrich Schütz
Baroque Aria	*Glück*	Georg Philipp Telemann
Baroque Aria	*Haus des Herrn*	Georg Philipp Telemann
Baroque Aria	*Himmelstochter, Ruh der Seelen*	C.P.E Bach
Baroque Aria	*Hört, ihr Augen, auf zu weinen*	J.S. Bach
Baroque Aria	*I Love and I Must*	Henry Purcell
Baroque Aria	*Ich ende behende*	J.S. Bach
Baroque Aria	*Ich sehe dich in deinem Worte*	Georg Philipp Telemann
Baroque Aria	*In Euch, Ihr grünen Auen*	Georg Philipp Telemann
Baroque Aria	*Israel, hoffe auf den Herren*	Dietrich Buxtehude
Baroque Aria	*Jesu, deine Gnadenblicke* (BWV 11)	J.S. Bach
Baroque Aria	*Komm! Ach Komm! O süsse Tod*	Johann Theile
Baroque Aria	*Komm, süßer Schlaf*	Georg Philipp Telemann
Baroque Aria	*Lasst hier Gesang und Saiten schallen*	Georg Philipp Telemann
Baroque Aria	*Le Carpillon*	André Campra
Baroque Aria	*Liebster Herr Jesu*	Dietrich Buxtehude
Baroque Aria	*Mortels, Que Vous Sert-il*	André Campra
Baroque Aria	My Lovely Celia	George Munro
Baroque Aria	*Nun sich der Tag geendet hat*	Adam Krieger

Baroque Aria	*Nun scheint in vollem Glanze der Himmel*	Joseph Haydn
Baroque Aria	Hush, no more, be silent	Henry Purcell
Baroque Aria	*O Del Ben*	Antonio Cesti
Baroque Aria	*Pupille Amate*	Giovanni Bononcini
Baroque Aria	*Schafe können sicher weiden* (BWV 208)	J.S. Bach
Baroque Aria	*Se pietade in te non trovi*	Domenico Manzolo
Baroque Aria	*Seltenes Glück*	Georg Philipp Telemann
Baroque Aria	*Sen core l'agnelletta*	Domenico Sarri
Baroque Aria	Thou Doting Fool	Henry Purcell
Baroque Aria	*Tout cede à vos doux appas*	Pascal Collasse
Baroque Aria	*Tu, Ch'hai le penne, Amore*	Giulio Caccini
Baroque Aria	*Vergiß dich selbst, mein schönster Engel!*	Georg Philipp Telemann
Baroque Aria	*Vo' far guerra*	G. F. Handel
Baroque Aria	*Was mich auf dieser Welt betrubt*	Dietrich Buxtehude
Baroque Aria	*Weep No More*	G. F. Handel
Baroque Aria	*Wenn der Schulmeister Singet*	G.P. Telemann
Baroque Aria	When Daisies Pied	Thomas Augustine Arne
Baroque Aria	*Ziehet hin und forschet*	Heinrich Schütz
Beginning Bass	A-Roving	Sir Richard Runciman Terry (arr.)
Beginning Bass	*Adieu!*	August Heinrich von Weyrauch (Attributed to Schubert)
Beginning Bass	All Along the Mother Volga	Alan Ord (arr.)
Beginning Bass	*Amor, ch'attendi*	Giulio Caccini
Beginning Bass	*Aria da cantar stanze*	Cosimo Bottegari
Beginning Bass	*Bois épais*	Jean Baptiste Lully
Beginning Bass	*Chevaliers de la table ronde*	Jay Althouse (arr.)
Beginning Bass	Come Ye Blessed	John Prindle Scott
Beginning Bass	Deep River	Moses Hogan (arr.)
Beginning Bass	*Der Leiermann*	Franz Schubert
Beginning Bass	Down Among the Dead Men	Traditional, 1715
Beginning Bass	Edelweiss	Rodgers & Hammerstein
Beginning Bass	Eldorado	Richard H. Walthew
Beginning Bass	*Gioite al canto mio*	Jacopo Peri
Beginning Bass	*Gleich Merlin, dem eitlen Weisen*	Fanny Mendelssohn Hensel
Beginning Bass	Hear! Ye Gods of Britain	Henry Purcell
Beginning Bass	*Hör' ich das Liedchen klingen*	Robert Schumann
Beginning Bass	*In grünem Wald ich neulich sass*	Friedrich von Spee
Beginning Bass	Leave Me, Loathsome Light	G.F. Handel
Beginning Bass	*Les Poissons*	Alan Menken
Beginning Bass	*Mädchen mit dem Roten Mundchen*	Robert Franz
Beginning Bass	*Maledetto sia l'aspetto*	Claudio Monteverdi
Beginning Bass	*Meeresleuchten*	Carl Loewe
Beginning Bass	My Cup Runneth Over	Harvey Schmidt
Beginning Bass	*Nel Riposo e nel contento*	G.F. Handel
Beginning Bass	*Pupille Nere*	G.B. Buononcini
Beginning Bass	*Reiterlied*	Carl Loewe
Beginning Bass	*Se nel ben sempre incostante*	Alessandro Stradella
Beginning Bass	Should You Ever Find Her Complying	T.A. Arne, arr. Bush

Beginning Bass	Soldier, Soldier, Will You Marry Me?	American Folksong, Arranged by Brian Dean
Beginning Bass	Sometimes I Feel Like a Motherless Child	Arr. H.T. Burleigh
Beginning Bass	Song of the Old Man	Modest Mussorgsky
Beginning Bass	Strike the Viol	Henry Purcell
Beginning Bass	The Christmas Tree	Elizabeth Sprague Coolidge
Beginning Bass	The Owl is Abroad	Henry Purcell
Beginning Bass	The Pretty Creature	Stephen Storace
Beginning Bass	The Self-Banished	John Blow
Beginning Bass	Waitin' for the Light to Shine	Roger Miller
Characterization	A Dog's Life	Michael Head
Characterization	A Real Low Down Basso Am I	Geoffrey O'Hara
Characterization	Agnes	Thomas Pasatieri
Characterization	Art Is Calling for Me (The Prima Donna Song)	Victor Herbert
Characterization	*Aufträge*	Robert Schumann
Characterization	Buffalo Gals	Ernest Bacon
Characterization	Captain Stratton's Fancy	Peter Warlock
Characterization	Cowboy Songs	Libby Larsen
Characterization	*Das irdische Leben*	Gustav Mahler
Characterization	*Der arme Peter*	Robert Schumann
Characterization	*Die Kartenlegerin*	Robert Schumann
Characterization	*Die Männer sind méchant*	Franz Schubert
Characterization	*Die Soldatenbraut*	Robert Schumann
Characterization	Epitaph on a Wife	Richard Hundley
Characterization	Four Plus One	Eldon Udell Black
Characterization	*Hans und Grethe*	Gustav Mahler
Characterization	*hist...whist*	John Duke
Characterization	I Bought Me a Cat	Aaron Copland (arr.)
Characterization	*Ich möchte wohl der Kaiser sein*	W.A. Mozart
Characterization	*In uomini, in soldati*	W.A. Mozart
Characterization	Is My Team Ploughing?	George Butterworth
Characterization	Jimmie's Got a Goil	Marc Blitzstein
Characterization	*Le Bestiaire*	Francis Poulenc
Characterization	*Lob des hohen Verstands*	Gustav Mahler
Characterization	Love in the Dictionary	Celius Dougherty
Characterization	Memories	Charles Ives
Characterization	Money, O	Michael Head
Characterization	*Muttertänderlei*	Richard Strauss
Characterization	*Nel cor più non mi sento*	Giovanni Paisiello
Characterization	O No, John!	Wolff (arr.)
Characterization	*Och Moder, ich well en Ding han*	Johannes Brahms
Characterization	*Rheinlegendchen*	Gustav Mahler
Characterization	*Schwesterlein, Schwesterlein*	Johannes Brahms
Characterization	*Se tu m'ami*	Alessandro Parisotti
Characterization	*Seligkeit*	Franz Schubert
Characterization	The Circus Band	Charles Ives
Characterizatio	The Black Oak Tree	John Jacob Niles (arr.)
Characterization	The Deaf Old Woman	Katherine K. Davis
Characterization	The Nightingale	C. Shaw (arr.)

Characterization	The Seal Man	Rebecca Clarke
Characterization	The Side Show	Charles Ives
Characterization	To My Neighbor at the Concert	Anthony Donato
Characterization	*Trost im Unglück*	Gustav Mahler
Characterization	*Un bacio di mano*	W.A. Mozart
Characterization	*Una donna a quindici anni*	W.A. Mozart
Characterization	*Vedrai carino*	W.A. Mozart
Characterization	*Vergebliches Ständchen*	Johannes Brahms
Characterization	*Verlorne Müh*	Gustav Mahler
Easier operatic arias for baritone	*Ah! Eccellenza!* from *Nina, o sia la pazza per amore*	Giovanni Paisiello
Easier operatic arias for baritone	*Ambo nati in questa valle* from *Linda di Chamounix*	Gaetano Donizetti
Easier operatic arias for baritone	*Aria di Buonafede* from *Il Monda della Luna*	Joseph Haydn
Easier operatic arias for baritone	*Guerrier sognai vittoria* from *Don Sebastiano*	Gaetano Donizetti
Easier operatic arias for baritone	*Non cambierei, lo guiro... Vedo quell'albero* from *Il filosofo di campagna*	Baldassarre Galuppi
Easier operatic arias for baritone	*Scorsi già molti paesi* from *Il barbiere di Siviglia*	Giovanni Paisiello
Easier operatic arias for baritone	*Signori... ascoltino le mie ragioni...* from *I promessi sposi*	Errico Petrella
Easier operatic arias for baritone	*Taci, attendi e allor vedrai* from *Adelson e Salvini*	Vincenzo Bellini
Easier operatic arias for baritone	Whether I Grow Old or No from *Lyra Britannica Book 1, 1745*	William Boyce
Easier operatic arias for bass	*Befraget mich ein zartes Kind* from *Bastien und Bastienne*	W.A. Mozart
Easier operatic arias for bass	*Hat man nicht auch Gold beineben* from *Fidelio*	Ludwig van Beethoven
Easier operatic arias for bass	*Ho capito, Signor sì!* from *Don Giovanni*	W.A. Mozart
Easier operatic arias for bass	*La mia ragion è questa* from *Il filosofo di campagno*	Baldassare Galuppi
Easier operatic arias for bass	*Tutto or m'è noto... Al tuo trono, o sommo Iddio* from *I promessi sposi*	Amilcare Ponchielli
Easier operatic arias for bass	*Ubriaco non son io* from *Ubriaco non son io*	W. A. Mozart
Easier operatic arias for bass	*Udite, tutti udite!* from *Il matrimonio segreto*	Domenico Cimarosa
Easier operatic arias for bass	*Veramente ho torto, è vero* from *Il barbiere di Siviglia*	Giovanni Paisiello
Easier operatic arias for mezzo	*Ah! Se tu dormi svegliati* from *Giulietta e Romeo*	Nicola Vaccai
Easier operatic arias for mezzo	*Bel Nume che adoro* from *Pigmalione*	Giovanni Battista Cimadoro
Easier operatic arias for mezzo	*Connais-tu le pays* from *Mignon*	Ambroise Thomas

Easier operatic arias for mezzo	Questa mano (Eurilda's aria) from Le Pescatrici	Joseph Haydn
Easier operatic arias for mezzo	Immagine gradita from Adelson e Salvini	Vincenzo Bellini
Easier operatic arias for mezzo	La Rachelina from La molinara	Giovanni Paisiello
Easier operatic arias for mezzo	Must the Winter Come So Soon? from Vanessa	Samuel Barber
Easier operatic arias for mezzo	Nella fatal di Rimini from Lucrezia Borgia	Gaetano Donizetti
Easier operatic arias for mezzo	O Luna Lucente from Il Monda della Luna	Joseph Haydn
Easier operatic arias for mezzo	Resta in pace, idolo mio from Gli Orazi e i Curiazi	Domenico Cimarosa
Easier operatic arias for mezzo	Silenzio, tacete from L'ajo nell'imbarazzo	Gaetano Donizetti
Easier operatic arias for mezzo	Un bocconcin d'amante from La grotta di Trofonio	Antonio Salieri
Easier operatic arias for soprano	Anch'io son giovine from La cambiale di matrimonio	Gioachino Rossini
Easier operatic arias for soprano	Canto di una Guècha from Iris	Pietro Mascagni
Easier operatic arias for soprano	Di questa poverella from Il filosofo di campagna	Baldassare Galuppi
Easier operatic arias for soprano	Donne vaghe… from La serva padrona	Giovanni Paisiello
Easier operatic arias for soprano	Dunque per un infido… S'arresta il sangue nelle vene from L'italiana in Londra	Domenico Cimarosa
Easier operatic arias for soprano	Gasparina's aria from La canterina	Joseph Haydn
Easier operatic arias for soprano	Giusto ciel, che conoscete from Il barbiere di Siviglia	Giovanni Paisiello
Easier operatic arias for soprano	Kiss Me Not Goodbye from The Mighty Casey	William Schuman
Easier operatic arias for soprano	L'ho perduta, me meschina from Le nozze di Figaro	W.A. Mozart
Easier operatic arias for soprano	Laurie's Song from The Tender Land	Aaron Copland
Easier operatic arias for soprano	Marito vorrei from La finta semplice	W.A. Mozart
Easier operatic arias for soprano	O fior del giorno from Edgar	Giacomo Puccini
Easier operatic arias for soprano	Papà, non mi lasciar from Il cappello di paglia di Firenze	Nino Rota
Easier operatic arias for soprano	Quando si trovano le basse femmine from Il mondo della luna	Baldassare Galuppi
Easier operatic arias for soprano	Se come voi piccina io fossi from Le Villi	Giacomo Puccini
Easier operatic arias for soprano	Wenn mein Bastien einst im Scherze from Bastien und Bastienne	W.A. Mozart
Easier operatic arias for tenor	Aria di Ecclitico from Il Monda della Luna	Joseph Haydn
Easier operatic arias for tenor	Aria di Nencio from L'infedeltà delusa	Joseph Haydn
Easier operatic arias for tenor	Aria di Sempronio from Lo speziale	Joseph Haydn

Easier operatic arias for tenor	*Crea in quegli occhi il lampo d'un desìo* from *Iris*	Pietro Mascagni
Easier operatic arias for tenor	*Ecco il fatal recinto... Ad ogni istante sembrami vederla* from *I promessi sposi*	Amilcare Ponchielli
Easier operatic arias for tenor	*Fanciullette ritrosette* from *La finta semplice*	W.A. Mozart
Easier operatic arias for tenor	*Fu di notte come in sogno* from *Amelia al ballo*	Gian Carlo Menotti
Easier operatic arias for tenor	*In quegl'anni in cui val poco* from *Le nozze di Figaro*	W.A. Mozart
Easier operatic arias for tenor	*Meiner Liebsten schönen Wangen* from *Bastien und Bastienne*	W.A. Mozart
Easier operatic arias for tenor	*Mentre l'erbetta pasce l'agnella* from *Il Flaminio*	Giovanni Battista Pergolesi
Easier operatic arias for tenor	*Nelle guerre d'amore* from *La finta semplice*	W.A. Mozart
Easier operatic arias for tenor	*Saper bramate* from *Il Barbiere di Seviglia*	Giovanni Paisiello
Easier operatic arias for tenor	*Sciocca ragion... Amina vile, ingrata* from *Il filosofo di campagna*	Baldassare Galuppi
Easier operatic arias for tenor	*Stringhe e ferri da calzette* from *La gazza ladra*	Gioachino Rossini
Easier operatic arias for tenor	*Venti volte in vita mia* from *L'italiana in Londra*	Domenico Cimarosa
Easier songs by important composers	*Adieu!*	August Heinrich von Weyrauch (Attributed to Schubert)
Easier songs by important composers	*An mein Klavier*	Franz Schubert
Easier songs by important composers	*Da unten im Tale*	Johannes Brahms
Easier songs by important composers	*Das Kinderspiel*	W.A. Mozart
Easier songs by important composers	*Der Gleichsinn*	Joseph Haydn
Easier songs by important composers	*Der Kreüzzug*	Franz Schubert
Easier songs by important composers	*Der Mond*	Felix Mendelssohn
Easier songs by important composers	*Der Nußbaum*	Robert Schumann
Easier songs by important composers	*Des Sennen Abschied*	Robert Schumann
Easier songs by important composers	*Die Forelle*	Franz Schubert
Easier songs by important composers	*Die Landlust*	Joseph Haydn
Easier songs by important composers	*Die Mainacht*	Franz Schubert
Easier songs by important composers	*Diggi, daggi, shurry, murry*	W.A. Mozart
Easier songs by important composers	*Ei, wie schmeckt der Coffee süße*	J.S. Bach
Easier songs by important composers	*Frühlingsglaube*	Franz Schubert
Easier songs by important composers	*Gruß*	Felix Mendelssohn
Easier songs by important composers	*Hat man nicht auch Gold beineben*	Ludwig van Beethoven
Easier songs by important composers	*Jasminenstrauch*	Robert Schumann
Easier songs by important composers	*Legend*	Pyotr Ilyich Tchaikovsky
Easier songs by important composers	*Liebes Mädchen, hör' mir zu*	Joseph Haydn
Easier songs by important composers	*Litanei*	Franz Schubert
Easier songs by important composers	*Lo Postouro delaissado*	Joseph Canteloube
Easier songs by important composers	*Lust der Sturmnacht*	Robert Schumann
Easier songs by important composers	*Mein Garten*	Robert Schumann
Easier songs by important composers	*Mein Mädel hat einen Rosemund*	Johannes Brahms

Easier songs by important composers	*Minnelied*	Johannes Brahms
Easier songs by important composers	More Love or More Disdain	Henry Purcell
Easier songs by important composers	*Non, je n'irai plus au bois*	Arranged by J.B. Weckerlin
Easier songs by important composers	*O Rest in the Lord* (Elijah)	Felix Mendelssohn
Easier songs by important composers	*Oiseaux si tous les ans*	W.A. Mozart
Easier songs by important composers	*Sehnsucht nach dem Frühlinge*	W.A. Mozart
Easier songs by important composers	*Sonntag*	Johannes Brahms
Easier songs by important composers	The Lovely Lass of Inverness	Ludwig van Beethoven
Easier songs by important composers	The Sandman	Johannes Brahms
Easier songs by important composers	*Tischlied*	Franz Schubert
Easier songs by important composers	*Volksleid*	Felix Mendelssohn
Easier songs by important composers	*Wanderers Nachtlied*	Franz Schubert
Easier songs by important composers	Who ever thinks or hopes of love	John Dowland
Easier songs by important composers	*Wiegenlied*	Franz Schubert
Harmonic Interest	Ann Street	Charles Ives
Harmonic Interest	Come away death	Madeleine Dring
Harmonic Interest	I Can Smell the Sea Air	Andre Previn
Harmonic Interest	Jazz Songs	Betty Roe
Harmonic Interest	Pull My Daisy	David Amram
Harmonic Interest	Take o Take	Madeleine Dring
Harmonic Interest	The Children's Hour	Charles Ives
Harmonic Interest	Under the Greenwood Tree	Madeleine Dring
Humorous Piece	A Song of Perfect Propriety	Seymour Barab
Humorous Piece	A Word on My Ear	Flanders & Swann
Humorous Piece	Amor	William Bolcom
Humorous Piece	Another New Voice Teacher	Gene Scheer and Andrew Thomas
Humorous Piece	Art is Calling for Me (The Prima Donna Song)	Victor Herbert
Humorous Piece	*Ballade des gros dindons*	Emmanuel Chabrier
Humorous Piece	C'est moi	Lerner & Loewe
Humorous Piece	Ching-a-ring chaw	Aaron Copland (arr.)
Humorous Piece	Content to Be Behind Me	Ben Moore
Humorous Piece	I Love Teaching Voice	Ben Moore
Humorous Piece	If You've Only Got a Moustache	Stephen Foster
Humorous Piece	I'm Glad I'm Not a Tenor	Ben Moore
Humorous Piece	Inventory	Seymour Barab
Humorous Piece	*L'Offrande*	Francis Poulenc
Humorous Piece	*Les Poissons*	Alan Menken
Humorous Piece	Lime Jello-Marshmallow Cottage Cheese Surprise	William Bolcom
Humorous Piece	Little Bunny Hop Hop Hop	Peter Schickele (aka P.D.Q. Bach)
Humorous Piece	Lord! I married me a wife!	Benjamin Britten (arr.)
Humorous Piece	Money, O!	Michael Head
Humorous Piece	My Wife is a Most Knowing Woman	Stephen Foster
Humorous Piece	Open Sesame Seeds	Peter Schickele (aka P.D.Q. Bach)
Humorous Piece	Renunciation	Seymour Barab
Humorous Piece	Rory O'Moore	Traditional
Humorous Piece	Sexy Lady	Ben Moore
Humorous Piece	Someone is Sending Me Flowers	David Baker arr. By Roger Vignoles
Humorous Piece	Song of a Nightclub Proprietress	Madeleine Dring

Humorous Piece	Sugar in the Cane	Paul Bowles
Humorous Piece	Sweethearts and Wives	Michael Head
Humorous Piece	Tale of the Oyster	Cole Porter
Humorous Piece	Tally-Ho!	Franco Leoni
Humorous Piece	Tobacco	Tobias Hume
Humorous Piece	The Audience Song	Ben Moore
Humorous Piece	The Foggy, Foggy Dew	Benjamin Britten (arr.)
Humorous Piece	The Green Dog	Herbert Kingsley
Humorous Piece	The Lords of Creation Men we call	Arthur Loesser, arr. Alfred Kugel
Humorous Piece	The Passionate Trencherwoman	Donald Swann
Humorous Piece	The Masochism Tango	Tom Lehrer
Humorous Piece	The Saga of Jenny	Kurt Weill
Humorous Piece	The Serpent	Lee Hoiby
Humorous Piece	The Shape of Things	Sheldon Harnick
Humorous Piece	There are Fairies at the Bottom of our Garden	Liza Lehmann
Humorous Piece	*Trinklied*	Traditional German
Humorous Piece	*Villanelle des petits canards*	Emmanuel Chabrier
Humorous Piece	Wagner Roles	Ben Moore
Rhythmic Interest	Bartholomew Green	Richard Hundley
Rhythmic Interest	Could Be	John Musto
Rhythmic Interest	Cycle of Light	Joel Martinson
Rhythmic Interest	Down to the Rivah	Richard MacGimsey
Rhythmic Interest	I Hate Music	Leonard Bernstein
Rhythmic Interest	In the dark pinewood	Samuel Barber
Rhythmic Interest	Intermezzo	Robert Schumann
Rhythmic Interest	Jabberwocky	Lee Hoiby
Rhythmic Interest	Jonah and the Whale	Richard MacGimsey
Rhythmic Interest	*La Pastorella*	Franz Schubert
Rhythmic Interest	*Les cloches*	Claude Debussy
Rhythmic Interest	*Le Violette*	Alessandro Scarlatti
Rhythmic Interest	Litany	John Musto
Rhythmic Interest	*Mattinata*	Ruggiero Leoncavallo
Rhythmic Interest	Of that so sweet imprisonment	Samuel Barber
Rhythmic Interest	Seashore Girls	Richard Hundley
Rhythmic Interest	Shadrach, Meshach and Abednego	Richard MacGimsey
Rhythmic Interest	Six Songs on the Poems of W. Pillin	Sharon Davis
Rhythmic Interest	Sweet chance, that led my steps	Michael Head
Rhythmic Interest	Sweet Suffolk Owl	Richard Hundley
Rhythmic Interest	The Astronomers	Richard Hundley
Rhythmic Interest	The Flute of Interior Time	John Harbison
Rhythmic Interest	The Lady of the Harbor	Lee Hoiby
Rhythmic Interest	The Seal Man	Rebecca Clarke
Rhythmic Interest	*Tout gai!*	Maurice Ravel
Rhythmic Interest	Under the Greenwood Tree	Thomas Augustine Arne
Rhythmic Interest	*Von ewiger Liebe*	Johannes Brahms
Rhythmic Interest	When to her lute	Lee Hoiby

A Selected Bibliography of Reference Sources: American, British, French, German, Italian, Russian & Spanish Art Songs and Arias, Musical Theatre, and Composers

Abbott, Helen. *Between Baudelaire and Mallarmé: Voice, Conversation and Music.* Farnham, Surrey: Ashgate Publishing, 2009.

Bernac, Pierre. *Francis Poulence: The Man and his Songs.* New York: W. W. Norton & Co., 1977

Bernac, Pierre. *The Interpretation of French Song.* New York: W. W. Norton & Co., 1978.

Bloom, Ken. *American Song: The Complete Musical Theatre Companion.* New York: Schirmer Books, 1996.

Boldrey, Richard. *Guide to Operatic Roles and Arias.* Michigan: Pst... Inc., 1994.

Carman, Judith E. and William K. Gaeddert, Rita M. Resch and Gordon Meyers. *Art Song in the United States 1759-1999: an Annotated Bibliography.* Lanham, MD: Scarecrow, 2001.

Chalis, Natalia. *The Singer's* Rachmaninoff. New York: Pelion Press, 1989.

Clark, Mark Ross. *Guide to the Aria Repertoire.* Bloomington, IN: Indiana University Press, 2007.

Cobb, Margaret. *The Poetic Debussy: A Collection of his song texts and selected letters.* Rochester, NY: University of Rochester Press, 1994.

Cockburn, Jacqueline and Richard Stokes. *The Spanish Song Companion.* Lanham, MD: Scarecrow Press, 2006.

Coffin, Berton and Ralph Errolle, Werner Singer and Pierre Delattre. *Phonetic Readings of Songs and Arias.* Lanham, MD: Scarecrow Press, Inc., 1982.

Coffin, Berton. *Singer's Repertoire: Part I: Coloratura Soprano Lyric Soprano and Dramatic Soprano.* New York, The Scarecrow Press, Inc.: 1960.

Coffin, Berton. *Singer's Repertoire: Part II: Mezzo Soprano and Contralto.* New York, The Scarecrow Press, Inc.: 1960.

Coffin, Berton. *Singer's Repertoire: Part III: Lyric and Dramatic Tenor.* New York, The Scarecrow Press, Inc.: 1960.

Coffin, Berton. *Singer's Repertoire: Part IV: Baritone and Bass.* New York, The Scarecrow Press, Inc.: 1960.

Coffin, Berton. *Singer's Repertoire: Part V: Program Notes for the Singer's Repertoire.* New York, The Scarecrow Press, Inc.: 1962.

Coffin, Berton and Werner Singer and Pierre Delattre. *Word-by-Word Translations of Songs and Arias: Part I- German and French.* Lanham, MD: Scarecrow Press, Inc., 1966.

Coffin, Berton and Arthur Schoep and Daniel Harris. *Word-by-Word Translations of Songs and Arias: Part II- Italian.* Lanham, MD: Scarecrow Press, Inc., 1972.

Cooke, Mervyn (ed). *The Cambridge Companion to Benjamin Britten.* Cambridge, UK: Cambridge University Press, 1999.

Copley, I.A.. *The Music of Peter Warlock: a critical Survey.* London: D. Dobson, 1979.

Daniel, Keith W. *Francis Poulenc: His Artistic Development and Musical Style.* Ann Arbor: UMI Research Press, 1982.

Daykin, Frank, editor, *The Encyclopedia of French Art Song: Fauré, Debussy, Ravel, Poulenc.* Hillsdale, NY: Pendragon Press, 2013.

DeVenney, David P. *The Broadway Song Companion: An Annotated Guide to Musical Theatre Literature.* Lanham, MD: The Scarecrow Press, 1998.

Elliott, Martha. *Singing in Style: A guide to vocal performance practices.* New Haven: Yale University Press, 2006.

Emmons, Shirley and Stanley Sonntag. *The Art of the Song Recital.* New York: Schirmer Books, 1979.

Emmons, Shirley and Wilbur Watkins Lewis. *Researching the Song: A Lexicon.* New York: Oxford University Press, Inc., 2006.

Espina, Noni. *Repertoire for the Solo Voice: A Fully Annotated Guide to Works for the Solo Voice Published in Modern Editions and Covering Material from the 13th Century to the Present (2 volumes).* New York: Scarecrow Press, Inc., 1997.

Everett, William A. *The Musical: A Research & Information Guide.* New York: Routledge, 2004.

Finson, Jon W, *Robert Schumann: The Book of Songs.* Cambridge, MA: Harvard University Press, 2008.

Fischer-Dieskau, Dietrich. *The Fischer-Dieskau Book of Lieder.* Revised Ed. New York, NY: Limelight Editions, 1995.

Fischer-Dieskau, Dietrich. *Schubert's Songs, A biographical study.* New York: Limelight Editions, 1984.

François-Sappey and Gilles Cantagrel. *Guide de la Mélodie et du Lied.* Paris: Librairie Arthème Fayard, 1994.

Friedberg, Ruth C. *American Art Song and American Poetry (3 volumes).* London: Scarecrow Press, 1981.

Gartside, Robert. *Interpreting the Songs of Gabriel Fauré.* Geneseo, New York: Leyerle Publications, 1996.

Gartside, Robert. *Interpreting the Songs of Maurice Ravel.* Geneseo, New York: Leyerle Publications, 1992.

Gordon, Rae Beth. *Ornament, Fantasy, and Desire in the Nineteenth-Century French Literature.* Princeton, NJ: Princeton University Press, 1992.

Gorrell, Lorraine. *The Nineteenth-Century German Lied.* Portland, Oregon: Amadeus Press, 1993.

Greene, Harry Plunket, *Interpretation in Song.* New York: The Macmillan Company, 1912.

Grubb, Thomas. *Singing in French: A Manuel of French Diction and French Vocal Repertoire.* New York: Schirmer Books, 1979.

Hart, Elizabeth, editor and author, *Anthology for Beginning American Singers.* Baltimore, MD: H.E.R.S. Publishing, 2009.

Hall, James. H. *The Art Song.* Norman: University of Oklahoma Press, 1974.

Hallmark, Rufus. *The Genesis of Schumann's Dichterliebe: A Source Study.* Ann Arbor, MI: University Microfilms International, 1979

Harwood, Earl of: *The New Kobbé's Complete Opera Book.* New Material: New York: G. P. Putnam's Sons, 1976.

Hoover, Maya. *A Guide to the Latin American Art Song Repertoire: An Annotated Catalog of Twentieth-Century Art Songs for Voice and Piano.* Bloomington, IN: Indiana University Press, 2010.

Hovland, Michael. *Musical Settings of American Poetry: A Bibliography.* New York: Greenwood, 1986.

Hunter, David. *Understanding French Verse: A Guide for Singers.* New York: Oxford University Press, 2005.

Irvine, Demar. *Massenet: A Chronicle of His Life and Times.* Oregon: Amadeus Press, 1994.

Ivey, Benjamin, *Francis Poulenc.* London: Phaidon Press Limited, 1996.

Ivey, Donald. *Song: Anatomy, Imagery and Styles.* New York: The Frees Press, 1970.

Jefferson, Alan. *The Lieder of Richard Strauss.* London: Cassell, 1971.

Johnson, Graham and Richard Stokes. *A French Song Companion.* New York: Oxford University Press, 2000.

Johnson, Graham and Richard Stokes. *Gabriel Fauré: The Songs and their Poets.* Farnham, Surrey: Ashgate Publishing Limited, 2009.

Johnson, Graham: *Britten, Voice and Piano: Lectures on the Vocal Music of Benjamin Britten.* Farnham, Surrey: Ashgate Publishing Limited, 2009.

Kagen, Sergius. *Music for the Voice.* Bloomington: Indiana University Press, 1968.

Kagen, Sergius. *On Studying Singing.* New York: Dover Publications, Inc., 1950.

Kimball, Carol. *Song: A Guide to Literature and Style.* Redmond, Washington: Pst...Inc., 2000.

Kimball, Carol. *Song: A Guide to Literature and Style.* Revised ed. Milwaukee, WI: Hal Leonard, 2006.

Komar, Arthur. *Robert Schumann: Dichterliebe, An Authoritative Score; Historical Background; Essays in Analysis; Views and Comments.* New York: W.W. Norton & Company, Inc. 1971

Le Massena, C.C. *The Songs of Schubert; A Guide for Singers, Teachers, Students and Accompanists.* New York: G. Schirmer, Inc, 1928.

Lakeway, Ruth. *Italian Art Song.* New York: Indiana University Press, 1989.

Lehmann, Lotte. *More than Singing: The Interpretation of Songs.* New York: Boosey & Hawkes, Inc., 1945; reprint ed., New York: Dover Publications, Inc., 1985.

Lesure, François, *Debussy Letters.* Cambridge, MA: Harvard University Press, 1987.

Lesure, François. Trans. Richard Langham Smith. *Debussy on Music: The Critical Writings of the Great French Composer Claude Debussy.* Ithaca, NY: Cornell University Press, 1988.

LeVan, Timothy. *Masters of the French Art Song.* Landham, MD: Scarecrow Press, Inc., 2001.

Little, Roger. *Guillaume Apollinaire.* London: The Athlone Press, University of London, 1976.

Mann, William, *The Operas of Mozart.* New York: Oxford University Press, 1977.

Manning, Jane. *New Vocal Repertoire.* Oxford: Carendon Press, 1998.

Marbry, Sharon. *Exploring Twentieth-Century Vocal Music: A Practical Guide to Innovations in Performance and Repertoire.* New York: Oxford University Press Inc., 2002.

Marissen, Michael. *Bach's Oratorios; The Parallel German-English Texts with Annotations.* New York: Oxford University Press. 2008

McGinnis, Pearl Yeadon. *The Opera Singer's Career Guide: Understanding the European Fach System.* Lanham, MD: Scarecrow Press, 2006.

Meister, Barbara. *An Introduction to the Art Song.* New York: Taplinger Publishing Company, 980.

Meister, Barbara. *Nineteenth Century French Song: Fauré, Chausson, Duparc and Debussy.* Bloomington, Indiana: Indiana University Press, 1980.

Mellers, Wilfrid. *Francis Poulenc.* New York: Oxford University Press, 1993.

Miller, Philip L. *The Ring of Words: An Anthology of Song Texts.* New York: W.W. Norton & Company, 1963.

Moore, Gerald. *The Schubert Song Cycles.* London: Hamish Hamilton Ltd., 1975

Nectoux, Jean-Michel. Trans Roger Nichols. *Gabriel Fauré: A Musical Life.* Cambridge: Cambridge University Press, 1991.

Nectoux, Jean-Michel. Trans J.A. Underwood. *Gabriel Fauré: His Life Through his Letters.* New York: Marion Boyars Publishers, 1984.

Nichols, Roger. *Debussy.* London: Oxford University Press, 1972.

Northcoat, Sydney. *The Songs of Henri Duparc.* Reprint Services Corp, 1949.

Noske, Fritz. *French Song from Berlioz to Duparc.* New York: Dover Publications, 1970.
Ord, Alan J. *Songs for Bass Voice: An Annotated Guide to Works for Bass Voice.* Lanham, MD: The Scarecrow Press, Inc., 1994.
Ord, Alan J. *Songs for Beginning Bass Voice: With Annotated Guide to Works for Beginning Bass Voice.* Lanham, MD: The Scarecrow Press, Inc., 2002.
Orenstein, Arbie. *Ravel: Man and Music.* New York: Columbia University Press, 1975.
Orenstein, Arbie. *A Ravel Reader: Correspondence, Articles, and Interviews.* New York: Columbia University Press, 1990.
Osborne, Charles. *Schubert and his Vienna.* New York: Alfred A. Knopf, 1985.
Parsons, James. *The Cambridge Companion to the Lied.* United Kingdom: Cambridge University Press, 2004
Petersen, Barbara A. *Ton und Wort, The Lieder of Richard Strauss.* Ann Arbor, MI: University Microfilms International, 1989.
Phillips, Lois. *Lieder Line by Line.* Revised ed. New York, NY: Oxford University Press Inc., 1996.
Piatak, Jean and Regina Avrashov. *Russian Songs and Arias.* Dallas: Pst… Inc., 1991.
Pilkington, Michael. *British solo song: a guide for singers, teachers, librarians and the music trade of songs currently available.* Norwich: Thames/Eikin, 2003.
Pilkington, Michael. *Gurney, Ireland, Quilter and Warlock.* Bloomington: Indiana University Press, 1989.
Poulenc, Francis. *Diary of my Songs* (dual language edition). London: Victor Gollancz Ltd., 1985.
Prawer, S.S. *The Penguin Book of Lieder.* Baltimore, MD: Penguin Books, Inc. 1964.
Reed, John. *The Schubert Song Companion.* London, England: Faber and Faber, 1993
Retzlaff, Jonathan and Cheri Montgomery. *Exploring Art Song Lyrics*. New York: Oxford University Press, 2012.
Rohinsky, Marie-Claire. *The Singer's Debussy.* Rosen Publishing Group, 1987.
Rosenthal, Harold, Warrack, John. *Concise Oxford Dictionary of Opera.* London: Oxford University Press, 1979.
Ross, Alex. *The Rest Is Noise: Listening to the Twentieth Century.* New York: Macmillan, 2007.
Sadie, Stanley. *The Grove Book of Operas, Second Edition.* New York: Oxford University Press, 2006.
Sams, Eric. *The Songs of Hugo Wolf.* London: Eulenburg Books, 1983.
Sams, Eric. *The Songs of Johannes Brahms.* New Haven, Conn: Eulenburg Books, 1983.
Sams, Eric. *The Songs of Robert Schumann.* London: Yale University Press, 1993.
Schoep, Arthur; Harris, Daniel. *Word by Word Translations of Songs and Arias, Part II Italian.* Metuchen, NJ: The Scarecrow Press, Inc. 1972.
Shephard, Philip. *What the Fach?! The Definitive Guide for Opera Singers Auditioning and Working in Germany, Austria, and Switzerland, 2nd Edition.* Create Space Independent Publishing Platform, 2010.
Simas, Rich. *The Musical No One Came To See.* New York: Garland Publishing, 1987.
Singer, Martial. *An Interpretive Guide to Operatic Arias; A Handbook for Singers, Coaches, Teachers and Students.* University Park, Pennsylvania: The Pennsylvania State University Press, 1983.
Smith, Barry, ed. *The Collected Letters of Peter Warlock.* Rochester, NY: Boydell Press, 2005.
Sobrer, Josep Miquel and Edmon Colomer. *The Singer's Anthology of 20th Century Spanish Songs.* New York: Pelion Press, 1987.
Spicker, Max, editor, *Celebrated Opera Arias* (4 volumes - all voice types). New York: Patelson's Music House LTD, reprinted 1985.
Stevens, Denis (ed.). *A History of Song.* New York: W.W. Norton & Company, 1950.
Stokes, Richard. *The Book of Lieder, the original texts of over 1000 songs.* London, England: Faber and Faber Ltd., 2005.
Suskin, Steven. *Show Tunes: The Songs, Shows and Careers of Broadway's Major Composers.* New York: Oxford University Press, 2000.
Sylvester, Richard D. *Tchaikovsky's Complete Songs: A Companion with Texts and Translations.* Bloomington, IN: Indiana University Press, 2002.
Thompson, Oscar. *Debussy: Man and Artist.* New York: Dover Publications, Inc., 1967.
Trezise, Simon (ed). *The Cambridge Companion to Debussy.* Cambridge, UK: Cambridge University Press, 2003.
Uris, Dorothy. *To Sing In English, A Guide to Improved Diction.* New York: Boosey and Hawkes, 1971.
Upton, William Treat. *Art-Song in America: A Study in the Development of American Music.* Boston: Ditson, 1969.

Valla, Léon. Trans. Marie and Grace O'Brien. *Claude Debussy: His life and Works.* London: Oxford University Press, 1933.

Villamil, Victoria Etnier. *A Singer's Guide to the American Art Song 1870-1980.* London: Scarecrow, 1993.

Vuillermoz, Arthur B. *Claude Debussy and the Poets.* Berkley, CA: University of California Press, 1976.

Whittaker, W. Gillies. *The Cantatas of Johann Sebastian Bach, Sacred and Secular; Volume I and II.* London: Oxford University Press, 1978.

A Selected Bibliography of Reference Sources: Online Resources

20th Century Song Foundation
http://www.songfoundation.com

American Art Song
http://www.americanartsong.org/default.htm
(Includes a page with links to many current composer's websites)
http://www.songofamerica.net/cgi-bin/iowa/home/index.html

American Guild of Musical Artists
http://musicalartists.org

American Theater Web
http://americantheaterweb.com

Analysis of Song
http://humanities.uchicago.edu/classes/zbikowski/seminar.html

Aria Database (diverse collection of information on over 1000 operatic arias, with translations, aria texts and MIDI files)
http://www.aria-database.com

Art Song
http://theartsongproject.com
http://www.artsong.eu
http://artsongcentral.com
(Limited list of free, printable sheet music with IPA transcription)

Bach Cantatas
http://www.bach-cantatas.com

British songs database (from the end of the 16th century to present)
http://cfaonline.cfa.asu.edu/hoffer/

Classical MIDI with words
http://www.recmusic.org/midi/

Classical Vocal Reprints
http://www.classicalvocalrep.com/

Contributions to Lieder Repertoire
http://www.pjb.com.au/mus/lieder_writers.html

DRAM (scholarly resource of recordings, including CD quality audio, liner notes and essays from New World, Composers Recordings and other important labels)
http://www.dramonline.org

French Melodie
    http://www.melodiefrancaise.com
    http://www.melodie.talktalk.net

Heinrich Heine
    http://www.library.umass.edu/hosted-projects/heine/

The International Music Score Library Project (a virtual library of public domain music)
    http://IMSLP.org

International Phonetic Alphabet Source
    http://www.ipasource.com/home

Internet Broadway Database (the official database for Broadway theater information. IBDB provides records of productions from the beginnings of New York theater until today)
    http://www.ibdb.com/index.php

Kurt Weill Foundation for Music
    http://www.kwf.org/kwf/

Latin American Art Song Alliance
    http://www.laasa.org

REC Music Foundation (to promote new classical music composers, primarily through the development of new computer tools [Artsconverge, The Lied & Song Text & Classical Midi with Words])
    http://www.recmusic.org

    The Lied, Art Song, and Choral Texts Archive Page is an archive of texts used in Lieder and other classical art songs, as well as in many choral works and other types of classical vocal pieces.
    http://www.recmusic.org/lieder

Lieder and Melodie
    http://liedmelo.free.fr

Musical Heaven (celebrating the musicals of yesterday and today)
    http://www.musicalheaven.com

Musicals 101
    http://musicals101.com

National Association of Teachers of Singing
    http://nats.org

New York Singing Teachers Association
    http://nyst.org/

Online Musical Scores
    http://www.dlib.indiana.edu/variations/scores/

Opera
    http://www.gopera.com
    http://opera.standford.edu
    http://www.operissimo.com/

Rare Art Songs
    http://www.lawrence.edu/fast/koopmajo/unsung.html

Russian Art Song (Includes recordings of native speakers reading texts)
  http://www.russianartsong.com/index.html

Schubert
  http://home1.swipnet.se/~w-18046/schub.html
  http://www.schubertline.co.uk/home.htm
  http://www.franzschubert.org.uk
  http://www.schubertlied.de/index.php/en/

The Singer's Repertoire Parts I – IV, by Berton Coffin is fully available online
  http://archive.org/stream/singersrepertoir027233mbp#page/n3/mode/2up

The Sybaritic Singer
  http://sybariticsinger.com/2013/02/05/day5/
    (Plan a Recital – Blog by music critic Tim Smith
    Practical advice on how to assess audience, order program, etc)

Theatermania- theater news
  http://theatermania.com

Unsung Songs
  http://www2.lawrence.edu/fast/KOOPMAJO/unsung.html

Voice Categories
  http://www.cantabile-subito.de/Categories/categories.html

Wolf, Hugo
  http://www.hugo-wolf-akademie.de

Song & Aria Title Index

100 Years 196	Ondrasik, J.
A Birthday 190	Davis, Sharon
A Brisk Young Sailor 126, 194	Butterworth, George
A Dog's Life 199	Michael Head
A Legend 181, 202	Tchaikovsky, Pyotr Ilyich
A Minor Bird 188	Dougherty, Celius
A Real Low Down Basso Am I 199	O'Hara, Geoffrey
A Song of Perfect Propriety 203	Barab, Seymour
A Word on My Ear 203	Flanders & Swann
A-Roving 198	Terry, Sir Richard Runciman (arr.)
A-tisket A-tasket 190	Fitzgerald, Ella & Van Alexander
A... 146, 196	Sabaté, Felipe Pedrell
Ach, dass ich Wassers gnug hatte 197	Bach, Johann Christoph
Ach, reiner Geist! 197	Telemann, Georg Philipp
Adieu 96, 188	Fauré, Gabriel
Adieu! 166, 198, 202	Weyrauch, August Heinrich von (Attr. to Schubert)
Agita de' venti dall'onte 186	Vivaldi, Antonio
Agnes 199	Pasatieri, Thomas
Ah! Eccellenza! from *Nina, o sia la pazza per amore* 200	Paisiello, Giovanni
Ah! Qu'on daigne du moins 156, 197	Rameau, Jean-Phillippe
Ah! Se tu dormi svegliati from *Giulietta e Romeo* 200	Vaccai, Nicola
All Along the Mother Volga	Ord, Alan (arr.)
All At Once 188	Weill, Kurt
Almen se non poss'io 116, 192	Bellini, Vincenzo
Almen se non poss'io 190	Bellini, Vincenzo
Amazing Grace 194	Althouse, Jay (arr.)
Ambo nati in questa valle from *Linda di Chamounix* 200	Donizetti, Gaetano
Amor 203	Bolcom, William
Amor mi tiene in pugno 146, 196	Donaudy, Stefano
Amor, ch'attendi 198	Caccini, Giulio
Amour d'antan 147, 196	Chausson, Ernest
An Chloe 188	Mozart, W.A.
An den Mond 188	Schubert, Franz
An mein Klavier 176, 202	Schubert, Franz
An Sylvia 189	Schubert, Franz
Anch'io son giovine from *La cambiale di matrimonio* 201	Rossini, Gioachino
Ann Street 203	Ives, Charles
Another New Voice Teacher 203	Scheer, Gene & Andrew Thomas
Anthem 86, 187	Rice, Anderson & Ulvaeus
Après un Rêve 77	Fauré, Gabriel
Aria da cantar stanze 166, 198	Bottegari, Cosimo
Aria di Agratina 188	Haydn, Franz Joseph
Aria di Buonafede from *Il Monda della Luna* 200	Haydn, Franz Joseph
Aria di Ecclitico rom *Il Monda della Luna* 201	Haydn, Franz Joseph
Aria di Nencio from *L'infedeltà delusa* 201	Haydn, Franz Joseph
Aria di romanesca 186	Caccini, Giulio
Aria di Rosina 188	Haydn, Franz Joseph

Aria di Sempronio	
from *Lo speziale* 201	Haydn, Franz Joseph
Arie aus dem Spiegel von Arcadien 86, 187	Schoenberg, Arnold
Arm, Arm Ye Brave 190	Handel, G.F.
Art Is Calling for Me (The Prima Donna Song) 199, 203	Herbert, Victor
As Joseph Was A-walking 195	Thiman, Eric
As when the dove 156, 197	Handel, G.F.
Ash Grove, The 194	Quilter, Roger (arr.)
Ashgrove, The 189	Britten, Benjamin (arr.)
Asleep 194	Coolidge, Elizabeth Sprague
Astronomers, The 204	Hundley, Richard
At Sea 106, 190	Ives, Charles
At the River 189, 193	Copland, Aaron
Audience Song, The 204	Moore, Ben
Auf Flügeln des Gesanges 188, 190	Mendelssohn, Felix
Auf geheimem Waldespfade 147, 196	Franz, Robert
Aufträge 186, 199	Schumann, Robert
Aureole, The 192	Chadwick, George Whitefield
Ave Maria (su due note) 116, 192	Rossini, Gioacchino
Away to Twiver 187	Warlock, Peter
Bäche von gesalznen Zaehren 197	Bach, J.S.
Ballade des gros dindons 96, 188, 203	Chabrier, Emmanuel
Bartholomew Green 204	Hundley, Richard
Batti, batti 186	Mozart, W.A.
Beautiful Dreamer 126, 194	Foster, Stephen
Befraget mich ein zartes Kind	
from *Bastien und Bastienne* 200	Mozart, W.A.
Beggar's Song 186	Barber, Samuel
Behold, a Virgin Shall Be with Child 195	LaMontaine, John
Bei der Wiege 66, 187, 190	Mendelssohn, Felix
Bekennen will ich seinen Namen 197	Bach, J.S.
Bel Nume che adoro	
from *Pigmalione* 200	Cimadoro, Giovanni Battista
Belle Hermione, Hèlas! 106, 190	Lully, Jean-Baptiste
Bellezza che s'ama 197	Scarlatti, Alessandro
Bergere legere 196	Anonymous
Berglied 127, 194	Zelter, Carl Friederich
Best Things Happen While You're Dancing, The 194	Berlin, Irving
Birds No More Shall Sing, The 195	Handel, G.F.
Bist du bei mir 188, 197	Bach, J.S.
Bitte 196	Franz, Robert
Black Coffee 190	Burke and Webster
Black Dress, The 189	Niles, John Jacob (arr.)
Black Oak Tree, The 199	Niles, John Jacob (arr.)
Blackberry Winter 190	Wilder, Alec
Blessing of the Boats 107, 190	Gordon, Ricky Ian
Blind 97, 188	Ireland, John
Blow, Blow Thou Winter Wind 190	Dring, Madeleine
Blow, Blow Thou Winter Wind 190	Quilter, Roger
Bois Epais 117, 167, 192, 198	Lully, Jean-Baptiste
Boy Next Door, The 192	Martin and Blane
Bread and Cherries 87, 187	Gurney, Ivor
Buffalo Gals 199	Bacon, Ernest
C'est à ce joli mois de May 195	Anonymous
C'est moi 203	Lerner & Loewe
Canary Cantata 197	Telemann, Georg Philipp
Cantique 87, 187	Boulanger, Nadia

Canto di una Guècha from *Iris* 201	Mascagni, Pietro
Canzonetta (Tu fai la superbetta) 136, 195	Fesch, Willlem de
Captain Stratton's Fancy 199	Warlock, Peter
Caro Mio Ben 55, 60, 188	Giordani, Giuseppe
Cavatina di Alcina 188	Haydn, Franz Joseph
Ch'io mai vi possa 58, 186, 190	Handel, G.F.
Chanson d'Automne 189	Berger, Jean
Chant Breton 117, 192	Lalo, Edouard
Charmant Papillon 186	Campra, André
Charming Chloë 196	Unknown
Che cangi tempra 188, 190	Donizetti, Gaetano
Che faro senza Euridice? 190	Gluck, Christoph Willibald
Che fiero costume 187	Legrenzi, Giovanni
Che t'ho fatt'io 188	Caccini, Francesca
Chevaliers de la table ronde 167, 198	Althouse, Jay (arr.)
Chi mi confort'ahime! 186	Caccini, Giulio
Children's Hour, The 203	Ives, Charles
Ching-a-ring chaw 187, 203	Copland, Aaron (arr.)
Christbaum 187	Cornelius, Peter
Christmas Tree, The 199	Coolidge, Elizabeth Sprague
Circus Band, The	Ives, Charles
Cloak, the Boat and the Shoes, The 192	Moore, Ben
Come Again, Sweet Love 97, 188	Dowland, John
Come and Trip It 186, 197	Handel, G.F.
Come Away Death 148, 190, 196	Finzi, Gerald
Come Away Death 190, 203	Dring, Madeleine
Come Away Death 22, 187	Quilter, Rodger
Come Down from the Tree 136, 195	Flaherty, Stephen
Come in Morning 190	Weill, Kurt
Come Live With Me 186	Handel, G.F.
Come Ready and See Me 190	Hundley, Richard
Come Sorrow Come 157, 197	Morley, Thomas
Come Ye Blessed 198	Scott, John Prindle
Come, Cheerful Day 195	Campion, Thomas
Comedy Tonight 188	Sondheim, Stephen
Compensation 127, 194	Lloyd, Charles Jr.
Connais-tu le pays from *Mignon* 200	Thomas, Ambroise
Content to Be Behind Me 203	Moore, Ben
Could Be 204	Musto, John
Cowboy Songs 199	Larsen, Libby
Crea in quegli occhi il lampo d'un desìo from *Iris* 202	Mascagni, Pietro
Create In Me A Clean Heart 192	Mueller, Carl F.
Cuckoo, The 186	Dring, Madeleine
Cuckoo, The 192	Dring, Madeleine
Cycle of Light 204	Martinson, Joel
Da unten im Tale 176, 188, 202	Brahms, Johannes
Daisies, The 189, 194	Barber, Samuel
Danza, danza, fanciulla 187	Durante, Francesco
Das Fischermädchen 196	Schubert, Franz
Das irdische Leben 199	Mahler, Gustav
Das Kinderspiel 177, 202	Mozart, W.A.
Das Veilchen 188	Liszt, Franz
Das Veilchen 195	Mozart, W.A.
Date abbiento al mio dolore 98, 188	Donaudy, Stefano
De Gospel Train 190	Burleigh, Harry

Deaf Old Woman, The 199	Davis, Katherine K.
Dear Prudence 196	Lennon, John and Paul McCartney
Declaration of Independence 118, 192	Dougherty, Celius
Dedication 194	Franz, Robert
Deep River 168, 198	Hogan, Moses (arr.)
Deh, rendetemi 16, 187	Provenzale, Francesco
Dein Angesicht 148, 188, 196	Schumann, Robert
Dein Blaues Auge 196	Brahms, Johannes
Dem Schutzengel 107, 190	Brahms, Johannes
Der arme Peter 199	Schumann, Robert
Der Frühling 128, 194	Brahms, Johannes
Der funfundzwanzigste Psalm 197	Bach, C.P.E.
Der Gleichsinn 177, 202	Haydn, Franz Joseph
Der Jager im Walde 190	Brahms, Johannes
Der kleine Sandman bin ich 190	Humperdinck, Englebert
Der König in Thule 108, 190	Zelter, Carl Friedrich
Der Kreüzzug 202	Schubert, Franz
Der Leiermann 198	Schubert, Franz
Der Lindenbaum 196	Schubert, Franz
Der Mond 178, 190, 202	Mendelssohn, Felix
Der Neurigiere 190	Schubert, Franz
Der Nussbaum 190, 192 , 202	Schumann, Robert
Der Tod und das Madchen 190	Schubert, Franz
Der wahren Tugend Gegenstreit 157, 197	Dedekind, Constantin Christian
Der Zauberer 188	Mozart, W.A.
Des Liebsten Schwur 195	Brahms, Johannes
Des Reichtums Glanz auf weiter Erden 197	Bach, J.S.
Des Sennen Abschied 178, 202	Schumann, Robert
Di questa poverella from *Il filosofo di campagna* 201	Galuppi, Baldassare
Diaphenia 108, 191	Pilkington, Francis
Diaphenia 187	Argento, Dominick
Die Armen will der Herr umarmen (Cantata 191) 197	Bach, J.S.
Die beiden Grenadiere 187	Schumann, Robert
Die Elenden sollen essen 197	Bach, J.S.
Die Forelle 186, 194, 202	Schubert, Franz
Die Kartenlegerin 199	Schumann, Robert
Die Landlust 179, 202	Haydn, Franz Joseph
Die Lotosblume 188, 190	Schumann, Robert
Die Mainacht 190	Brahms, Johannes
Die Mainacht 202	Schubert, Franz
Die Männer sind méchant 195, 199	Schubert, Franz
Die Post 186	Schubert, Franz
Die Soldatenbraut 199	Schumann, Robert
Die Sonne scheint nicht mehr 191	Brahms, Johannes
Die Spröde 137, 195	Zelter, Carl Friderich
Dieu Tout Puissant 158, 197	Destouches, André
Diggi, daggi, shurry, murry 179, 202	Mozart, W.A.
Dimmi, ben mio 193	Beethoven, Ludwig van
Dirge 187	Argento, Dominick
Dolce Amor, Bendato Dio 195	Bruni, Francesco
Dolce Scherza 109, 191	Perti, Giacomo Antonio
Don't get around much anymore 196	Ellington, Duke
Don't put your daughter on the Stage, Mrs. Worthington 191	Coward, Sir Noël
Donna haser senza amore 158, 197	Puliti, Gabriello

Donne vaghe… from *La serva padrona* 201	Paisiello, Giovanni
Douce dame jolie 109, 191	Machaut, Guillaume de
Down Among the Dead Men 168, 198	Traditional, 1715
Down By the Sally Gardens 188, 196	Donovan, Richard arr.
Down to the Rivah 204	MacGimsey, Richard
Dream a Little Dream 191	Schwandt, Wilbur & Andre
Dream Valley 137, 195	Quilter, Roger
Drink to Me Only with Thine Eyes 98, 188	Mellish, Colonel (arr. Quilter)
Du bist wie eine blume 191	Schumann, Robert
Du Ring an meinem Finger 193	Schumann, Robert
Dunque per un infido… S'arresta il sangue nelle vene from *L'italiana in Londra* 201	Cimarosa, Domenico
E l'uccellino 133, 195	Puccini, Giacomo
Early in the Morning 88, 187	Rorem, Ned
Ecco il fatal recinto… Ad ogni istante sembrami vederla from *I promessi sposi* 202	Ponchielli, Amilcare
Ecco, che pur baciate 159, 197	Obizzi, Domenico
Edelweiss 81, 198	Rodgers, Richard
Ei, wie schmeckt der Coffee süße 180, 202	Bach, J.S.
Eile, mich, Gott, zu erretten 197	Schütz, Heinrich
Eileen Aroon 193	Traditional
Ein goldenes Kettlein 40, 187	Marx, Joseph
El Caballito 88, 187	Revueltas, Silvestra
El tra la la y el punteado 89, 187	Granados, Enrique
Eldorado 169, 198	Walthew, Richard H.
Elégie 188	Massenet, Jules
En las montañas de Asturias 110, 191	Rodrigo, Joaquin
English Songs, The 189	Haydn, Franz Joseph
Envoi de Fleurs 118, 193	Gounod, Charles
Epitaph on a Wife 199	Hundley, Richard
Erfreue dich Seele 197	Bach, J.S.
Erlaube mir feins Mädchen 191	Brahms, Johannes
Erstes Grün 191	Schumann, Robert
Es hat die Rose sich beklagt 128, 194	Franz, Robert
Es ist ein' Ros'entsprungen 197	Traditional
Es muss ein wunderbares sein 188	Liszt, Franz
Esser mesto il mio cor 191	Flotow, Friedrich von
Estribillio 191	Rodrigo, Joaquin
Eurilda's aria (*Questa mano*) from *Le Pescatrici* 201	Haydn, Franz Joseph
Everything Else 194	Kitt, Tom
Ev'ry time We Say Goodbye 129, 194	Porter, Cole
Fa così lodoletta che fuggi 188	Vinci, Leonardo
Fain Would I, Chloris 129, 194	Blow, John
Faithfu'Johnnie 191	Beethoven, Ludwig van
Fanciullette ritrosette from *La finta semplice* 202	Mozart, W.A.
Fere Selvaggie 195	Caccini, Giulio
Figlia mia 191	Handel, G.F.
Figlia mia 149, 196	Handel, G.F.
Filli, Non T'amo Piu 191	Carissimi, Giacomo
Fleurs 110, 191	Poulenc, Francis
Flute of Interior Time, The 204	Harbison, John
Foggy, Foggy Dew, The 204	Britten, Benjamin (arr.)
For Your Delight 188, 190	Hundley, Richard
Four Nights 191	Williams, Ralph Vaughan
Four Plus One 199	Black, Eldon Udell

From the Land of the Sky-Blue Water 99, 188	Cadman, Charles Wakefield
Frühlingsglaube 190, 202	Schubert, Franz
Fu di notte come in sogno from *Amelia al ballo* 202	Menotti, Gian Carlo
Fürchte dich nicht 197	Bach, J.S.
Fürchtet euch nicht 197	Schütz, Heinrich
Fußreise 187	Wolf, Hugo
Gasparina's aria from *La canterina* 201	Haydn, Franz Joseph
Gia il sole dal Gange 186	Scarlatti, Alessandro
Gioite al canto mio 169, 198	Peri, Jacopo
Giusto ciel, che conoscete from *Il barbiere di Siviglia* 201	Paisiello, Giovanni
Give me your hand 194	Duke, John
Gleich Merlin, dem eitlen Weisen 170, 198	Hensel, Fanny Mendelssohn
Glück 197	Telemann, Georg Philipp
Go 'way from my Window 195	Niles, John Jacob (arr.)
Go Down in the Lonesome Valley 190	Burleigh, Harry
Gott ist gerecht 196	Bach, J.S.
Gottes Macht und Vorsehung 130, 194	Beethoven, Ludwig
Grablied für die Mutter 99, 188	Schubert, Franz
Grandma 119, 193	Chanler, Theodore
Green Dog, The 204	Kingsley, Herbert
Green Finch and Linnet Bird 89, 187	Sondheim, Stephen
Greensleeves 69	Kern, Philip
Gruß 180, 202	Mendelssohn, Felix
Guerrier sognai vittoria from *Don Sebastiano* 200	Donizetti, Gaetano
Gute Nacht 119, 193	Franz, Robert
Hands, Eyes and Heart 100, 188	Williams, Ralph Vaughan
Hans und Grethe 199	Mahler, Gustav
Happy Working Song 191	Menken, Alan
Hat man nicht auch Gold beineben from *Fidelio* 200	Beethoven, Ludwig van
Hat man nicht auch Gold beineben 181, 202	Beethoven, Ludwig van
Haus des Herrn 197	Telemann, Georg Philipp
Have you seen but a white lily grow 191	Unknown
Hawk and Buckle 194	Gurney, Ivor
Hear! Ye Gods of Britain 198	Purcell, Henry
Heidenröslein 188	Schubert, Franz
Himmelstochter, Ruh der Seelen 159, 197	Bach, C.P.E.
hist…whist 199	Duke, John
Ho capito, Signor sì! from *Don Giovanni* 200	Mozart, W.A.
Hochlandisches Wiegenlied 191	Schumann, Robert
Hope 188	Ireland, John
Hör' ich das Liedchen klingen 170, 198	Schumann, Robert
Hört, ihr Augen, auf zu weinen 197	Bach, J.S.
How Sweet the Moonlight Sleeps 194	Head, Michael
How unhappy's the nymph 195	Boyce, William
Hush, no more, be silent 191, 198	Purcell, Henry
Hymn 187	Argento, Dominick
I Am in Need of Music 28, 193	Moore, Ben
I Bought Me a Cat 90, 187, 199	Copland, Aaron (arr.)
I Can Smell the Sea Air 203	Previn, Andre
I Could Have Danced All Night 120, 193	Loewe, Frederick
I Feel Pretty 90, 187	Bernstein, Leonard & Stephen Sondheim

I Hate Music 204	Bernstein, Leonard
I Have a Fawn 195	Davis, Katherine K.
I Heard a Blackbird in a Tree 186	Arlen, Albert
I Heard the Voice of Jesus Say 195	Harriss, Charles
I Know that My Redeemer Liveth 193	Handel, G.F.
I Like It Here 100, 188	Wilder, Alec
I Love all graceful things 133, 195	Thiman, Eric
I Love and I Must 160, 197	Purcell, Henry
I Love Teaching Voice 203	Moore, Ben
I Remember 191	Sondheim, Stephen
I Whistle a Happy Tune 91, 187	Rodgers, Richard
I Wish it so 68, 193	Blitzstein, Marc
I'm Glad I'm Not a Tenor 203	Moore, Ben
Ich ende behende 197	Bach, J.S.
Ich folge dir gleichfalls 186	Bach, J.S.
Ich liebe dich 193	Beethoven, Ludwig van
Ich liebe dich 193	Grieg, Edvard
Ich möchte wohl der Kaiser sein 199	Mozart, W.A.
Ich sehe dich in deinem Worte 197	Telemann, Georg Philipp
If he really knew me 130, 194	Sager, Carole Bayer & Marvin Hamlisch
If You've Only Got a Moustache 203	Foster, Stephen
Il Bacio 186, 193	Arditi, Luigi
Il Giglio e la Rosa 187	Donizetti, Gaetano
Im Sturme 187	Loewe, Johann Karl Gottfried
Im Wunderschönen Monat Mai 188	Schumann, Robert
Imagine 196	Lennon, John
Immagine gradita from *Adelson e Salvini* 201	Bellini, Vincenzo
Immer leiser wird mein Schlummer 120, 193	Brahms, Johannes
In a Myrtle Shade 188	Griffes, Charles
In a simple way I love you 191	Ford, Nancy
In der Fremde 149, 196	Brahms, Johannes
In einem Kühlen Grunde 191	Traditional
In Euch, Ihr grünen Auen 197	Telemann, Georg Philipp
In grünem Wald ich neulich sass 198	Spee, Friedrich von
In my own little Corner 89	Rodgers, Richard
In quegl'anni in cui val poco from *Le nozze di Figaro* 202	Mozart, W.A.
In stiller Nacht 188	Brahms, Johannes
In the dark pinewood 191, 204	Barber, Samuel
In the Springtime 191	King, Betty Jackson
In uomini, in soldati 199	Mozart, W.A.
Intermezzo 204	Schumann, Robert
Inventory 203	Barab, Seymour
Is it Really Me? 191	Schmidt, Harvey
Is My Team Ploughing? 199	George Butterworth
Israel, hoffe auf den Herren 197	Buxtehude, Dietrich
It must be so 196	Bernstein, Leonard
It Was a Lover and His Lass 191	Dring, Madeleine
Jabberwocky 204	Hoiby, Lee
Jasminenstrauch 202	Schumann, Robert
Jazz Songs 203	Roe, Betty
Je te veux 139, 195	Satie, Erik
Jeanie With the Light Brown Hair 150, 196	Foster, Stephen
Jeg elsker Dig 111, 191	Grieg, Edvard
Jesse James 196	Siegmeister, Arr. Elie
Jesu, deine Gnadenblicke 197	Bach, J.S.

Title	Page(s)	Composer
Jesus, the Very Thought of Thee	195	Thiman, Eric
Jimmie's Got a Goil	199	Blitzstein, Marc
Johanna	189	Sondheim, Stephen
Jonah and the Whale	204	MacGimsey, Richard
Joshua fit the Battle of Jericho	194	Anonymous
June on Castle Hill	139, 195	Finzi, Gerald
Karen	191	Ives, Charles
Kiss Me Not Goodbye from *The Mighty Casey*	201	Schuman, William
Komm, Jesu, komm zu deiner Kirche	150, 196	Bach, J.S.
Komm, süßer Schlaf	197	Telemann, Georg Philipp
Komm! Ach Komm! O süsse Tod	160, 197	Theile, Johann
Kommen und Scheiden	34, 187	Mendelssohn, Fanny Hensel
L'Amour s'envole	195	Weckerlin, J.B. (arr.)
L'esule	112, 191	Verdi, Giuseppe
L'ho perduta, me meschina from *Le nozze di Figaro*	201	Mozart, W.A.
L'Offrande	203	Poulenc, Francis
L'Ora è tarda	191	Tosti, Francesco Paolo
La belle table est mise	191	Arms Fischer, William (arr.)
La Brise	121, 193	Saint-Saëns, Camille
La Diva de L'Empire	111, 191	Satie, Erik
La Fortuna	131, 194	Scarlatti, Alessandro
La Maison Grise	112, 191	Messager, André
La Mañana	191	Ginastera, Alberto
La mia ragion è questa from *Il filosofo di campagno*	200	Galuppi, Baldassare
La Pastorella	204	Schubert, Franz
La Pastorella delle Alpi	186	Rossini, Gioacchino
La Rachelina from *La molinara*	201	Paisiello, Giovanni
La Rose (Ode anacréontique)	151, 196	Fauré, Gabriel
La sauterelle	121, 193	Poulenc, Francis
La Serenata	189	Tosti, Francesco Paolo
La Solitundine (2nd aria)	186	Handel, G.F.
La statue de bronze	196	Satie, Erik
Lachen und Weinen	189	Schubert, Franz
Lads in their Hundreds, The	188	Butterworth, George
Lady of the Harbor, The	204	Hoiby, Lee
Lagrimetta alle pupille	186	Vivaldi, Antonio
Lamb, The	125, 193	Chanler, Theodore
Lass From Low Countree, The	105, 189	Niles, John Jacob (arr.)
Lass With the Delicate Air, The	186	Arne, Michael
Lasst hier Gesang und Saiten schallen	197	Telemann, Georg Philipp
Lasst mich ruhen	131, 194	Liszt, Franz
Last Rose of Summer, The	155, 191, 196	Britten, Benjamin (arr.)
Laurie's Song from *The Tender Land*	201	Copland, Aaron
Le Bestiaire	199	Poulenc, Francis
Le Carpillon	161, 197	Campra, André
Le Chanson du Tambourine	193	Unknown
Le charme	140, 195	Chausson, Ernest
Le Charme	191	Chausson, Ernest
Le Fils de la Femme Poisson	191	Trenet, Charles
Le Mariage des Roses	140, 195	Franck, César
Le Soir	122, 193	Gounod, Charles
Le Violette	193, 204	Scarlatti, Alessandro

Leave Me, Loathsome Light	171, 190, 198	Handel, G.F.
Les cloches	204	Debussy, Claude
Les matelots	189	Fauré, Gabriel
Les Poissons	171, 198, 203	Menken, Alan
Liebes Mädchen hör' mir zu	194, 202	Haydn, Franz Joseph
Liebhaber in allen Gestalten	194	Schubert, Franz
Lieblingsplätzchen	101, 189	Mendelssohn, Felix
Liebst du um Schönheit	187	Schumann, Clara Wieck
Liebster Herr Jesu	197	Buxtehude, Dietrich
Lime Jello-Marshmallow Cottage Cheese Surprise	203	Bolcom, William
Linden Lea	189, 190	Williams, Ralph Vaughan
Lion Tamer	91, 187	Schwartz, Stephen
Litanei	182, 202	Schubert, Franz
Litany	204	Musto, John
Little Bunny Hop Hop Hop	203	Schickele, Peter (aka P.D.Q. Bach)
Lo Postouro delaissado	202	Canteloube, Joseph
Lob des hohen Verstands	199	Mahler, Gustav
Look for the Silver Lining	194	Kern, Jerome
Lord! I married me a wife!	203	Britten, Benjamin (arr.)
Lord's Prayer, The	190	Malotte, Albert Hay
Lords of Creation Men we call, The	204	Loesser, Arthur (arr. Alfred Kugel)
Lost chord, The	192	Sullivan, Arthur
Love Has Eyes	191	Bishop, Henry
Love in the Dictionary	199	Dougherty, Celius
Love is a plaintive song	187	Sullivan, Arthur
Love Look Away	191	RRodgers, Richard
Love's Philosophy	187	Quilter, Roger
Loveliest of Trees	191	Butterworth, George
Loveliest of Trees	141, 191, 195	Duke, John
Lovely Lass of Inverness, The	203	Beethoven, Ludwig van
Luck	194	Gordon, Ricky Ian
Lust der Sturmnacht	202	Schumann, Robert
Lydia	56, 63, 191	Fauré, Gabriel
Ma rendi pur contento	101, 189, 193	Bellini, Vincenzo
Mädchen mit dem Rothen Mundchen	57, 198	Franz, Robert
Madrigal	132, 194	d'Indy, Vincent
Mai	187	Fauré, Gabriel
Maiden Snow	190	Hundley, Richard
Make Someone Happy	195	Styne, Jule, Betty Comden and Adolph Green
Maledetto sia l'aspetto	172, 198	Monteverdi, Claudio
Malurous qu'o uno fenno	141, 195	Canteloube, Joseph
Man is for the Woman Made	193	Purcell, Henry
Mandoline	186	Fauré, Gabriel
Mandoline	187	Debussy, Claude
Many a New Day	51	Rogers, Richard
Margot	151, 196	Romberg, Sigmund
Marie	152, 196	Franz, Robert
Marito vorrei from *La finta semplice*	201	Mozart, W.A.
Marmotte	113, 191	Beethoven, Ludwig van
Masochism Tango, The	204	Lehrer, Tom
Mattinata	204	Leoncavallo, Ruggiero
Meeresleuchten	172,	Loewe, Carl
Mein Garten	182, 202	Schumann, Robert
Mein Mädel hat einen Rosemund	202	Brahms, Johannes
Meine Liebe is grün	187	Brahms, Johannes

Meiner Liebsten schönen Wangen from *Bastien und Bastienne* 202	Mozart, W.A.
Memories 199	Ives, Charles
Menelaus 191	Williams, Ralph Vaughan
Mentre l'erbetta pasce l'agnella from *Il Flaminio* 202	Pergolesi, Giovanni Battista
Metropolitan Tower, The 71, 193	Laitman, Lori
Minnelied 203	Brahms, Johannes
Mirth Admit Me 187	Handel, G.F.
Mock Turtle's Song, The 194	Duke, John
Money, O 199, 203	Head, Michael
Moonlight's Watermelon 193	Hundley, Richard
More Love or More Disdain 183, 203	Purcell, Henry
Mortels, Que Vous Sert-il 161, 197	Campra, André
Mr. Snow 92, 187	Rodgers, Richard
Much More 191	Schmidt, Harvey
Music for a While 190, 193	Purcell, Henry
Music When Soft Voices Die 195	Quilter, Roger
Must the Winter Come So Soon? from *Vanessa* 201	Barber, Samuel
Muttertänderlei 199	Richard Strauss
My Cup Runneth Over 198	Schmidt, Harvey
My German Boyfriend 113, 191	Thomas, Richard Pearson
My Heart is Like a Singing Bird 190	Parry, C.H.H.
My Love Rode By 195	Calbreath, Mary Evelene
My Lovely Celia 197	Munro, George
My Romance 194	Rodgers, Richard
My Wife is a Most Knowing Woman 203	Foster, Stephen
Nel cor più non mi sento 199	Paisiello, Giovanni
Nel pur ardor 191	Peri, Jacopo
Nel Riposo e nel contento 198	Handel, G.F.
Nella fatal di Rimini from *Lucrezia Borgia* 201	Donizetti, Gaetano
Nelle guerre d'amore from *La finta semplice* 202	Mozart, W.A.
Newborn 189	Ireland, John
Nightingale, Charm'd by the Rose, The 192	Rimsky-Korsakov, Nicolai
Nightingale, The 199	Arr. C. Shaw
Nine of the Clock 92, 187	Gurney, Ivor
Nocturne 189	Fauré, Gabriel
Non cambierei, lo guiro... Vedo quell'albero from *Il filosofo di campagna* 200	Galuppi, Baldassarre
Non piango e non sospiro 189	Caccini, Giulio
Non posso disperar 193	Bononcini, Giovanni Battista
Non vogl'io se non vederti 64	Giordani, Giuseppe
Non, je n'irai plus au bols 183, 203	Weckerlin, J.B. (arr.)
Non, je ne crois pas 191	Unknown
Nos plaisirs seront peu durables 193	Handel, G. F.
Now Sleeps the Crimson Petal 190	Quilter, Roger
Nun lass uns Frieden Schliessen 93, 187	Wolf, Hugo
Nun scheint in vollem Glanze der Himmel 162, 198	Haydn, Franz Joseph
Nun sich der Tag geendet hat 197	Krieger, Adam
Nymphs and Shepherds 193	Purcell, Henry
O Cessate di Piagarmi 193	Scarlatti, Alessandro
O che odor di buono 193	Donaudy, Stefano
O chiome belle 191	Caccini, Francesca
O crudel che il mio pianto non vedi 192	Bellini, Vincenzo

O Del Ben 162, 198	Cesti, Antonio
O del mio amato ben 190	Donaudy, Stefano
O del mio dolce ardor 193	Gluck, Christoph Willibald
O di tua man 190	Vivaldi, Antonio
O do not love too long 122, 193	Rorem, Ned
O fior del giorno from *Edgar* 201	Puccini, Giacomo
O Isis und Osiris 190	Mozart, W.A.
O Leggiadri Occhi Belli 189	Anonymous
O Luna lucente 189	Haydn, Franz Joseph
O Luna Lucente from *Il Monda della Luna* 201	Haydn, Franz Joseph
O Mistress Mine 189, 190	Quilter, Roger
O No, John! 199	Arr. Wolff
O pargoletto arciero 189	Pasquini, Bernardo
O Rest in the Lord 203	Mendelssohn, Felix
O servi, volate	Vivaldi, Antonio
O servi, volate 186	Vivaldi, Antonio
O tu ch'innanzi morte 132, 194	Monteverdi, Claudio
O Waly, Waly 189	Britten, Benjamin (arr.)
Och Moder, ich well en Ding han 199	Brahms, Johannes
Of that so sweet imprisonment 204	Barber, Samuel
Ogni, amatore 142, 195	Piccinni, Niccolo
Oh Fair to See 187	Finzi, Gerald
Oiseaux si tous les ans 184, 203	Mozart, W.A.
Ol' Man River 193	Kern, Jerome
Old Sir Faulk 193	Walton, William
Oliver Cromwell 187	Britten, Benjamin (arr.)
On the Seashore of Endless Worlds 142, 195	Carpenter, John Alden
On The Street Where You Live 196	Loewe, Frederick
Once Upon a Dream 192	Fain, Sammy & Jack Lawrence
Only Child, The 189	Ireland, John
Open Sesame Seeds 203	Schickele, Peter (aka P.D.Q. Bach)
Or che il cielo a me ti rende 195	Righini, Vincenzo
Ouvre tes yeux bleus 189	Massenet, Jules
Owl is Abroad, The 199	Purcell, Henry
Padre, addio 143, 195	Lotti, Antonio
Papà, non mi lasciar from *Il cappello di paglia di Firenze* 201	Rota, Nino
Par min dirti 186	Vivaldi, Antonio
Parla piu piano 102, 189	Rota, Nino
Parting 192	Pasatieri, Thomas
Passepied 186	Delibes, Léo
Passing By 152, 196	Purcell, Edward
Passing By 102, 189	Warlock, Peter
Passionate Trencherwoman, The 204	Swann, Donald
Path to the Moon 195	Thiman, Eric
Peace Crowned with Roses 190	Handel, G.F.
Per pianto la mia carne 114, 192	Orsini, Eleonora
Per pietà 187	Stradella, Alessandro
Per pieta bell'idol mio 93, 187	Bellini, Vincenzo
Persin le bimbe vengono da be 187	Mozart, W.A.
Petit Oiseau 94, 187	Berlioz, Hector
Petite Abeille 187	Bacilly, Bertrand de
Phantasie 192	Mahler, Gustav
Phillis Has Such Charming Graces 153, 196	Young, Anthony
Piango, gemo, sospiro 190	Vivaldi, Antonio

Piercing Eyes 195	Haydn, Franz Joseph
Pilgrim's Home, The 193	Handel, G. F.
Places to Live 189	Bolcom, William
Plaisir d'amour 133, 194	Martini, Jean-Paul
Posate, dormite 123, 193	Bassani, Giovanni Battista
Pretty Creature, The 199	Storace, Stephen
Pria che spunti in ciel l'aurora 153, 196	Cimarosa, Domenico
Printemps qui commence 194	Saint-Saëns, Camille
Prison 123, 193	Fauré, Gabriel
Pull My Daisy 203	Amram, David
Pupille Amate 163, 198	Bononcini, Giovanni
Pupille Nere 198	Buononcini, G.B.
Pur dicesti, o bocca bella 186	Lotti, Antonio
Pur Ritorno 189	Handel, G.F.
Quando si trovano le basse femmine from *Il mondo della luna* 201	Galuppi, Baldassare
Quella fiamma che m'accende 75	Marcello, Benedetto
Questa mano e questo cuore 189	Haydn, Franz Joseph
Qui veut chaser une migraine 173	Bataille, Gabriel
Quien amores ten 192	Milan, Luis de
Reiterlied 173, 198	Loewe, Carl
Renunciation 203	Barab, Seymour
Resta in pace, idolo mio from *Gli Orazi e i Curiazi* 201	Cimarosa, Domenico
Rheinlegendchen 199	Mahler, Gustav
Romance 190, 192	Debussy, Claude
Rory O'Moore 203	Traditional
Rosefrail 193	Moeran, Ernest John
Rugiadose, Odorose 196	Scarlatti, Alessandro
S'il est un charmant gazon 189	Liszt, Franz
Saga of Jenny, The 204	Weill, Kurt
Sailor's Song 187	Haydn, Franz Joseph
Salley Gardens, The 189	Britten, Benjamin
Sandman, The 203	Brahms, Johannes
Santa Lucia 143, 195	Traditional Neapolitan Song
Saper bramate from *Il Barbiere di Seviglia* 186, 202	Paisiello, Giovanni
Sapphische Ode 190	Brahms, Johannes
Schafe können sicher weiden 198	Bach, J.S.
Schlummerlied 195	Franz, Robert
Schwesterlein, Schwesterlein 199	Brahms, Johannes
Sciocca ragion... Amina vile, ingrata from *Il filosofo di campagna* 202	Galuppi, Baldassare
Scorsi già molti paesi from *Il barbiere di Siviglia* 200	Paisiello, Giovanni
Se bel rio 103, 189	Rontani, Raffaello
Se cerca, se dice 187	Vivaldi, Antonio
Se come voi piccina io fossi from *Le Villi* 201	Puccini, Giacomo
Se nel ben sempre incostante 174, 195, 198	Stradella, Alessandro
Se parto, se resto 186	Vivaldi, Antonio
Se pietade in te non trovi 163, 198	Manzolo, Domenico
Se tu m'ami 199	Parisotti, Alessandro
Sea Fever 187, 189	Ireland, John
Sea-Shell 103, 189	Engel, Carl
Seal Man, The 200, 204	Clarke, Rebecca
Seashore Girls 204	Hundley, Richard
Sebben crudele 51, 193	Caldara, Antonio

Segui, segui dolente core 154, 196	Falconieri, Andrea
Sehnsucht nach dem Frühlinge 184, 203	Mozart, W.A.
Seit ich ihn gesehen 124, 193	Schumann, Robert
Self-Banished, The 199	Blow, John
Seligkeit 199	Schubert, Franz
Seltenes Glück 198	Telemann, Georg Philipp
Selve amiche, ombrose piante 194	Caldara, Antonio
Selve, voi che le speranze 192	Rosa, Salvator
Sen core l'agnelletta 164, 198	Sarri, Domenico
September Song 124, 193	Weill, Kurt
Serenade 104, 189	Haydn, Josef
Sérénade Florentine 154, 196	Duparc, Henri
Sérénade Italienne 192	Chausson, Ernest
Serpent, The 204	Hoiby, Lee
Sexy Lady 203	Moore, Ben
Shadrach, Meshach and Abednego 204	MacGimsey, Richard
Shall I compare thee? 104, 189	Paulus, Stephen
Shape of Things, The 204	Sheldon Harnick
Shenandoah 194	Althouse, Jay (arr.)
Shepherd! Thy Demeanour Vary 186	Brown, Thomas
Should He Upbraid 186	Bishop, Henry Rowley
Should You Ever Find Her Complying 198	Arne, T.A. arr. Bush
Si dolce è'l tormento 133, 194	Monteverdi, Claudio
Si mes vers avaient des ailes 193	Hahn, Reynaldo
Si, tra I ceppi 65	Handel, G.F.
Side Show, The 200	Ives, Charles
Signori... ascoltino le mie ragioni... from *I promessi sposi* 200	Petrella, Errico
Silent Noon 193	Williams, Ralph Vaughan
Silenzio, tacete from *L'ajo nell'imbarazzo* 201	Donizetti, Gaetano
Silvia, now your scorn 189	Purcell, Henry
Simple Gifts 187	Traditional
Six Songs on the Poems of W. Pillin 204	Davis, Sharon
Sleep 188	Argento, Dominick
Sleep That Flits on Baby's Eyes, The 195	Carpenter, John Alden
Slitheree-Dee, The 192	Silverstein, Shel
Smile 192, 194	Chaplan, Charles (Charlie)
So Shall the Lute and Harp 186	Handel, G.F.
Sogno d'infanzia 192, 193	Bellini, Vincenzo
Soldier, Soldier, Will You Marry Me? 174, 199	Dean, Brian (arranged by)
Someone is Sending Me Flowers 203	Baker, David (arr. By Roger Vignoles)
Sometimes a day goes by 125, 193	Kander, John
Sometimes I Feel Like a Motherless Child 189, 192	Anonymous
Sometimes I Feel Like a Motherless Child 199	Burleigh, (arranged by)
Song at Night 193	Hold, Trevor
Song of a Nightclub Proprietress 203	Dring, Madeleine
Song of the Old Man 199	Mussorgsky, Modeste
Sonntag 185, 196, 203	Brahms, Johannes
Sorge il sol! Che fait tu? 192	Donaudy, Stefano
Sound of Music, The 192	Rodgers, Richard
Spesso vibra per suo gioco 186	Scarlatti, Alessandro
Spick and Span 94, 188	Chanler, Theodore
Spriate pur, spirate 186	Donaudy, Stefano
Spring 188	Argento, Dominick
Spring Day 192	McArthur, Edwin
Spring is Singing in the Garden 195	Anderson, W.A.

Strike the Viol 175, 199	Purcell, Henry
Stringhe e ferri 189	Rossini, Gioacchino
Stringhe e ferri da calzette	
from *La gazza ladra* 202	Rossini, Gioachino
Strings in the Earth and Air 192	Hundley, Richard
Sugar in the Cane 204	Bowles, Paul
Suleika 192	Mendelssohn, Felix
Suo-gan 144, 195	Welsh folk song
Sweet chance, that led my steps 204	Head, Michael
Sweet Suffolk Owl 204	Hundley, Richard
Sweethearts and Wives 204s	Head, Michael
Taci, attendi e allor vedrai	
from *Adelson e Salvini* 200	Bellini, Vincenzo
Take, O take those lips away 192, 203	Dring, Madeleine
Tale of the Oyster 204	Porter, Cole
Tally-Ho! 204	Leoni, Franco
Tea for Two 193	Youmans, Vincent & Irving Caesar
That's him 192	Weill, Kurt
There are Fairies at the Bottom of our Garden 204	Liza Lehmann
There is a lady sweet and kind 114, 192	Warlock, Peter
There the Brisk, Sparkling Nectar 186	Handel, G.F.
They All Laughed 188	Gershwin, George
They Call the Wind Maria 189	Lerner and Loewe
They Can't Take That Away From Me 192	Gershwin, George
Think No More Lad 186	Butterworth, George
This Little Rose 195	Roy, William
Thoroughly Modern Millie 195	Heusen, James "Jimmy" Van
Those Evening Bells 192	Ives, Charles
Thou Doting Fool 198	Purcell, Henry
Ti sento 186	Vivaldi, Antonio
Till There was You 195	Willson, Meredith
Tirana del Tripili 145, 195	Lasema, Blas de (attributed to)
Tired 189	Williams, Ralph Vaughan
Tischlied 203	Schubert, Franz
To My Neighbor at the Concert 200	Donato, Anthony
Tobacco 204	Hume, Tobias
Toglietemi la vita ancor 95, 188	Scarlatti, Alessandro
Tonight at Eight 188	Bock, Jerry & Sheldon Harnick
Tout cede à vos doux appas 164, 198	Collasse, Pascal
Tout Gai! 134, 194, 204	Ravel, Maurice
Trees They Grow So High, The 144, 195	Britten, Benjamin (arr.)
Trinklied 204	Traditional German
Trost im Unglück 200	Mahler, Gustav
Tu mancavi a tormentarmi 135, 194	Cesti, Antonio
Tu, Ch'hai le penne, Amore 198	Caccini, Giulio
Tutto or m'è noto… Al tuo trono, o sommo Iddio	
from *I promessi sposi* 200	Amilcare Ponchielli
Ubriaco non son io	
from *Ubriaco non son io* 200	W. A. Mozart
Udite, tutti udite!	
from *Il matrimonio segreto* 200	Cimarosa, Domenico
Um Mitternacht 186	Zelter, Carl Friederich
Un bacio di mano 200	Mozart, W.A.
Un bocconcin d'amante from *La grotta di Trofonio* 201	Antonio Salieri
Un certo non so che 193	Vivaldi, Antonio
Un Momento di Contento 186	Handel, G.F.
Un moto di gioia 186	Mozart, W.A.

Una donna a quindici anni 200	Mozart, W.A.
Under the Greenwood Tree 192, 203	Dring, Madeleine
Under the Greenwood Tree 204	Arne, Thomas Augustine
Utro (Morning) 115, 192	Rachmaninoff, Sergei
Vaga luna 193	Bellini, Vincenzo
Vanilla Ice Cream 188	Bock, Jerry
Vanne, segu'il mio desio 145, 196	Handel, G. F.
Vedrai carino 200	Mozart, W.A.
Venti volte in vita mia from *L'italiana in Londra* 202	Cimarosa, Domenico
Veramente ho torto, è vero from *Il barbiere di Siviglia* 200	Paisiello, Giovanni
Verborgenheit 189	Wolf, Hugo
Verdi prati 193	Handel, G. F.
Vergebliches Ständchen 200	Brahms, Johannes
Vergiß dich selbst, mein schönster Engel! 165, 198	Telemann, Georg Philipp
Verlorne Müh 200	Mahler, Gustav
Vezzosette e care pupillette 105, 189	Falconieri, Andrea
Vieni, o mio diletto 192	Vivaldi, Antonio
Vilia 194	Lehar, Franz
Villanelle des petits canards 204	Chabrier, Emmanuel
Virgin's Cradle-Hymn, The 192	Fryer, Herbert
Vittoria, Vittoria 83, 186, 194	Carissimi, Giacomo
Vo' far guerra 198	Handel, G.F.
Volkslied 203	Mendelssohn, Felix
Von ewiger Liebe 204	Brahms, Johannes
Wagner Roles 204	Moore, Ben
Waitin' for the Light to Shine 175, 199	Miller, Roger
Wanderers Nachtlied 185, 203	Schubert, Franz
Was mich auf dieser Welt betrubt 198	Buxtehude, Dietrich
Water is Wide , The 189, 195	Hayes, Mark (arr.)
Water Mill, The 134, 194	Williams, Ralph Vaughan
Water of Tyne, The (Ma Bonny Lad) 195	Atkinson, (arr.)
Water Parted from the Sea 155, 196	Ame, T.A.
Way to Your Heart, The 194	Geller, Mandy
Wayfaring Stranger 192	Niles, John Jacob (arr.)
Weep No More 165, 198	Handel, G.F.
Weihnachtlisches Wiegenlied 115, 192	Pärt, Arvo
Wenn der Schulmeister Singet 198	Telemann, Georg Philipp
Wenn mein Bastien einst im Scherze from *Bastien und Bastienne* 201	Mozart, W.A.
Wer hat dies Liedlein erdacht 186	Mahler, Gustav
When a felon's not engaged in his employment 192	Sullivan, Arthur
When Daisies Pied 198	Arne, Thomas Augustine
When I Bring to Your Colour'd Toys 196	Carpenter, John Alden
When I Have Sung My Songs 189	Charles, Ernest
When I Was a Lad 194	Sullivan, Arthur
When I was One and Twenty 192	Butterworth, George
When one has a Sweetheart 189	Rogers, Clara Kathleen
When to her lute 204	Hoiby, Lee
Wher'er You Walk 189, 194	Handel, G.F.
Whether I Grow Old or No from *Lyra Britannica Book 1*, 200	William Boyce
Who ever thinks or hopes of love 203	Dowland, John
Widmung 188	Schumann, Robert
Widmung 73, 190, 196	Franz, Robert
Wiegenlied 203	Schubert, Franz

Wind of the Western Sea 192	Peel, Graham
Windy Nights 194	Barab, Seymour
Winter 188	Argento Dominick
With Rue My Heart is Laden 189	Butterworth, George
Wo die schönen Trompeten blasen 135, 194	Mahler, Gustav
Wohin? 188, 196	Schubert, Franz
Year's at the Spring, The 189	Beach, Amy
You don't know this man 192	Brown, Jason Robert
Young And Foolish 192	Horwitt, Arnold B. & Albert Hague
Zéphyr 95, 188	Debussy, Claude
Ziehet hin und forschet 198	Schütz, Heinrich
Życzenie 192	Chopin, Fryderyk

Composer Index

Althouse, Jay (arr.)
    Amazing Grace 194
    Chevaliers de la table ronde 167, 198
    Shenandoah 194
Amram, David
    Pull My Daisy 203
Anderson, W.A.
    Spring is Singing in the Garden 195
Anonymous
    Bergere legere 196
    C'est à ce joli mois de May 195
    Charming Chloë 196
    Have you seen but a white lily grow 191
    Joshua fit the Battle of Jericho 194
    Le Chanson du Tambourine 193
    Non, je ne crois pas 191
    O Leggiadri Occhi Belli 189
    Sometimes I Feel Like a Motherless Child 189
Arditi, Luigi
    Il Bacio 186, 193
Argento Dominick
    Diaphenia 187
    Dirge 187
    Hymn 187
    Sleep 188
    Spring 188
    Winter 188
Arlen, Albert
    I Heard a Blackbird in a Tree 186
Arms Fischer, William (arr.)
    La belle table est mise 191
Arne, Michael
    The Lass With the Delicate Air 186
Arne, Thomas Augustine
    Should You Ever Find Her Complying 198
    Under the Greenwood Tree 204
    Parted from the Sea 155, 196
    When Daisies Pied 198
Atkinson, (arr.)
    Water of Tyne, The (Ma Bonny Lad) 195
Bach, C.P.E.
    Der funfundzwanzigste Psalm 197
    Himmelstochter, Ruh der Seelen 159, 197
Bach, J.S.
    Bäche von gesalznen Zaehren 197
    Bekennen will ich seinen Namen 197
    Bist du bei mir 188
    Bist du Bei Mir 197
    Des Reichtums Glanz auf weiter Erden 197
    Die Armen will der Herr umarmen (Cantata 191) 197
    Die Elenden sollen essen 197
    Ei, wie schmeckt der Coffee süße 180, 202
    Erfreue dich Seele 197
    Fürchte dich nicht 197
    Gott ist gerecht 196
    Hört, ihr Augen, auf zu weinen 197
    Ich ende behende 197
    Ich folge dir gleichfalls 186
    Jesu, deine Gnadenblicke 197
    Komm, Jesu, komm zu deiner Kirche 150, 196
    Schafe können sicher weiden 198
Bach, Johann Christoph
    Ach, dass ich Wassers gnug hatte 197
Bacilly, Bertrand de
    Petite Abeille 187
Bacon, Ernest
    Buffalo Gals 199
Baker, David (arr. By Roger Vignoles)
    Someone is Sending Me Flowers 203
Barab, Seymour
    A Song of Perfect Propriety 203
    Inventory 203
    Renunciation 203
    Windy Nights 194
Barber, Samuel
    Beggar's Song 186
    Daisies, The 189, 194
    In the dark pinewood 191, 204
    Must the Winter Come So Soon?
        from *Vanessa* 201
    Of that so sweet imprisonment 204
Bassani, Giovanni Battista
    Posate, dormite 123, 193
Bataille, Gabriel
    Qui veut chaser une migraine 173
Beach, Amy
    Year's at the Spring, The 189
Beethoven, Ludwig van
    Dimmi, ben mio 193
    Faithfu'Johnnie 191
    Gottes Macht und Vorsehung 130, 194
    Hat man nicht auch Gold beineben 181, 202
        from *Fidelio* 200
    Ich liebe dich 193
    Marmotte 113, 191
    The Lovely Lass of Inverness 203
Bellini, Vincenzo
    Almen se non poss'io 116, 192
    Almen se non poss'io 190
    Ma rendi pur contento 193
    Ma rendi pur contento 101, 189
    O crudel che il mio pianto non vedi 192
    Per pieta bell'idol mio 93, 187
    Sogno d'infanzia 192
    Sogno d'infanzia 193
    Taci, attendi e allor vedrai
        from *Adelson e Salvini* 200
    Vaga luna 193
    Immagine gradita
        from *Adelson e Salvini* 201
Berger, Jean
    Chanson d'Automne 189
Berlin, Irving
    Best Things Happen While You're Dancing, The 194
Berlioz, Hector
    Petit Oiseau 94, 187

Bernstein, Leonard
  I Feel Pretty 90, 187
  I Hate Music 204
  It must be so 196
Bishop, Henry Rowley
  Love Has Eyes 191
  Should He Upbraid 186
Black, Eldon Udell
  Four Plus One 199
Blitzstein, Marc
  I Wish it so 68, 193
  Jimmie's Got a Goil 199
Blow, John
  Fain Would I, Chloris 129, 194
  Self-Banished, The 199
Bock, Jerry
  Vanilla Ice Cream 188
Bock, Jerry & Sheldon Harnick
  Tonight at Eight 188
Bolcom, William
  Amor 203
  Lime Jello-Marshmallow Cottage Cheese Surprise 203
  Places to Live 189
Bononcini, Giovanni Battista
  Non posso disperar 193
  Pupille Amate 163, 198
Bottegari, Cosimo
  Aria da cantar stanze 166, 198
Boulanger, Nadia
  Cantique 87, 187
Bowles, Paul
  Sugar in the Cane 204
Boyce, William
  How unhappy's the nymph 195
Brahms, Johannes
  Da unten im Tale 176, 202
  Dein Blaues Auge 196
  Dem Schutzengel 107, 190
  Der Frühling 128, 194
  Der Jager im Walde 190
  Des Liebsten Schwur 195
  Die Mainacht 190
  Die Sonne scheint nicht mehr 191
  Erlaube mir feins Mädchen 191
  Immer leiser wird mein Schlummer 120, 193
  In der Fremde 149, 196
  In stiller Nacht 188
  Meine Liebe is grün 187
  Mein Mädel hat einen Rosemund 202
  Minnelied 203
  Och Moder, ich well en Ding han 199
  Sapphische Ode 190
  Schwesterlein, Schwesterlein 199
  Sonntag 185, 203
  Sonntag 196
  The Sandman 203
  Vergebliches Ständchen 200
  Von ewiger Liebe 204
  Da unten im Tale 188
Britten, Benjamin
  Ashgrove, The 189
  Last Rose of Summer, The 155, 196
  Lord! I married me a wife! 203
  O Waly, Waly 189
  Oliver Cromwell 187
  Salley Gardens, The 189
  The Foggy, Foggy Dew 204
  The last rose of summer 191
  Trees They Grow So High, The 144, 195
Brown, Jason Robert
  You don't know this man 192
Brown, Thomas
  Shepherd! Thy Demeanour Vary 186
Bruni, Francesco
  Dolce Amor, Bendato Dio 195
Buononcini, G.B.
  Pupille Nere 198
Burke and Webster
  Black Coffee 190
Burleigh, Harry
  De Gospel Train 190
  Go Down in the Lonesome Valley 190
  Sometimes I Feel Like a Motherless Child 199
Butterworth, George
  A Brisk Young Sailor 126, 194
  Is My Team Ploughing? 199
  Lads in Their Hundreds, The 188
  Loveliest of Trees 191
  Think No More Lad 186
  When I was One and Twenty 192
  With Rue My Heart is Laden 189
Buxtehude, Dietrich
  Israel, hoffe auf den Herren 197
  Liebster Herr Jesu 197
  Was mich auf dieser Welt betrubt 198
Caccini, Francesca
  Che t'ho fatt'io 188
  O chiome belle 191
Caccini, Giulio
  Amor, ch'attendi 198
  Aria di romanesca 186
  Chi mi confort'ahime! 186
  Fere Selvaggie 195
  Non piango e non sospiro 189
  Tu, Ch'hai le penne, Amore 198
Cadman, Charles Wakefield
  From the Land of the Sky-Blue Water 99, 188
Calbreath, Mary Evelene
  My Love Rode By 195
Caldara, Antonio
  Sebben crudele 51, 193
  Selve amiche, ombrose piante 194
Campion, Thomas
  Come, Cheerful Day 195
Campra, André
  Charmant Papillon 186
  Le Carpillon 161, 197
  Mortels, Que Vous Sert-il 161, 197
Canteloube, Joseph
  Lo Postouro delaissado 202
  Malurous qu'o uno fenno 141, 195
Carissimi, Giacomo
  Filli, Non T'amo Piu 191

Carissimi, Giacomo
    Vittoria, Vittoria 78, 186, 194
Carpenter, John Alden
    On the Seashore of Endless Worlds 142, 195
    Sleep That Flits on Baby's Eyes, The 195
    When I Bring to Your Colour'd Toys 196
Celius Dougherty
    Love in the Dictionary 199
Cesti, Antonio
    O Del Ben 162, 198
    Tu mancavi a tormentarmi 135, 194
Chabrier, Emmanuel
    Ballade des gros dindons 96, 188, 203
    Villanelle des petits canards 204
Chadwick, George Whitefield
    Aureole, The 192
Chanler, Theodore
    Grandma 119, 193
    Lamb, The 125, 193
    Spick and Span 94, 188
Chaplan, Charles (Charlie)
    Smile 192, 194
Charles, Ernest
    When I Have Sung My Songs 189
Chausson, Ernest
    Amour d'antan 147, 196
    Le charme 140, 195
    Sérénade Italienne 192
Chopin, Fryderyk
    Życzenie 192
Cimadoro, Giovanni Battista
    Bel Nume che adoro
        from *Pigmalione* 200
Cimarosa, Domenico
    Dunque per un infido… S'arresta il sangue nelle vene
        from *L'italiana in Londra* 201
    Pria che spunti in ciel l'aurora 153, 196

    Resta in pace, idolo mio
        from *Gli Orazi e i Curiazi* 201
    Udite, tutti udite!
        from *Il matrimonio segreto* 200
    Venti volte in vita mia
        from *L'italiana in Londra* 202
Clarke, Rebecca
    The Seal Man 200, 204
Collasse, Pascal
    Tout cede à vos doux appas 164, 198
Coolidge, Elizabeth Sprague
    Asleep 194
    Christmas Tree, The 199
Copland, Aaron
    Ching-a-ring chaw 187, 203
    I bought me a cat 90, 187, 199
    Laurie's Song
        from *The Tender Land* 201
    Shall We Gather at the River 189, 193
Cornelius, Peter
    Christbaum 187

Coward, Sir Noël
    Don't put your daughter on the Stage, Mrs. Worthington 191
d'Indy, Vincent
    Madrigal 132, 194
Davis, Katherine K.
    I Have a Fawn 195
    The Deaf Old Woman 199
Davis, Sharon
    A Birthday 190
    Six Songs on the Poems of W. Pillin 204
Dean, Brian (arr.)
    Soldier, Soldier, Will You Marry Me? 174, 199
Debussy, Claude
    Les cloches 204
    Mandoline 187
    Romance 190, 192
    Zéphyr 95, 188
Dedekind, Constantin Christian
    Der wahren Tugend Gegenstreit ruhrt von der Erden Eitelkeit 157, 197
Delibes, Léo
    Passepied 186
Destouches, André
    Dieu Tout Puissant 158, 197
Donato, Anthony
    To My Neighbor at the Concert 200
Donaudy, Stefano
    Amor mi tiene in pugno 146, 196
    Date abbiento al mio dolore 98, 188
    O che odor di buono 193
    O del mio amato ben 190
    Sorge il sol! Che fait tu? 192
    Spriate pur, spirate 186
Donizetti, Gaetano
    Ambo nati in questa valle
        from *Linda di Chamounix* 200
    Che cangi tempra 188
    Che cangi tempra 190
    Guerrier sognai vittoria
        from *Don Sebastiano* 200
    Il Giglio e la Rosa 187
    Nella fatal di Rimini
        from *Lucrezia Borgia* 201
    Silenzio, tacete
        from *L'ajo nell'imbarazzo* 201
Donovan, Richard
    Down by the Sally Gardens 188, 196
Dougherty, Celius
    A Minor Bird 188
    Declaration of Independence 118, 192
Dowland, John
    Come Again, Sweet Love 97, 188
    Who ever thinks or hopes of love 203
Dring, Madeleine
    Blow, Blow Thou Winter Wind 190
    Come Away Death 190, 203
    Cuckoo, The 186, 192
    It Was a Lover and His Lass 191
    Song of a Nightclub Proprietress 203
    Take, O Take those Lips Away 192, 203
    Under the Greenwood Tree 192, 203

Duke, John
    Give me your hand   194
    hist...whist   199
    Loveliest of Trees   141, 191, 195
    Mock Turtle's Song, The   194

Duparc, Henri
    Sérénade Florentine   154, 196

Durante, Francesco
    Danza, danza, fanciulla   187

Ellington, Duke
    Don't get around much anymore   196

Engel, Carl
    Sea-Shell   103, 189

Errico Petrella
    Signori... ascoltino le mie ragioni...
        from *I promessi sposi*   200

Fain, Sammy & Jack Lawrence
    Once Upon a Dream   192

Falconieri, Andrea
    Segui, segui dolente core   154, 196
    Vezzosette e care pupillette   105, 189

Fauré, Gabriel
    Adieu   96, 188
    Après un Rêve   77
    La Rose (Ode anacréontique)   151, 196
    Les matelots   189
    Lydia   56, 63, 191
    Mai   187
    Mandoline   186
    Nocturne   189
    Prison   123, 193

Fesch, Willlem de
    Canzonetta (Tu fai la superbetta)   136, 195

Finzi, Gerald
    Come Away Death   190
    Come away, come away, death   148, 196
    June on Castle Hill   139, 195
    Oh Fair to See   187

Fitzgerald, Ella & Van Alexander
    A-tisket A-tasket   190

Flaherty, Stephen
    Come Down from the Tree   136, 195

Flanders & Swann
    A Word on My Ear   203

Flotow, Friedrich von
    Esser mesto il mio cor   191

Ford, Nancy
    In a simple way I love you   191

Foster, Stephen
    Beautiful Dreamer   126, 194
    If You've Only Got a Moustache   203
    Jeanie With the Light Brown Hair   150, 196
    My Wife is a Most Knowing Woman   203

Franck, César
    Le Mariage des Roses   140, 195

Franz, Robert
    Widmung   190
    Auf geheimem Waldespfade   147, 196
    Bitte   196
    Dedication   194
    Es hat die Rose sich beklagt   128, 194
    Gute Nacht   119, 193
    Mädchen mit dem Rothen Mundchen   57, 198
    Marie   152, 196
    Schlummerlied   195
    Widmung   73, 196

Fryer, Herbert
    Virgin's Cradle-Hymn, The   192

Galuppi, Baldassare
    Di questa poverella
        from *Il filosofo di campagna*   201
    La mia ragion è questa
        from *Il filosofo di campagno*   200
    Quando si trovano le basse femmine
        from *Il mondo della luna*   201
    Sciocca ragion... Amina vile, ingrata
        from *Il filosofo di campagna*   202
    Non cambierei, lo guiro... Vedo quell'albero
        from *Il filosofo di campagna*   200

Geller, Mandy
    Way to Your Heart, The   194

Gershwin, George
    They All Laughed   188
    They Can't Take That Away From Me   192

Ginastera, Alberto
    La Mañana   191

Giordani, Giuseppe
    Caro Mio Ben   55, 60, 188
    Non vogl'io se non vederti   64

Gluck, Christoph Willibald
    Che faro senza Euridice?   190
    O del mio dolce ardor   193

Gordon, Ricky Ian
    Blessing of the Boats   107, 190
    Luck   194

Gounod, Charles
    Envoi de Fleurs   118, 193
    Le Soir   122, 193

Granados, Enrique
    El tra la la y el punteado   89, 187

Grieg, Edvard
    Ich liebe dich   193
    Jeg elsker Dig   111, 191

Griffes, Charles
    In a Myrtle Shade   188

Gurney, Ivor
    Bread and Cherries   87, 187
    Hawk and Buckle   194
    Nine of the Clock   92, 187

Hahn, Reynaldo
    Si mes vers avaient des ailes   193

Handel, G. F.
    Ch'io mai vi possa   58, 190
    Nos plaisirs seront peu durables   193
    Pilgrim's Home, The   193
    Vanne, segu'il mio desio   145, 196
    Verdi prati   193
    Where e'er you walk   *194*
    Arm, Arm Ye Brave   190
    As when the dove   156, 197
    Birds No More Shall Sing, The   195
    Ch'io mai vi possa   58, 186
    Come and Trip It   186, 197

Come Live With Me 186
Figlia mia 149, 191, 196
I Know that My Redeemer Liveth 193
La Solitundine (2nd aria) 186
Leave Me 190
Leave Me, Loathsome Light 171, 198
Mirth Admit Me 187
Nel Riposo e nel contento 198
Peace Crowned with Roses 190
Pur Ritorno 189
Si, tra I ceppi 65
So Shall the Lute and Harp 186
There the Brisk, Sparkling Nectar 186
Un Momento di Contento 186
Vo' far guerra 198
Weep No More 165, 198
Wher'er You Walk 189
Where'er You Walk 194

Harbison, John
    The Flute of Interior Time 204

Harriss, Charles
    I Heard the Voice of Jesus Say 195

Haydn, Franz Joseph
    Aria di Agratina 188
    Aria di Buonafede
        from *Il Monda della Luna* 200
    Aria di Ecclitico
        from *Il Monda della Luna* 201
    Aria di Nencio
        from *L'infedeltà delusa* 201
    Aria di Rosina 188
    Aria di Sempronio
        from *Lo speziale* 201
    Cavatina di Alcina 188
    Der Gleichsinn 177, 202
    Die Landlust 179, 202
    English Songs, The 189
    Eurilda's aria (Questa mano)
        from *Le Pescatrici* 201
    Gasparina's aria
        from *La canterina* 201
    Liebes Mädchen hör' mir zu 194
    Liebes Mädchen, hör' mir zu 202
    Nun scheint in vollem Glanze der Himmel 162, 198
    O Luna lucente 189
    O Luna Lucente
        from *Il Monda della Luna* 201
    Piercing Eyes 195
    Questa mano e questo cuore 189
    Sailor's Song 187
    Serenade 104, 189

Hayes, Mark (arr.)
    Water is Wide, The 189, 195

Head, Michael
    A Dog's Life 199
    How Sweet the Moonlight Sleeps 194
    Money, O 199, 203
    Sweet chance, that led my steps 204
    Sweethearts and Wives 204s

Hensel, Fanny Mendelssohn
    Gleich Merlin, dem eitlen Weisen 170, 198
    Kommen und Scheiden 34, 187

Herbert, Victor
    Art Is Calling for Me 199, 203

Heusen, James "Jimmy" Van
    Thoroughly Modern Millie 195

Hogan, Moses (arr.)
    Deep River 168, 198

Hoiby, Lee
    Jabberwocky 204
    The Lady of the Harbor 204
    The Serpent 204
    When to her lute 204

Hold, Trevor
    Song at Night 193

Horwitt, Arnold B. & Albert Hague
    Young And Foolish 192

Hume, Tobias
    Tobacco 204

Humperdinck, Englebert
    Der kleine Sandman bin ich 190

Hundley, Richard
    Astronomers, The 204
    Bartholomew Green 204
    Come Ready and See Me 190
    Epitaph on a Wife 199
    For Your Delight 188, 190
    Maiden Snow 190
    Moonlight's Watermelon 193
    Seashore Girls 204
    Strings in the Earth and Air 192
    Sweet Suffolk Owl 204

Ireland, John
    Blind 97, 188
    Hope 188
    Newborn 189
    Only Child, The 189
    Sea Fever 187
    Sea Fever 189

Ives, Charles
    Ann Street 203
    At Sea 106, 190
    Children's Hour, The 203
    Circus Band, The
    Karen 191
    Memories 199
    Side Show, The 200
    Those Evening Bells 192

Kander, John
    Sometimes a day goes by 125, 193

Kern, Jerome
    Look for the Silver Lining 194
    Ol' Man River 193

Kern, Philip
    Greensleeves 69

King, Betty Jackson
    In the Springtime 191

Kingsley, Herbert
    The Green Dog 204

Kitt, Tom
    Everything Else 194

Krieger, Adam
    Nun sich der Tag geendet hat 197

Laitman, Lori
    Metropolitan Tower, The 71, 193
Lalo, Edouard
    Chant Breton 117, 192
LaMontaine, John
    Behold, a Virgin Shall Be with Child 195
Larsen, Libby
    Cowboy Songs 199
Lasema, Blas de (attr. to)
    Tirana del Tripili 145, 195
Legrenzi, Giovanni
    Che fiero costume 187
Lehar, Franz
    Vilia 194
Lehrer, Tom
    The Masochism Tango 204
Lennon, John
    Imagine 196
Lennon, John and Paul McCartney
    Dear Prudence 196
Leoncavallo, Ruggiero
    Mattinata 204
Leoni, Franco
    Tally-Ho! 204
Liszt, Franz
    Das Veilchen 188
    Es muss ein wunderbares sein 188
    Lasst mich ruhen 131, 194
    S'il est un charmant gazon 189
Liza Lehmann
    There are Fairies at the Bottom of our Garden 204
Lloyd, Charles Jr.
    Compensation 127, 194
Loesser, Arthur (arr. Alfred Kugel)
    The Lords of Creation Men we call 204
Loewe, Carl
    Meeresleuchten 172,
    Reiterlied 173, 198
Loewe, Frederick
    C'est moi 203
    I Could Have Danced All Night 120, 193
    On The Street Where You Live 196
    They Call the Wind Maria 189
Loewe, Johann Karl Gottfried
    Im Sturme 187
Lotti, Antonio
    Padre, addio 143, 195
    Pur dicesti, o bocca bella 186
Lully, Jean-Baptiste
    Belle Hermione, Hèlas! 106, 190
    Bois Epais 117, 167, 192, 198
MacGimsey, Richard
    Down to the Rivah 204
    Jonah and the Whale 204
    Shadrach, Meshach and Abednego 204
Machaut, Guillaume de
    Douce dame jolie 109, 191
Mahler, Gustav
    Das irdische Leben 199
    Hans und Grethe 199
    Lob des hohen Verstands 199
    Phantasie 192
    Rheinlegendchen 199
    Trost im Unglück 200
    Verlorne Müh 200
    Wer hat dies Liedlein erdacht 186
    Wo die schönen Trompeten blasen 135, 194
Malotte, Albert Hay
    The Lord's Prayer 190
Manzolo, Domenico
    Se pietade in te non trovi 163, 198
Marcello, Benedetto
    Quella fiamma che m'accende 75
Martin and Blane
    Boy Next Door, The 192
Martini, Jean-Paul
    Plaisir d'amour 133, 194
Martinson, Joel
    Cycle of Light 204
Marx, Joseph
    Ein goldenes Kettlein 40, 187
Mascagni, Pietro
    Canto di una Guècha
        from *Iris* 201
    Crea in quegli occhi il lampo d'un desìo
        from *Iris* 202
Massenet, Jules
    Elégie 188
    Ouvre tes yeux bleus 189
McArthur, Edwin
    Spring Day 192
Mellish, Colonel (arr. Quilter)
    Drink to Me Only with Thine Eyes 98, 188
Mendelssohn, Felix
    Auf Flügeln des Gesanges 190
Mendelssohn, Felix
    Auf Flüglen des Gesanges 188
    Bei der Wiege 190
    Bei der Wiege 66, 187
    Der Mond 178, 202
    Der Mond 190
    Gruß 180, 202
    Lieblingsplätzchen 101, 189
    O Rest in the Lord 203
    Suleika 192
    Volksleid 203
Menken, Alan
    Happy Working Song 191
    Les Poissons 171, 198, 203
Menotti, Gian Carlo
    Fu di notte come in sogno
        from *Amelia al ballo* 202
Messager, André
    La Maison Grise 112, 191
Milan, Luis de
    Quien amores ten 192
Miller, Roger
    Waitin' for the Light to Shine 175, 199
Moeran, Ernest John
    Rosefrail 193

Monteverdi, Claudio
    Maledetto sia l'aspetto 172, 198
    O tu ch'innanzi morte 132, 194
    Si dolce è'l tormento 133, 194
Moore, Ben
    Audience Song, The 204
    Cloak, the Boat and the Shoes, The 192
    Content to Be Behind Me 203
    I Am in Need of Music 28, 193
    I Love Teaching Voice 203
    I'm Glad I'm Not a Tenor 203
    Sexy Lady 203
    Wagner Roles 204
Morley, Thomas
    Come Sorrow Come 157, 197
Mozart, W.A.
    An Chloe 188
    Batti, batti 186
    Befraget mich ein zartes Kind
        from *Bastien und Bastienne* 200
    Das Kinderspiel 177, 202
    Das Veilchen 195
    Der Zauberer 188
    Diggi, daggi, shurry, murry 179, 202
    Fanciullette ritrosette
        from *La finta semplice* 202
    Ho capito, Signor sì!
        from *Don Giovanni* 200
    Ich möchte wohl der Kaiser sein 199
    In quegl'anni in cui val poco
        from *Le nozze di Figaro* 202
    In uomini, in soldati
        From *Cosi fan tutte* 199
    L'ho perduta, me meschina
        from *Le nozze di Figaro* 201
    Marito vorrei
        from *La finta semplice* 201
    Meiner Liebsten schönen Wangen
        from *Bastien und Bastienne* 202
    Nelle guerre d'amore
        from *La finta semplice* 202
    O Isis und Osiris
        from *The Magic Flute* 190
    Oiseaux si tous les ans 184, 203
    Persin le bimbe vengono da be 187
    Sehnsucht nach dem Frühlinge 184, 203
    Ubriaco non son io
        from *Ubriaco non son io* 200
    Un bacio di mano 200
    Un moto di gioia 186
    Una donna a quindici anni 200
    Vedrai carino 200
    Wenn mein Bastien einst im Scherze
        from *Bastien und Bastienne* 201
Mueller, Carl F.
    Create In Me A Clean Heart 192
Munro, George
    My Lovely Celia 197
Mussorgsky, Modest
    Song of the Old Man 199
Musto, John
    Could Be 204
    Litany 204

Niles, John Jacob
    Black Dress, The 189
    Black Oak Tree, The 199
    Go 'way from my Window 195
    Lass From Low Countree, The 105, 189
    Wayfaring Stranger 192
O'Hara, Geoffrey
    A Real Low Down Basso Am I 199
Obizzi, Domenico
    Ecco, che pur baciate 159, 197
Ondrasik, J.
    100 Years 196
Ord, Alan (arr.)
    All Along the Mother Volga
Orsini, Eleonora
    Per pianto la mia carne 114, 192
Paisiello, Giovanni
    Ah! Eccellenza!
        from *Nina, o sia la pazza per amore* 200
    Donne vaghe…
        from *La serva padrona* 201
    Giusto ciel, che conoscete
        from *Il barbiere di Siviglia* 201
    La Rachelina
        from *La molinara* 201
    Nel cor più non mi sento 199
    Saper bramate
        from *Il Barbiere di Seviglia* 186, 202
    Scorsi già molti paesi
        from *Il barbiere di Siviglia* 200
    Veramente ho torto, è vero
        from *Il barbiere di Siviglia* 200
Parisotti, Alessandro
    Se tu m'ami 199
Parry, C.H.H.
    My Heart is Like a Singing Bird 190
Pärt, Arvo
    Weihnachtlisches Wiegenlied 115, 192
Pasatieri, Thomas
    Agnes 199
    Parting 192
Pasquini, Bernardo
    O pargoletto arciero 189
Paulus, Stephen
    Shall I compare thee? 104, 189
Peel, Graham
    Wind of the Western Sea 192
Pergolesi, Giovanni Battista
    Mentre l'erbetta pasce l'agnella
        from *Il Flaminio* 202
Peri, Jacopo
    Gioite al canto mio 169, 198
    Nel pur ardor 191
Perti, Giacomo Antonio
    Dolce Scherza 109, 191
Piccinni, Niccolo
    Ogni, amatore 142, 195
Pilkington, Francis
    Diaphenia 108, 191

Ponchielli, Amilcare
   Ecco il fatal recinto... Ad ogni istante sembrami vederla
      from *I promessi sposi* 202
   Tutto or m'è noto... Al tuo trono, o sommo Iddio
      from *I promessi sposi* 200

Porter, Cole
   Ev'ry time We Say Goodbye   129, 194
   Tale of the Oyster   204

Poulenc, Francis
   Fleurs   110, 191
   La sauterelle   121, 193
   Le Bestiaire   199
   L'Offrande   203

Previn, Andre
   I Can Smell the Sea Air   203

Provenzale, Francesco
   Deh, rendetemi   16, 187

Puccini, Giacomo
   E l'uccellino   133, 195
   O fior del giorno
      from *Edgar* 201
   Se come voi piccina io fossi
      from *Le Villi* 201

Puliti, Gabriello
   Donna haser senza amore   158, 197

Purcell, Edward
   Passing By   152, 196

Purcell, Henry
   Hear! Ye Gods of Britain   198
   Hush, Be Silent   191
   Hush, no more, be silent   198
   I Love and I Must   160, 197
   Man is for the Woman Made   193
   More Love or More Disdain   183, 203
   Music for a While   190
   Music for a while   193
   Nymphs and Shepherds   193
   Owl is Abroad, The   199
   Silvia, now your scorn   189
   Strike the Viol   175, 199
   Thou Doting Fool   198

Quilter, Rodger
   Come Away Death   22, 187
   Ash Grove, The   194
   Blow, Blow Thou Winter Wind   190
   Dream Valley   137, 195
   Love's Philosophy   187
   Music When Soft Voices Die   195
   Now Sleeps the Crimson Petal   190
   O Mistress Mine   189
   O Mistress Mine   190

Rachmaninoff, Sergei
   Utro (Morning)   115, 192

Rameau, Jean-Phillippe
   Ah! Qu'on daigne du moins   156, 197

Ravel, Maurice
   Tout Gai!   134, 194, 204

Revueltas, Silvestra
   El Caballito   88, 187

Rice, Anderson & Ulvaeus
   Anthem   86, 187

Righini, Vincenzo
   Or che il cielo a me ti rende   195

Rimsky-Korsakov, Nicolai
   Nightingale, Charm'd by the Rose, The   192

Rodgers, Richard
   Edelweiss   81, 198
   I Whistle a Happy Tune   91, 187
   Mr. Snow   92, 187
   My Romance   194
   Sound of Music, The   192
   In my own little Corner   89
   Love Look Away   191
   Many a New Day   51

Rodrigo, Joaquin
   En las montañas de Asturias   110, 191
   Estribillio   191

Roe, Betty
   Jazz Songs   203

Rogers, Clara Kathleen
   When one has a Sweetheart   189

Romberg, Sigmund
   Margot   151, 196

Rontani, Raffaello
   Se bel rio   103, 189

Rorem, Ned
   Early in the Morning   88, 187
   O do not love too long   122, 193

Rosa, Salvator
   Selve, voi che le speranze   192

Rossini, Gioacchino
   Ave Maria (su due note)   116, 192
   La Pastorella delle Alpi   186
   Stringhe e ferri   189
   Anch'io son giovine
      from *La cambiale di matrimonio* 201
   Stringhe e ferri da calzette
      from *La gazza ladra* 202

Rota, Nino
   Papà, non mi lasciar from *Il cappello di paglia di Firenze*   201
   Parla piu piano   102, 189

Roy, William
   This Little Rose   195

Sabaté, Felipe Pedrell
   A...   146, 196

Sager, Carole Bayer & Marvin Hamlisch
   If he really knew me   130, 194

Saint-Saëns, Camille
   La Brise   121, 193
   Printemps qui commence   194

Salieri, Antonio
   Un bocconcin d'amante
      from *La grotta di Trofonio* 201

Sarri, Domenico
   Sen core l'agnelletta   164, 198

Satie, Erik
   Je te veux   139, 195
   La Diva de L'Empire   111, 191
   La statue de bronze   196

Scarlatti, Alessandro
- *Bellezza che s'ama* 197
- *Gia il sole dal Gange* 186
- *La Fortuna* 131, 194
- *Le Violette* 193
- *Le Violette* 204
- *O Cessate di Piagarmi* 193
- *Rugiadose, Odorose* 196
- *Spesso vibra per suo gioco* 186
- *Toglietemi la vita ancor* 95, 188

Scheer, Gene & Andrew Thomas
- Another New Voice Teacher 203

Schickele, Peter (aka P.D.Q. Bach)
- Little Bunny Hop Hop Hop 203
- Open Sesame Seeds 203

Schmidt, Harvey
- Is it Really Me? 191
- Much More 191
- My Cup Runneth Over 198

Schoenberg, Arnold
- *Arie aus dem Spiegel von Arcadien* 86, 187

Schubert, Franz
- *An den Mond* 188
- *An mein Klavier* 176, 202
- *An Sylvia* 189
- *Das Fischermädchen* 196
- *Der Kreüzzug* 202
- *Der Leiermann* 198
- *Der Lindenbaum* 196
- *Der Neurigiere* 190
- *Der Tod und das Madchen* 190
- *Die Forelle* 186, 194, 202
- *Die Mainacht* 202
- *Die Männer sind méchant* 195, 189
- *Die Post* 186
- *Frühlingsglaube* 190, 202
- *Grablied für die Mutter* 99, 188
- *Heidenröslein* 188
- *Lachen und Weinen* 189
- *La Pastorella* 204
- *Liebhaber in allen Gestalten* 194
- *Litanei* 182, 202
- *Seligkeit* 199
- *Tischlied* 203
- *Wanderers Nachtlied* 185, 203
- *Wiegenlied* 203
- *Wohin* 188, 196

Schuman, William
- Kiss Me Not Goodbye from *The Mighty Casey* 201

Schumann, Clara Wieck
- *Liebst du um Schönheit* 187

Schumann, Robert
- *Aufträge* 186, 199
- *Dein Angesicht* 148, 188, 196
- *Der arme Peter* 199
- *Der Nussbaum* 190, 192, 202
- *Des Sennen Abschied* 178, 202
- *Die beiden Grenadiere* 187
- *Die Kartenlegerin* 199
- *Die Lotosblume* 188, 190
- *Die Soldatenbraut* 199
- *Du bist wie eine blume* 191
- *Du Ring an meinem Finger* 193
- *Erstes Grün* 191
- *Hochlandisches Wiegenlied* 191
- *Hör' ich das Liedchen klingen* 170, 198
- *Im Wunderschönen Monat Mai* 188
- *Intermezzo* 204
- *Jasminenstrauch* 202
- *Lust der Sturmnacht* 202
- *Mein Garten* 182, 202
- *Seit ich ihn gesehen* 124, 193
- *Widmung* 188

Schütz, Heinrich
- *Eile, mich, Gott, zu erretten* 197
- *Fürchtet euch nicht* 197
- *Ziehet hin und forschet* 198

Schwandt, Wilbur & Andre
- Dream a Little Dream 191

Schwartz, Stephen
- Lion Tamer 91, 187

Scott, John Prindle
- Come Ye Blessed 198

Shaw, C. (arr.)
- The Nightingale 199

Sheldon Harnick
- The Shape of Things 204

Siegmeister, Elie
- Jesse James 196

Silverstein, Shel
- Slitheree-Dee, The 192

Sondheim, Stephen
- Comedy Tonight 188
- Green Finch and Linnet Bird 89, 187
- I Remember 191
- Johanna 189

Spee, Friedrich von
- *In grünem Wald ich neulich sass* 198
- Pretty Creature, The 199

Stradella, Alessandro
- *Per pietà* 187
- *Se nel ben sempre incostante* 174, 195, 198

Strauss, Richard
- *Muttertänderlei* 199

Styne, Jule, Betty Comden and Adolph Green
- Make Someone Happy 195

Sullivan, Arthur
- Love is a plaintive song 187
- Lost chord, The 192
- When a felon's not engaged in his employment 192
- When I Was a Lad 194

Swann, Donald
- The Passionate Trencherwoman 204

Tchaikovsky, Pyotr Ilyich
- A Legend 181, 202

Telemann, Georg Philipp
- *Ach, reiner Geist!* 197
- *Canary Cantata* 197
- *Glück* 197
- *Haus des Herrn* 197
- *Ich sehe dich in deinem Worte* 197
- *In Euch, Ihr grünen Auen* 197
- *Komm, süßer Schlaf* 197
- *Lasst hier Gesang und Saiten schallen* 197

  Seltenes Glück 198
  Vergiß dich selbst, mein schönster Engel! 165, 198
  Wenn der Schulmeister Singet 198
Terry, Sir Richard Runciman (arr.)
  A-Roving 198
Theile, Johann
  Komm! Ach Komm! O süsse Tod 160, 197
Thiman, Eric
  As Joseph Was A-walking 195
  I Love all graceful things 133, 195
  Jesus, the Very Thought of Thee 195
  Path to the Moon 195
Thomas, Ambroise
  Connais-tu le pays
    from *Mignon* 200
Thomas, Richard Pearson
  My German Boyfriend 113, 191
Tosti, Francesco Paolo
  La Serenata 189
  L'Ora è tarda 191
Traditional
  Down Among the Dead Men 168, 198
  Eileen Aroon 193
  Es ist ein' Ros'entsprungen 197
  In einem Kühlen Grunde 191
  Rory O'Moore 203
  Simple Gifts 187
  Sometimes I feel like a motherless child 192
Traditional German
  Trinklied 204
Traditional Neapolitan Song
  Santa Lucia 143, 195
Trenet, Charles
  Le Fils de la Femme Poisson 191
Vaccai, Nicola
  Ah! Se tu dormi svegliati
    from *Giulietta e Romeo* 200
Verdi, Giuseppe
  L'esule 112, 191
Vinci, Leonardo
  Fa così lodoletta che fuggi 188
Vivaldi, Antonio
  Agita de' venti dall'onte 186
  Lagrimetta alle pupille 186
  O di tua man 190
  O servi, volate
  O servi, volate 186
  Par min dirti 186
  Piango, gemo, sospiro 190
  Se cerca, se dice 187
  Se parto, se resto 186
  Ti sento 186
  Un certo non so che 193
  Vieni, o mio diletto 192
Walthew, Richard H.
  Eldorado 169, 198
Walton, William
  Old Sir Faulk 193

Warlock, Peter
  Away to Twiver 187
  Captain Stratton's Fancy 199
  Passing By 102, 189
  There is a lady sweet and kind 114, 192
Weckerlin, J.B. (arr.)
  L'Amour s'envole 195
  Non, je n'irai plus au bois 183, 203
Weill, Kurt
  All At Once 188
  Come in Morning 190
  September Song 124, 193
  That's him 192
  The Saga of Jenny 204
Welsh folk song
  Suo-gan 144, 195
Weyrauch, August Heinrich von (Attr. to Schubert)
  Adieu! 166, 198, 202
Wilder, Alec
  Blackberry Winter 190
  I Like It Here 100, 188
William Boyce
  Whether I Grow Old or No
    from *Lyra Britannica Book 1, 1745* 200
Williams, Ralph Vaughan
  Four Nights 191
  Hands, Eyes and Heart 100, 188
  Linden Lea 189, 190
  Menelaus 191
  Silent Noon 193
  Tired 189
  Water Mill, The 134, 194
Wilson, Meredith
  Till There was You 195
Wolf, Hugo
  Fußreise 187
  Nun lass uns Frieden Schliessen 93, 187
  Verborgenheit 189
Wolff (arr.)
  O No, John! 199
Youmans, Vincent & Irving Caesar
  Tea for Two 193
Young, Anthony
  Phillis Has Such Charming Graces 153, 196
Zelter, Carl Friederich
  Berglied 127, 194
  Die Spröde 137, 195
  Um Mitternacht 186
  Der König in Thule 108, 190

About the Author

Christopher Arneson is a professional voice trainer and vocologist. In 2003, he joined the voice faculty at Westminster Choir College of Rider University, where he is Director of Voice Pedagogy and teaches Voice, Voice Pedagogy, Literature for Teaching, and Speech for the Actor. He is co-director of Westminster's CoOPERAtive, a young artist program for singers.

Dr. Arneson is a frequent guest speaker regarding the training and care of the professional voice. He is a faculty member for the New York Singing Teachers Association's (NYSTA) professional development program, where he teaches classes in vocal repertoire and applied pedagogy. He is chair of the NATS Pedagogy Curriculum Committee and has recently published articles in the *Journal of Singing*: "Teaching Teachers" and "Performance Anxiety: A 21st Century Perspective."

Dr. Arneson was formerly the co-director of the Voice and Speech department in the MFA program at the renowned Actors Studio of the New School University in New York. In addition, he teaches Use and Care of the Professional Voice at the Mason Gross School of the Arts at Rutgers University in New Brunswick, New Jersey. Dr. Arneson completed vocology internships at the Grabscheid Voice Center at Mt. Sinai Hospital and the Vox Humana Laboratory at St. Luke's-Roosevelt Hospital, both in New York, and at Robert Wood Johnson University Hospital in New Jersey, where he continues to collaborate with otolaryngologists and speech-language pathologists in the remediation of voice disorders.

Dr. Arneson holds both Bachelor of Music and Master of Music in Opera degrees from Binghamton University, completed post-graduate studies at Cornell University, and earned a Doctor of Musical Arts degree from Mason Gross School of the Arts at Rutgers University. He is an editor for the NATS *Journal of Singing*, and served on the editorial board for the new revised edition of the Royal Conservatory of Music's Vocal Repertoire Collection, published by the Carnegie Hall Achievement Program. He is a member of the American Academy of Teachers of Singing, was designated as Master Teacher for the NATS Teaching Intern Program, and served as Program Chair for the 2014 NATS National Conference.

Arneson was an editor of *Fundamentals of Great Vocal Technique: The Teachings of Michael Trimble*, published in 2013 by Inside View Press. He resides in Yardley, Pennsylvania with his Labrador Retrievers, Wally, Wilma, and Wayman.

Lauren Athey-Janka, editorial assistant and soprano, is a professional singer and voice teacher in New Jersey and Pennsylvania. Her students have successfully competed and placed in NATS, Classical Singer, and Schmidt vocal competitions each year and have performed in off-Broadway, regional and local theaters. Lauren's students are also involved in professional, All Eastern, All State and All South Jersey Choirs. She frequently gives masterclasses for schools, choirs and festivals on the changing voice, vocal health and performance techniques and serves as a vocal consultant for both professional and children's choirs and theater companies. Lauren has studied voice science, voice pedagogy and voice disorders with leading professionals in speech pathology and vocal pedagogy. She has a Master of Music degree in Voice Performance and Pedagogy from Westminster Choir College and a Bachelor of Music in Voice Performance from Boston University. Lauren and her husband Vinny reside in New Jersey with their rescue puppies.